Praise for
From the Sahara to Samarkand

"*From the Sahara to Samarkand* not only covers the travels of Rosita Forbes. It reveals the extraordinary courage mixed with knowledge and humour that were keynotes in Sita's remarkable life. Margaret Bald in her excellent introduction captures with splendid detail Sita's break from the traditions of "What Women Did" in the 1920s and 1930s. Sita travelled through desert sand by camel or on foot. She visited mosques and temples in dangerous places and met heroes in the process. She wrote with style and beautiful language. Margaret Bald's introduction, the photo album, and the travel writings themselves are elegant summaries of the splendid diversities in Sita's life."

—Lord Renton of Mount Harry,
nephew of Rosita Forbes and author of
*Chief Whip: People, Power and
Patronage in Westminster*

"What an astonishing book this is! Rosita Forbes was not just intrepid, but extremely intelligent; not just adventurous, but deeply curious; not just a fine writer, but a shrewd and sympathetic observer as well. It's rare to find a person at once so iconoclastic, unconventional and fearless, and yet so attuned to her fellow human beings across the globe."

—Rosemary Mahoney, author of
Down the Nile: Alone in a Fisherman's Skiff

"Oh, how captivating are the details of her descriptions, the gutsiness of her adventures, her disguises and lies as she moves through mostly Arabic/Islamic worlds where the English are unwelcome, women are hidden, and amenities are rare! Even with a whiff of colonialism, this is a unique and captivating view of the world, from 1919 to 1937, from a beautiful and memorable woman whose playfulness with words makes this great fun to read!"

—Rita Golden Gelman, author of
Tales of a Female Nomad: Living at Large in the World

"The world could do with a few more female explorers. No one better to lead the way than the undaunted Rosita Forbes. Praise to Margaret Bald for bringing back this great traveler and writer to the spotlight, where she belongs."

—Arita Baaijens, author of
Desert Songs: A Woman Explorer in Egypt and Sudan
and fellow of the Royal Gegraphical Society

From the Sahara to Samarkand

Selected Travel Writings of Rosita Forbes, 1919–1937

Edited with an Introduction by
Margaret Bald

From the Sahara to Samarkand

"A record of travel and adventure that sparkles with wit and humor, and at the same time throws into relief an intimate and unforgettable picture."

—*St. Louis Globe Democrat* on
Forbidden Road: Kabul to Samarkand

"'Colorful' is the word for her style, but she employs it with considerable skill. Thanks to her powers of observation and to a capacity for letting things happen to her, the story of which she is the not over-obtrusive heroine provides the reader with a picture that is instructive as well as animated."

—Peter Fleming, *The Times Literary Supplement* on
Forbidden Road: Kabul to Samarkand

"Miss Forbes is one of the most accurate, and incidentally most entertaining, of explorers."

—*Saturday Review of Literature*

Praise for the Writings of Rosita Forbes

"She has an intense and imaginative curiosity about her fellow-humans, makes friends with them everywhere, shares the most appalling living conditions with a gay heart. And she writes of all this with cleverness and a vibrant personal quality of vividness and wit."

—*The New York Times*

"She was a keen observer, a shrewd commentator on men and races, and a forceful and interesting writer. Vital, indefatigable, and immensely courageous, she was not only one of the leading women explorers of, at the very least, her own time but one of its most picturesque and entertaining personalities."

—*The Times of London* in Rosita Forbes's obituary

"By all odds the most absorbing narrative of dangerous adventuring in unknown regions since Shackleton's *South*."

—*The New York Tribune* on *The Secret of the Sahara: Kufara*

This book is dedicated to the memory of
PENELOPE SALLY ROSITA (POLLY) RENTON
(1970–2010), who exemplified the courage,
sense of adventure, and zest for life of
her great-aunt Rosita Forbes.

Axios Press
P.O. Box 118
Mount Jackson, VA 22842
888.542.9467   info@axiospress.com

Library of Congress Cataloging-in-Publication Data

Forbes, Rosita.
    From the Sahara to Samarkand : selected travel writings of Rosita Forbes, 1919–1937 / edited with an introduction by Margaret Bald.
    p. cm.
    ISBN 978-1-60419-030-4 (pbk.)
    1. Asia—Description and travel. 2. Middle East—Description and travel. 3. Asia—Social life and customs—20th century. 4. Middle East—Social life and customs—20th century. 5. Forbes, Rosita—Travel—Asia. 6. Forbes, Rosita—Travel—Middle East. 7. Women travelers—Biography. 8. Authors, English—20th century—Biography. I. Bald, Margaret. II. Title.

DS9.F67 2010

915.04'41092—dc22

[B]

2010006688

Contents

1924: Morocco: The Sultan of the Mountains

1925: A Thousand Miles of Abyssinia

1928: A Woman with the Legion—South of the Atlas, Morocco

1931: Interlude in Turkey, Iraq, and Persia

1937: From Kabul to Samarkand

Editor's Acknowledgments

My thanks go first to Lord Renton of Mount Harry and the Estate of Rosita Forbes for the kind permission to reprint her writing. I am especially grateful to Tim Renton for his generous encouragement and for taking time from the book he is writing about his Aunt Sita to patiently answer my questions and follow the progress of this book. Thank you also to Jill Hughes for her help. I'd like to acknowledge Emma Sweeney for seeing the merit in this project and Jody Banks and Glenda Selvage at Axios Press for their guidance and assistance in bringing it to fruition. I deeply appreciate the efforts of my first readers, who offered perceptive comments on the introduction: Jonathan Calvert, Ian A. Bald, and Ali Tufel. Thanks to my sons André MacLeod Calvert and Daniel Ian Calvert for important technological assistance, to Elizabeth Stuart Calvert for being the patron saint of writers and artists, to Stephanie Cowell for cheering me on, and to the staff of the Authors Guild for their advice. The loving support of my husband Jon, my traveling companion on our own long and remarkable journey, continues to inspire and sustain me and makes everything possible.

I am particularly indebted to the following sources for information on Rosita Forbes's career as a writer and traveler: Samuel J. Rogal's essay on Forbes in the *Dictionary of Literary Biography, Volume 19: British Travel Writers, 1910–1939*, edited by Barbara Brothers and Julia M. Gergits (The Gale Group, 1998); the entry on Rosita Forbes in *Orlando: Women's Writings in the British Isles from the Beginnings to the Present* (http://orlando.cambridge. org); Penelope Tuson's *Playing the Game: Western Women in Arabia* (London: I. B. Tauris, 2003); *Women's Voices on Africa: A Century of Travel Writings*, edited by Patricia W. Romero (Princeton, NJ: Markus Wiener Publishing, 1992); Margaret Cole's *Women of To-Day* (London: Nelson, 1938); and Duncan J. D. Smith's biographical essay on Rosita Forbes (www.duncanjdsmith.com). For information on Rosita Forbes's family and ancestry, David K. Renton's "The Rentons: A Family History" (www.dkrenton. co.uk) was an important reference.

Introduction

"I've slept on anything or nothing—on a sloping shelf of rock above the red cave city of Petra in the Hedjaz; on a table in a Tongan shed; on a native mat in Fiji; on an opium couch in Siam; on desert sands in Africa and Arabia; in the ammunition wagon of a Chinese troop-train; in an armoured car in Palestine; on the decks of innumerable junks, sampans and dhows; on the earthen floors of as many huts, stables and caves. Once I couldn't even wash my hands for seventeen days. Often I haven't had a bath for months. I've lived on dead camel, locusts, sea-worms grilled till they tasted like spinach, octopus floating on oil, its insides scooped out and filled with garlic, and once, in a Samoan isle, on what my German host described as 'a leetle sick horse,' which tasted like suckling pig."

—ROSITA FORBES

THE INCOMPARABLE ROSITA FORBES was a renowned explorer and travel writer during the years between the first and second world wars. In the 1920s, she explored the Libyan desert, sailed across the Red Sea to Yemen and Asir in Arabia, visited the mountain stronghold of the Moroccan brigand Raisuli, and trekked more than a thousand miles by mule and on horseback into remote Abyssinia. In the 1930s, she traveled from Turkey to Syria, Palestine, Iraq, and Persia; into the Andes and down the Amazon; to the principalities of India; and from Afghanistan to

Samarkand in Soviet Central Asia. Between 1919 and 1949, she wrote some thirty books about these and other journeys, as well as biographies, history, novels, and memoirs. She was a widely published journalist and commentator on international affairs, a popular lecturer, a documentary filmmaker, and the editor of a pioneering women's magazine. She was also a style icon, known as much for her beauty and glamour as for her daring trips to far-flung and perilous places. The story of this extraordinary woman deserves to be retold and her writing discovered by a new generation of readers.

Joan Rosita Torr, Sita to her family and friends, was born in 1890 (not 1893, as many references have it) to a family of landed gentry in Lincolnshire, England. One of five children, Sita was a voracious reader, a collector of maps, and an accomplished equestrienne. Her mother, Rosita Graham, who descended from Scots and from venturesome Spaniards who had sought gold in South America, was the daughter of a Conservative businessman. Sita's father, Herbert J. Torr, the son of a member of Parliament, was a Cambridge graduate and, unlike his fellow Lincolnshire squires, a Liberal social reformer who believed in women's emancipation and encouraged his daughters' education. Sita was taught languages and geography by a governess and studied in London and in Italy. She recalled always being conscious of feeling different from other people and "beset by the need of a destiny." Inspired by her half-Spanish grandmother who had ridden over the Andes on horseback with a tame monkey on her wrist, she longed for adventure. "Travel was synonymous with adventure and there were no fences, laws or inhibitions," she wrote.

In 1911, Sita fulfilled her dreams of escape when she married Colonel Ronald Forbes, a Scottish army officer bound for India. Together, they hunted tigers in Rajputana, climbed in the Himalayas, and spent time in the Australian outback and South Africa. The honeymoon was short-lived, however, as her new husband proved to be unfaithful and bad-tempered. When Colonel Forbes was recalled to London, Mrs. Forbes pawned her wedding ring and bought a horse, a revolver, and a camera. She set off alone to travel among the Zulus, as she explained in her memoirs, "searching for the beginning of me as an individual, not as the daughter of a brilliant and much troubled father or the wife of a good-looking highlander with whom for three preposterous years I was miserable."

When war broke out, Rosita Forbes returned to London and enlisted as an ambulance driver for the Société de Secours aux Blessés Militaires. She served on the front in France for two years and was decorated twice for bravery. In 1917, having caused a family scandal by divorcing Colonel Forbes, she and a friend, Armorel Meinertzhagen, both "ready for anything," set off to see the world. Forbes's first book, *Unconducted Wanderers* (1919), chronicled her year-long sojourn with Armorel (called "Undine" in the book) in the United States, the Pacific Islands, and Asia.

Critics took note of this amusing and unpretentious tale of two ingénues larking their way across Asia and the debut of Rosita Forbes as a new and appealing voice in the genre of travel writing, which was burgeoning again as Britons sought to escape the restrictions and dreariness of the war years. "A particularly cheerful volume of unusual happenings, keen observation, and piquant narration," said *The Nation*. "The difference between 'Unconducted Wanderers' and the travel-books of a generation ago, is quite obvious," wrote *The Bookman*. "In past periods if two unchaperoned young women started forth on an unconducted series of desultory wanderings through the mysterious East (which, by the way, they wouldn't), any book written by one of them would be a pompous, dull affair, compact with the obvious things and pugnacious with gentile bigotry. Rosita Forbes's attitude is quite different. She was guided by extreme curiosity, and drank in the vivid qualities of the Orient through senses wholly open to their values."

Forbes continued to travel in the Maghreb, the Horn of Africa, and the Middle East, where she came to know many of the region's major political figures and developed a passionate interest in Arab and Islamic cultures, the cause of Arab independence—and desert exploration. "The curly red lines across African deserts had the fascination of a magnet," she wrote, "and I hoped fervently that the pioneers who were writing their names over the blank spaces, would leave just one small desert for me."

Her "small desert" was the Sahara. In February 1921, Forbes made international headlines when she survived an arduous four-month expedition by camel caravan to Kufara (or Kufra), a group of oases in the heart of the Libyan desert beyond the frontiers of Italian occupation. She was disguised as Sitt Khadija, an Egyptian widow on a pilgrimage to Kufara, and was accompanied by Ahmed Mohammed Bey Hassanein, a dashing young clerk in the Ministry of the Interior in Cairo. For generations, explorers had been tantalized by the idea of finding Kufara and the closed sacred city of the Senussi, a fundamentalist Muslim sect that had a history of hostility to foreigners. Forbes and Hassanein were the first since a disastrous German expedition some 40 years earlier to attempt to reach Kufara. In 1878–79, the German explorer Friedrich Gerhard Rohlfs and his party had approached the oasis but had barely escaped with their lives after the Senussi took them prisoner, looted their camp, and destroyed their scientific records.

Unlike Rohlfs, Forbes and Hassanein carried with them a valuable letter of introduction from the pro-British Senussi emir, Sayed Idris al-Senussi (later King Idris of Libya). But their trip proved to be no less risky than the German's. During their journey from the port of Benghazi to Kufara and back to the Siwa Oasis in Egypt, they were beset by sandstorms, tormented by lice and sand rash, lost their way, ran out of food, and nearly died of thirst. Hostile tribesmen held them prisoner, and they escaped a murder plot by a treacherous guide. After two grueling months, they reached the palm groves and salt marshes of Kufara and spent ten days in the sacred city of Taj as guests of Senussi brethren before embarking on their return trip, in which they charted a new route to Egypt, crossing a waterless stretch of three hundred miles.

During the final days of their journey, Hassanein broke his collarbone in a fall from a camel and was unable to continue. Forbes left the caravan with a Bedouin to get help, heading east toward the Siwa Oasis with a container of water and food for four days. She found a British patrol that her friend Field-Marshall Lord Allenby had sent out to look for the expedition, and the "preposterous adventure," as Forbes called it, came to an end.

Upon her return to Cairo, and then to London, Forbes, much to her surprise, became the woman of the hour. She was waylaid by reporters, who trumpeted the expedition's success and the story of the intrepid young Englishwoman. In London, King George V and Queen Mary received her at Buckingham Palace, and she was made a fellow of the august Royal Geographical Society, the bastion of British male explorers. European geographical societies awarded her medals, and she lectured to sold-out halls. Forbes's account of the journey, *The Secret of the Sahara: Kufara* (1921), adapted from her daily journals and illustrated by photographs she took with a Kodak hidden under her robes, was a runaway success and ranks among the classic accounts of desert exploration.

The contribution of Hassanein, however, the scion of a highly distinguished Cairo family, an Oxford graduate, and an Olympian in fencing, was eclipsed by the attention paid to Forbes. In Cairo, while she was being wined and dined by the press, Hassanein was bedridden. The British government was eager to claim Forbes's feat as a great achievement for the empire, and the public was fascinated. Some press coverage of the trip barely mentioned Hassanein or left the impression that he was a hired servant.

Although Forbes referred to "my expedition" in her book, she did dedicate *The Secret of the Sahara* to Hassanein, called him her "co-explorer" or "fellow explorer," and spoke of his "invaluable" contributions to the expedition, including his experience as secretary in 1916 to the Italian-British mission that had negotiated a treaty with the Senussi. But she portrayed him as a bit of a dandy and poked fun, for example, at the Balliol College blazer, L'Heure Bleue bath salts, and patent leather shoes he had packed in "opulent" luggage for his desert "rest cure." The effect of these and other humorous asides, if unintentionally so, was demeaning to Hassanein, a proud, sensitive, and ambitious man.

In November 1921, Hassanein claimed in a lecture to the Scottish Geographical Society in Edinburgh, then in a letter to *The Scotsman*, that in contrast to Forbes's account, he had actually led the expedition, and she "took of necessity a subordinate part." Hassanein said that he had conceived of the trip in 1916, long before Forbes came into the picture. He was going to travel with his Oxford classmate, Francis Rodd, who dropped out of the expedition and suggested in 1920 that Forbes join the party. Forbes countered that although Hassanein had long wished to search for Kufara, "he had done nothing practical to translate ambition into achievement." She had been working since 1919 to organize her own expedition, she wrote to *The Scotsman*, and "Hassanein Bey most kindly consented to accompany me in my journey at the very last moment and had nothing whatsoever to do either with originating or organising [it]. . . . He came as my most valued and helpful guest."

As prominent supporters of Forbes declared in letters to *The Times* of London, all the preparations for the expedition were left in her hands, including procuring supplies and equipment, and she paid the expenses, including Hassanein's. She dedicated six months to the planning and, in addition to improving her faltering Arabic, learned surveying, acquired maps, and obtained essential letters of introduction to the Senussi emir from former King Faisal of Syria (later king of Iraq), whom she visited in his exile in Italy, and to the Italian governor of Cyrenaica from a British official.

Regardless of who led the expedition, it is clear that both explorers were responsible for its success. As Forbes acknowledged, Hassanein's familiarity with the language, religion, and customs of the region, as well as his contacts among the Senussi, were crucial. According to Forbes, however, the Senussi saw it as in their interests to approve a British expedition. "They liked and admired Hassanein Bey," Forbes wrote, "but they admired and believed in Britain. They wanted us to secure them from Italy. If a British alliance was impossible, they hoped for an Egyptian one." Rather than being a passenger, as Hassanein's partisans implied, Forbes clearly made decisions en route. And while Hassanein might have believed that he was in charge, "subordinate" was never a word that could be used to describe Rosita Forbes.

Hassanein was vindicated in his quest for recognition and respect when he returned to the desert in 1923 to lead an expedition supported by Egypt's King Fuad. He traveled some 2,000 miles from the Mediterranean coast of Egypt to Darfur and found the lost oases of Arkenu and Uweinat in southwestern Egypt. This time, upon his return to Cairo, he was lionized, and in London he received the prestigious Founder's Medal of the Royal Geographical Society. He went on to serve Egypt as a diplomat and prominent royal adviser. But the controversy about the credit for the Kufara expedition and Forbes's portrayal of Hassanein's role lingered on and is discussed even today.

"I think the truth of the matter was that too much fuss had been made over my Kufra journey," Forbes admitted in her memoirs. "It had caught the people's imagination—and held it for altogether too long. . . . And in that ill-balanced decade, the popular press behaved as if 'woman' was herself a prodigy and anything she contrived to do, however unimportant, a symptom of evolution." It would have been better, she wrote, if the world had "accepted the Kufra journey as a good adventure and a pleasantly moderate achievement, instead of distorting it by extremes of carping or of praise."

For better or worse, Forbes's life was never the same after Kufara. The tall, slender, and photogenic "lady explorer" became a darling of the media. "Bride in Black" headlined the *New York Times* in December 1921 when she wed her second husband, Colonel Arthur T. McGrath, an Irishman on the general staff of the British War Office. She was "attired completely in black and carrying a walking stick instead of a bouquet," the *Times* reported. Forbes wore black, she later explained, to symbolize the death of her previous life. Besides, "I looked my best in black, so why not wear it?" she wrote. "All this was intended to be a private joke. Instead there were headlines on two continents, and when—later that winter—I lectured about North Africa and the Middle East, reporters were far more interested in the quite ordinary black dress I had worn for what was supposed to be the quietest of weddings, than in the Arabs. This caused me much heart-searching and I began to suspect myself of charlatanism."

At a time when desert romance novels and films featuring lecherous Arabs, such as *The Sheik* starring Rudolph Valentino, were all the rage, Forbes said that she recounted her experiences with Arabs to correct false Western ideas of their character. "The Arabs are not an amorous, brutal, savage race, but a grave, intellectual, self-contained, intensely religious people," she told *The Washington Post*. Yet the publicity about her adventures reflected some of the very same "desert sheikh" stereotypes she hoped to debunk.

This contradiction between her serious purpose and the frivolous aspects of her celebrity image would continue to preoccupy Forbes. For during the era of the Jazz Age flappers, Rosita Forbes, or Mrs. McGrath, as she was now known in private life, made for great newspaper copy on both sides of the Atlantic. After all, she was not a redoubtable Victorian lady voyager in a sensible skirt wielding a parasol; rather, she epitomized the emancipated, modern "new woman" of the postwar era—*en voyage* swathed in Bedouin robes or clad in riding breeches, boots, and a leather jacket; dressed on the lecture tour in Parisian couture and dramatic hats, wearing make-up, her hair fashionably bobbed.

Forbes's exploits were chronicled avidly in British and American dailies and magazines, which serialized her travel pieces, ran breathless features on the elegant "adventuress," and chronicled her comings and goings in the society pages and gossip columns. "Daring Death in the Desert: How a White Woman Entered and Escaped From the Secret City of the Sahara," read a typical headline. "Rosita a Bad Girl! Says Sheeks Homely, Wrinkled," declared one article. "Her Own Story of Experiences Thrilling and Amusing, with Ferocious Cannibals and Naked Zulus—as the Guest of Raisuli, the Desert Bandit Chief—in the Queen of Sheba's Land and Other Strange Places," promised another.

The articles about Forbes frequently drew a contrast between her frail and feminine appearance and her reputation as "a woman who has braved deserts and the mountain fastness where untamed bandits hold sway," as one American paper put it. The reporters "expected a combination of whipcord and leather," Forbes wrote of her experiences in New York on a lecture tour. "I wore vermillion under a pencil-slim fur coat. When my unassuming figure was pointed out to the representative of the *Herald*, he exclaimed, 'That girl rode camels? Smokes them, you mean!'" Although such publicity opened doors for Forbes, she was frustrated by the exaggerated focus on her gender and her looks. "It was an era of unbalanced personality worship," she wrote, "and in the case of a woman, it was reduced to humiliating sentimentality."

Forbes did, in fact, break new ground for women, although that was not what motivated her. She was an irrepressible and independent traveler who took risky and difficult trips, braved the hostility of the colonial officials and bureaucrats of the British empire, and invaded the male preserve of exploration, using charm, *chutzpah*—and her extensive network of establishment connections—to get where she wanted to go. As historian Penelope Tuson explained in *Playing the Game: Western Women in Arabia*, lone women travelers such as Rosita Forbes "implicitly threatened the status quo, both at the domestic level of family life and also in the subtle, but carefully structured hierarchy of colonial and imperial administration." "In season and out of season," Forbes wrote, "I was told, 'You cannot go! It is impossible.' 'Yes, I see—of course,' I agreed, and went."

Forbes also defied convention and courted gossip by traveling at first as an unattached divorced woman and then without her husband Arthur (to whom she remained married for more than 40 years). Mrs. McGrath did sometimes travel with Mr. McGrath, with female friends, or alone, but she went on some of her most adventurous excursions in the company of male acquaintances.

"There must have been a man at the bottom of it," said one official, for example, of her Kufara expedition, and "doubtless he got his quid pro quo," referring to Hassanein. "In the circumstances of heat, sweat, dirt, thirst, starvation, and exhaustion to which, unconsciously, he referred," Forbes commented, "the suggestion was so ludicrous that I could only laugh." "There is much feeling," she wrote, "chiefly masculine, against a woman venturing into those spheres which, for centuries, have been marked 'strictly preserved. All feminine trespassers will be prosecuted.'"

In summer 1921, fresh from her Kufara triumph and inspired by the fervent desire to visit Mecca of the Bedouins she had known in the Sahara, Forbes set out from Egypt disguised as a Muslim on an ill-fated pilgrimage commissioned by *The Times* of London, which took her as far as Jedda in Arabia. She included the account of her misadventures in her 1928 book, *Adventure: Being a Gipsy Salad—Some Incidents, Excitements and Impressions of Twelve Highly-Seasoned Years*, a collection of magazine articles.

In 1922, Forbes published two novels, *The Jewel in the Lotus* and *Quest: The Story of Anne, Three Men and Some Arabs*, both set in North Africa and the Middle East, about the romantic dilemmas of young Englishwomen similar to herself. Forbes was to write nine more novels. Some were respectably reviewed and sold well, and two were adapted for films (Cecil B. DeMille's 1927 Hollywood production, *Fighting Love*, and British International Pictures' *The White Sheik* in 1928). But her novels were appreciated more for their artful and convincing descriptions of the foreign places and social scenes she knew than for their literary quality. The *New York Times* critic said it best: "We leave *The Extraordinary House* (a 1934 novel) with a preference for the author's travel books."

Forbes's bags never remained unpacked for long. In 1922, she mounted a two-month expedition to northern Yemen and to southern Asir, a verdant and mountainous tribal area bordering Yemen, today a province of Saudi Arabia. Few Westerners had been to Asir, and according to Forbes, no European woman had ever been seen there. Disguised again as Sitt Khadija and accompanied by Kamel Fahmi, an Egyptian Railways inspector, Forbes sailed for two weeks across the Red Sea in a *sambukh* to the port of Jizan and visited Asir's capital, Sabya, and the Tehama coastal plain. Historians still consider her detailed article about Asir, published in the Royal Geographical Society's journal in 1923, as an important source about this little-known region. A complete and more picaresque tale of the trip appeared in *Adventure*.

In 1923, the publisher Thornton Butterworth asked Forbes to write a biography of Morocco's Robin Hood, Sherif Moulai Ahmed ben Mohammed el-Raisuli—brigand, warrior, politician, and descendent of the Prophet—who had led a revolt of the Rif mountains tribesmen against Morocco's sultan in the early 1900s. In 1904, Raisuli had kidnapped American citizens from Tangier and held them for ransom and later fought the Spanish occupiers of northern Morocco. Forbes ventured into the rugged terrain of the Rif and stayed for eleven days with Raisuli and his family at his compound in Tazrut.

In *The Sultan of the Mountains: The Life Story of Raisuli* (1924), illustrated by rare photographs of the portly and aging Raisuli, she made the bold choice of telling the story of this legendary figure—a raconteur of epic proportions—in his own words and from his perspective. Her book was praised at the time as an essential authority for the student of Morocco and remains so today. John Milius's 1975 film, *The Wind and the Lion*, with Sean Connery as the charismatic Raisuli, was inspired in part by Forbes's portrait of the sherif and her relationship with him.

By the time her book on Raisuli was published, Forbes had finished a whirlwind and highly successful lecture tour of the United States, giving eighty-eight lectures in ninety-one days. She and the famed explorer Harry St. John Philby were planning an expedition bankrolled by London's *Daily Telegraph* to cross the Rub' al-Khali, Arabia's legendary sea of sand, known as the Empty Quarter. When British authorities in Aden refused to grant them the necessary permits, she set her sights instead on Abyssinia (Ethiopia). Eight years later, in 1932, Philby finally crossed the Empty Quarter without her.

In 1924–25, Forbes took cinematographer Harold Jones on a four-month journey of some 1,100 miles through Abyssinia to make a documentary. "We rode through a three-thousand-year-old country," she wrote in her memoirs, "saw the ruined capital of the Queen of Sheba and the underground red-rock city of Lalibela, fraternized with a tribe of leaden-skinned troglodytes living among the mountains, scrapped with brigands, outwitted crocodiles, and eventually emerged battered and in rags with a book of adventures and 1,000 feet of film."

From Red Sea to Blue Nile premiered in London with great fanfare in 1925 and was screened in Addis Ababa. Only a six-minute snippet of Forbes's silent film survives today in the British National Film Archives. She published a colorful and exhaustive account of the expedition in her 1925 book *From Red Sea to Blue Nile: Abyssinian Adventure*. It was reprinted in 1935 with a preface written by Forbes as the country stood on the brink of war and occupation by Italy. The Ethiopians, she wrote, "are a courageous people who have lived all their lives in the sixteenth century and who will, the day after war is declared, find themselves most tragically in the twentieth."

During the late 1920s and the 1930s, Forbes traveled extensively in Africa, South and Central America, Burma, India, and Western and Eastern Europe. She continued to lecture and to write scores of travel articles and thought pieces on international politics for newspapers, magazines, and geographical journals. She recounted her trip to South America in *Eight Republics in Search of a Future: Evolution and Revolution in South America* (1933) and published tales of incidents from her travels, some semi-fictionalized, in *Women Called Wild* (1935) and *These Are Real People* (1937).

Women Called Wild, in particular, did not sit well with some critics—and justifiably so. The book combined profiles of women she had met on her travels—such as Halide Edib Adivar (Turkey's champion of women's emancipation), Alexandra David-Néel (the French explorer of Tibet), Russian Bolsheviks, and Chinese Communists—with lurid, sensational, and undocumented stories about slavery in Abyssinia and Arabia, witchcraft, sorcery, and voodoo of the kind that made good copy in popular magazines. "Mrs. Forbes writes a story of weird and far-off places, as episodic and uneven as a fruit cake," said *The Washington Post*. "Using every device to shock and horrify her reader, the author . . . only succeeds in making the reader indifferent, reading about multiple atrocities incessantly recurrent, with a calm blandness. . . ." Forbes was always on firmer ground when she reported her experiences in a straightforward manner, rather than blending the real and the imaginary or straining to "goggle the eyes" of her readers, as one critic put it.

Forbes's most notable journeys of this era, chronicled in two outstanding books, were those that took her back to the Middle East at a pivotal moment of change and to Afghanistan and Soviet Central Asia. In 1929–30, Forbes traveled from Turkey, via Syria, Palestine, Iraq, and Persia (Iran), to the borders of Afghanistan and back again along the Russian frontier through Azerbaijan and Kurdistan. She told the story of this trip in *Conflict: Angora to Afghanistan* (1931), a *tour de force* of reporting and vivid observation. "I looked forward to seeing the effect of a decade of intensive modernization, imposed largely by force on people traditionally conservative," she wrote. "In every country I found a state of conflict, which included not only the inevitable racial, religious, and political disputes, but a more formidable antagonism between the educated and the ignorant; between sexes, classes and generations."

Her cast of characters included Turkey's President Mustafa Kemal, her long-time friend King Faisal of Iraq, and Reza Khan, the shah of Persia, as well as the students and professional women of Ankara and Tehran and the opium-smoking harem dwellers of

Qum; the insurgent Kurds of Mount Ararat, their women fighters toting rifles and babies; the embattled Druses in their mountain fiefdom in Lebanon; Zionist colonists and beleaguered Arab farmers in Palestine; young Iraqi nationalists from Baghdad, devout Shia pilgrims in the holy cities of Karbala and Najaf, and the Zoroastrians of Yezd. "The test of any civilization is its treatment of its minorities, racial, religious and political," she wrote, concerned that the emerging forces of nationalism, particularly in Turkey and Iraq, would threaten the survival of the diverse communities whose stories she told in the pages of *Conflict*.

In 1930, while Forbes was in the Persian city of Meshed, where "the Golden Road to Samarkand" begins, she watched fugitives from Soviet Turkmenistan drive by in their high-wheeled covered wagons, the "men's faces, dark and hard with flat cheekbones, and the enormous sheepskin hats like haloes." Like many wanderers before her, Forbes's imagination was captured by the idea of a journey to fabled Samarkand, one of the world's most ancient cities, the capital of Tamerlane's 14th-century empire, and then part of the Soviet Union. It took six years for Forbes to persuade the Russian embassy to give her a transit visa allowing her to cross the closed border between Afghanistan and Soviet Central Asia at the Amu Darya (the Oxus River that Alexander the Great had crossed in 329 BCE).

She began her journey in 1936 at Peshawar in India (Pakistan today) and traveled over the Khyber Pass and onward in a truck loaded with benzene along the nomad's road to Kabul, an earth-colored city, enclosed by mountain ramparts, "which has a beauty like nothing else on earth," as she wrote in *Forbidden Road: Kabul to Samarkand* (1937). She took a mail truck southwest on a side trip of some 600 hundred miles to the oasis town of Kandahar in the company of 53 patient, helpful, and good-tempered Afghans, "the best travelling companions I ever had."

From Kabul, she traveled northwest toward the border of Soviet Central Asia with Captain George Galloway, a British diplomat, and his temperamental orderly, Kuli Khan. Together they visited Bamiyan, where they gazed upon the ancient Buddha statues carved into niches in the cliff face that were destroyed by the Taliban in 2001, and passed over the Hindu Kush to the holy city of Mazar-i-Sharif, a mud-built town thronged with pilgrims and crowned by an exquisitely tiled sea-blue mosque. *Forbidden Road* is particularly moving to read today for its portrait of an Afghanistan that has been lost to the ravages of three decades of war.

Forbes continued alone over the border at the Amu Darya, traveling by train and truck to Bokhara and Samarkand in Uzbekistan, where she found both socialist progress and the glory of Tamerlane—Samarkand's facades of "sea and sand with sunshine caught between them," whose beauty she had dreamed of years before in Meshed.

In 1938, Forbes returned to India to write about its princely states in *India of the Princes* (1939). This was the last of her great journeys. Before the war, Forbes edited *Women of All Lands: Their Charm, Culture and Characteristics*, an unusual magazine that celebrated the customs and achievements of women of all races and many ethnic groups around the world. Its eighteen issues, copiously illustrated by the work of top photojournalists and art photographers, including glamour shots by the Hollywood photographer Hurrell, were collected in a book published in 1939. It serves as a veritable encyclopedia of vintage 1930s perspectives on feminism and femininity.

That year, Forbes visited the Bahamas and found her future "journey's end" on the island of Eleuthera, where she and her husband made plans to build their dream house, Unicorn Cay. She published *Unicorn in the Bahamas* (1939), the first of four books of travel and history she wrote about the West Indies and the

Caribbean, as well as *These Men I Knew* (1940), impressions of leaders she had interviewed or met on her travels, including Hitler, Stalin, Mussolini, Roosevelt, Gandhi, and Haile Selassie. During the war, she lectured tirelessly to soldiers and civilians in Britain, Canada, and the United States on behalf of the Allied war effort.

After the palatial home in London where she had entertained in grand style was destroyed in the Blitz, she and her husband moved to Eleuthera. There, she continued to write and published two volumes of memoirs, *Gypsy in the Sun* (1944) and *Appointment with Destiny* (1946), exhaustive year-by-year accounts of a lifetime of travel, "a fascinating monumental hodgepodge of travel, exploration, prophecy, hindsight, commentary and crusading," as the *New York Times* reviewer put it. By that time, she said, she had been to every known country, save Tibet and New Zealand. After Arthur McGrath's death in 1962, Forbes relocated to Bermuda, where she died in 1967 at the age of seventy-seven.

"Few women can have travelled so widely, seen so much, or produced a survey of the globe comparable with that comprised in her long series of books," wrote *The Times* of London in Forbes's obituary. "She was a keen observer, a shrewd commentator on men and races, and a forceful and interesting writer. Vital, indefatigable, and immensely courageous, she was not only one of the leading women explorers of, at the very least, her own time but one of its most picturesque and entertaining personalities."

By the time of Forbes's death, her most important travel books had long been out of print. With the revival in recent years of classic works of travel literature and the rediscovery of the neglected women travelers of the nineteenth and early twentieth centuries, there is new interest in Forbes, her accomplishments, and her writing.

Forbes's travel tales remain fresh and engaging. They are also valuable historical documents. She went to places that would be forever changed by war or revolution and whose histories are central to our understanding of the post-September 11 world. She told her readers what she saw, what she learned, and what it felt like to be there, in her own inimitable style—lively, witty, informative, and opinionated. And she conveyed the moments of terror and tedium, exhaustion and exhilaration, frustration and contentment of life on the road. "In real life," she wrote, "the big things and the little things are inextricably mixed up together, so in Libya at one moment, one worried because one's native boots were full of holes, and at the next, perhaps, one wondered how long one would be alive to wear them."

Forbes had a gift for eloquent descriptive writing: "Djibouti, white and neat and empty, looked as if it had just been washed and dumped out in the sun to dry." "The red sands of Marrakesh, sprawling at the foot of the Atlas like a wounded Leviathan. . . ." The dust of Addis Ababa "rose like golden pollen over flocks and herds." In Kurdistan, "the plain was alive with horses, whose tails, swishing a continual protest against hordes of insects, were like wind-driven grass. As for the warriors, they were splendid beyond description and as the spines of a hedgehog so were the arms with which they bristled." Her detailed descriptions of the color and design of the traditional dress of the people she observed—for example, a Kurdish woman's "flowing robe of semi-transparent apricot muslin powdered with mist-blue flowers" and "her long brocaded coat of sapphire and gold with tight sleeves . . . stiffened and lined with cramoisie, so that it stood out like court dresses of the Rennaisance"—are an ethnographer's and a fashionista's delight.

Forbes was a feminist *avant la lettre*—though she probably would have resisted this label, as she disliked being pigeonholed or confined by preconceived notions of how she should think or behave. Unlike most travel writers of her time, she paid special attention to women. She sought them out, wrote about their customs, their living conditions, and the state of their rights, and took pains to shine a spotlight on women of accomplishment.

Yet Forbes was as interested in the ordinary people she encountered on her travels as she was in the luminaries she wrote about, as comfortable breaking bread with Bedouins around a campfire as she was at cocktails on Fifth Avenue or in the great country houses of the British aristocracy. "She has an intense and imaginative curiosity about her fellow-humans," a reviewer wrote in the *New York Times* in 1939, "makes friends with them everywhere, shares the most appalling living conditions with a gay heart. And she writes of all this with cleverness and a vibrant personal quality of vividness and wit."

Forbes's travel writing did have flaws. Particularly in her earliest books, she used at times racially stereotyped language that was typical of the era but is no less disturbing to encounter. Her forays into writing traveler's tall tales that blurred fact and fiction were an unfortunate choice for a writer whose reputation was founded on her convincing accounts of her incredible real-life adventures. In fact, in her efforts to document her trips, she tended in her early books to "empty the notebook" and write overly long, discursive accounts. "Success had come to me so fast and with such unexpected violence that I had no time to learn to write," Forbes admitted in her memoirs. "I could not limit my impressions. I could not stop my sentences."

With experience, however, Forbes's writing became more economical. "Do you think 'Lizzie' would understand?" an American newspaper editor asked her early in her career as he scanned a complicated article on conditions in Palestine. Forbes did learn to consider the prototypical "Lizzie" in her writing but never acceded to the wishes of an English reader in Manchester, who wrote to her: "I do like reading your travel books, but, just when I am all excited over an adventure, I come upon pages of archaeology and geography. Please, Mrs Forbes, do write one book that is all adventure, with no information in it at all." Forbes found a happy medium of splendid adventure, captivating storytelling, and insightful reporting. She went everywhere, did everything, and had a devil of a fine time of it.

—MARGARET BALD

Editor's Note

This volume collects selections from Rosita Forbes's travel writing, excerpted from eight books: *Unconducted Wanderers* (1919), *The Secret of the Sahara: Kufara* (1921), *The Sultan of the Mountains: The Life Story of Raisuli* (1924), *From Red Sea to Blue Nile: Abyssinian Adventure* (1925), *Adventure: Being a Gipsy Salad—Some Incidents, Excitements and Impressions of Twelve Highly-Seasoned Years* (1928), *Conflict: Angora to Afghanistan* (1931), *Women Called Wild* (1935), and *Forbidden Road: Kabul to Samarkand* (1937). Because these books were published over two decades by a number of different publishers in Britain and the United States, there are inconsistencies in editorial style and in spelling of names of people and places. These, as well as archaic place names, have been left unchanged. When the original book contained a glossary, however, the definitions from the glossary have been placed in footnotes.

1919

Into Java and Sumatra

From Chapters IX and X of
Unconducted Wanderers (1919)

Java

ONE OF THE gymnastic Papuan mosquitoes must have accomplished his nefarious design, for the instant we arrived at Cairns—a desolate, galvanized iron township surrounded by blue gums and banana trees—I collapsed with dengue fever. However, Undine nursed me so strenuously that, in self-defence, I found it necessary to recover in spite of a delightful toy which she borrowed from the only chemist one hot dry day when I was babbling cheerfully of cannibals and caterpillars! It was called a Home Thermometer, and one's temperature either ran out altogether at one end past a scarlet notice which said, "Call a doctor at once," or sank despairingly to about 60, where "No danger" was written in sulphur yellow.

A dilatory steamer finally picked us up in the middle of a cyclone, carried us for three peaceful days north to Thursday Island, ringed with its fleet of pearl fishers, and forthwith plunged headlong with us into the North-West monsoon. For unnumbered days we lay in wet deck-chairs, lashed to any convenient rail, while the fo'c'sle plunged down into great breakers which broke right over the deck, covering the bridge in spray, and the propeller sailed triumphantly out of the water, and pretended it was an aeroplane. When I wasn't falling downstairs to the hermetically sealed saloon to have soup upset in my lap, and potatoes dribbled in my hair, I remember I chased elusive but very strong smells through cockroach-haunted passages, with a tin of Keating's powder, to the infinite fury of the chief steward, who generally followed with a broom.

How glad we were to reach Java, in spite of some delightful Australians, wounded in the war, who cheered our dripping hours on the unsteady deck with stories of Gallipoli as seen through the rose-coloured spectacles of the cheerful Anzacs! One, who had contributed a hand to the tragedy and the glory of Suvla Bay, reduced us to helpless mirth with his description of the kindly soul who visited him in the hospital, and exclaimed in impulsive pity, "Oh, my dear man, have you lost your hand for good?" One wonders what would be the correct answer—"Oh no, I left it in the bathroom by mistake," or, "Well, the doctor says it will grow again in a few months!"

Certainly the joys of civilization are great! We arrived at fascinating Batavia early in the morning, having motored up from the wharf ten miles away, alongside a canal full of odd-shaped barges and house-boats. We were deposited by various friends at an immense and ruinously expensive hotel, and instructed to follow the Dutch custom of sleeping all the afternoon. But, of course, we didn't. The town was much too attractive. We set forth on foot, and trotted over round uneven cobble-stones to the native bazaars, where we meant to buy silk stockings and Java straw hats, but the wily Hindu was too clever for us, and we soon found ourselves the unwilling possessors of so much ancient and heavy brassware that we were obliged to return in haste. The betel-nut sets are rather attractive, as they consist of great beaten brass bowls containing a jar for the leaves, two boxes for the nuts, a couple of bowls for the mixture when made, and a cup to hold the requisite chalk. The juice of the nut is squeezed out and mixed with chalk into a rose-pink paste, which is then sucked to the great detriment of the appearance.

We drank the most wonderful coffee in the world in the sitting-room veranda of our palatial rooms, and, having turned our backs carefully on the printed tariff—as we considered it discouraging—we watched very fat Dutchmen attired in violet-hued pyjamas and much adipose tissue asleep in deck-chairs, their bare feet tilted heavenwards, and sonorous grunts issuing from their unshaven faces. Afterwards we drove round the white well-ordered town in the smallest cart I've ever been in. It resembled the Indian ecca, or a hencoop with a tassled awning over it, and was drawn by a nine-hand pony almost hidden by his jingling, silver-decorated harness. The whole turn-out can be bought for a few shillings, and to hire it costs threepence an hour! Canals run down the centre of the main streets, and all the red-tiled paths are bordered with trees, under which sit brown Sudanese coolies in cartwheel hats and scarlet loin cloths, selling great bunches of furry-red leeches—which, stripped of their outer bark, taste like juicy grape-plums—and piles of pink, sticky "bullocks' hearts"— a shiny pear-like fruit.

We ended our day in an open-air café, where we sat in immense basket-chairs, drinking a fiery liqueur called a "paheit," which is guaranteed to remove all sense of discretion after three seconds, listening to the band and watching the population flow past, bare-headed, in toy victorias drawn by gaily decorated pairs of tiny ponies. They don't dine in Java till 9 or 10 PM, and then they wade through an eleven-course meal, eating roast veal and apricots together, black bread and cheese with their fish, and finishing with very rich cream cakes. It is a distressing fact that almost the first sentence we learned in Malay was, "Give me some more."

Next morning, we had to drag ourselves out of bed at 5 AM, and eat German sausage and black bread and cheese in darkness, in order to catch an early train. All Javanese trains seem to start about 6 AM, and they stop at nightfall, so travelling is tedious. When we left Batavia the streets were flooded a couple of feet deep after the heavy rain, and we almost swam over the delicate bridges, and through wide, shady avenues where each shop, with its white-columned veranda, stands back in its own spacious garden. We were going up to Soebang to stay with the assistant manager of a great block of British plantations, a kingdom within a kingdom, for it consists of 500,000 acres with a population of 250,000 natives who are taxed by the Tuan—king of the lands— one-fifth of their rice crop and one free day's work per week from every man between the age of fourteen and forty-five. The Company have their own police, their own harbour and forty miles of coast-line, and about one hundred white men superintending the work. Tea, sugar, rice, rubber, coffee, coco-nuts—you can see them all grown within a twenty-mile radius.

We left the crawling train at Pegadon Baru and finished our journey on a tiny one-cylinder trolley, which ran jerkily along narrow rails through endless rice-fields—where water buffaloes dragged primitive wooden ploughs—to the headquarters of the plantations, a white, old-fashioned Dutch building with wide, cool verandas wreathed in climbing orchids and yellow trumpet vines. Everything was *too* comfortable after the tin shacks of New Guinea. The beds were like small rooms, with a square mosquito frame ten or twelve feet above one's head, shutting one in completely, no sheet or coverlet of any kind, just a pillow lying forlornly on the immense stretch of white mattress and a "Dutch Wife," a sort of short bolster which I believe you are supposed to place across your shivering form so that the middle bit of you is warm! The house was run by soft-eyed Malays, who said to themselves, "The Tuan has bought two new wives; they must have been very expensive ones!"

For some days we scoured the country in a Hudson super-six, which I drove to the imminent danger of goats and dreamy water buffalo, but I could not rival the performance of the native chauffeur, who killed eleven and a half hens in quite a short run! The country was very green under the incessant rain, and thickly cultivated; blue, volcanic hills rise towards the centre of the island; herds of water buffalo wallow in the muddy rivers; tall cranes stand dejectedly in the rice fields; a few scarlet flame-trees blaze forth from a sheltered corner, but on the whole there are very few flowers.

Swarms of Malayans—imported labour—Sudanese from the north of the island, Javanese from the south, vie with each other in the vivid colours of their sarongs and the unwieldy vastness of their Chinese hats. Closed bullock-carts creak along the deeply rutted roads, looking like moving temples; while the small reed and lath houses look exactly like match-boxes. All this, in a cloudy rain-swept setting of intense green with skittish goats driven by small brown imps dressed in a golden straw hat and a smile, and yellow flying-foxes hanging head downward on the mango-trees as thick as gooseberries.

Java and Sumatra

ONE NIGHT WE all packed ourselves into the trolley and rattled down through the rice to Pegadon Baru to see a Malay harvest feast. We were met by scores of coolies with flaring torches, and carried across the deep mud, shoulder high, in huge chairs mounted on a dozen poles. Our arrival, in the brilliantly lit and gorgeously decorated hall, reminded me of the carefully timed entrance of the fairy queen and the principal boy in a Drury Lane pantomime.

I felt our muddy brogues and short tweed skirts were hardly equal to the occasion, especially as singing girls insisted on crouching at our feet, and wailing forth songs about our great grandeur. An amiable Dutchman, unskilled in the intricacies of the English tongue, translated one oft-repeated sentence as, "You are a very large English lady," which I thought unconsciously descriptive.

We ate many strange foods to the music of zithers and brass gongs, and watched graceful olive-skinned girls, with smooth back hair above their brooding Eastern eyes, posturing slowly and stiffly, with sinuous, thin arms and long double-jointed fingers, henna-stained at the tips. They wore short velvet jackets, gold embroidered, with orange floating scarves and heavy silken sarongs to their small jewelled feet. Alas, their singing voices are like fairy mice, squeaking monotonously in shrill, nerve-jarring tones. It is a most singular thread of sound, frail, attenuous, yet infinitely sharp. It never changes a semitone, and the singer is as immobile as the sphinx, scarcely even moving her lips.

The superlative Hudson took us right across the blue mountains to Bandoeng, where once again we fell in love with Dutch colonization, Dutch manners, and Dutch coffee. It is delightful to drive through the streets at night when all the population is drinking its pre-prandial paheits in the cafés, or on the brilliantly illuminated verandas of the stately white houses. I have come to the conclusion that the Dutch build the best colonial houses in the world. In Java and Sumatra, or in South Africa, it is always the same model—solid and white, with big, cool courts and lofty, columned *stoeps*, wreathed with orchids or vines according to the country. Inside, the floors are marble-tiled or of dark polished wood, and the great brass-bound oak chests and gleaming marqueterie bureaux fill my soul with envy!

We saw rubber trees dripping their white sap into little tin cups, and the sheets of evil-smelling gelatinous substance hanging out to dry. We saw pale Sudanese girls stamping far-famed Orange Pekoe into square cases for export—these girls are lotus flowers abloom at thirteen, and ancient, haggard grandmothers at thirty. We saw whole hillsides white with the coffee in bloom, and we made pigs of ourselves over ripe brown mangosteens, king of all tropical fruit. Then we spent a long hot day in a "schnell-trein"— obviously a corruption of snail-train—which chugged through exquisite hilly country in its own serpentine fashion, and finally dropped us at Djokjakarta among scarlet hibiscus and white, drooping Datura blossoms—the Hindu death-flower.

Of course we made a pilgrimage to the world-famed Borobadoer, driving out there in a toy cart drawn by four amazingly small and swift ponies. Suddenly, out of the pale green sugarcane of the exquisite Kedoe valley, rises the great grey temple against a background of feathery coco-nut palms with transparent lilac shadows on the jagged mountain range beyond. Legend tells that the colossal work was undertaken by an ancient king as a penance for marrying his own daughter. Seven great carved terraces rise one above the other, enclosing the summit of a hill, and at the top a contemplative Buddha, enthroned on a sacred lotus, sits within a cupola above a bottomless well, possibly used as a burial place for priests and kings of old. The seven terraces are supposed to represent the seven planes of man's existence, as he ascends from the material to the spiritual, and the walls of each terrace are elaborately carved with scenes from the Buddhist and Brahminic legends.

R. Friederich says:

> The mixture of Buddhism and Brahminism is best seen in the three upper and inner galleries of Boro Budur. In the first we see the history of Sakyamuni, from the annunciation of his descent from the heaven of Indra till his transformation into Buddha, with some scenes of his life. The first thirteen scenes in the second gallery likewise represent Buddha as a teacher with some of his pupils; after that it would seem as if a concordat had been formed between the different cults; we have first in three separate scenes Buddha, Vishnu (Batara Guru), and Siva all together, and other groups follow Buddhistic and Siviate without distinction. It is only in the fourth gallery that we again find Buddha dominant.

It is very interesting the way in which many famous temples in the East have been used as worshipping places for different cults, apparently at the same time. In the largest temple of Angkor in Cambodia there are statues of Buddha, of Siva the Destroyer, and of Krishna in the same court. In the Kutab Minar at Delhi there are relics of Hindu worship under the shadow of the Mohammedan Pillar of Victory. Even at ruined Saranath, one of the earliest Buddhist monasteries, where there is still a Jain temple, there are some small statues of Hindu deities. Curiously enough, though Brahminism ousted Buddhism, and became the ruling religion of India, the latter was the basis on which the former developed from "the creed of a caste to the religion of a nation."

As a matter of fact, the Hindu temples at Prambanan appealed to me more than the solid mass of the Borobadoer, which is dwarfed by the glorious peaks of Kedoe, purple above the fields of grain. There are three principal buildings, and half a dozen smaller ones, all standing together in a grassy field. They are cuneiform, and open at the top to show great statues of Krishna, Shiva, Vishnu, and the elephant-headed Ganesh, before whom fresh marigolds are laid. Hanumau, the monkey god, is provided with daily rice, and huge sacred cows are the carved guardians of his shrine. It reminded me of India and the sweet scent of crushed marigolds and ghee in the Golden Temple at Benares beside the holy Ganges.

The Djokjakarta also possesses a wondrous bazaar, where in close, crowded alleys, between wooden booths, you may buy anything, from a pair of Birmingham boot-laces to a battered silver cow-bell, or from a basket of strange, sticky sweetmeats to a colossal brass elephant or the admirably wrought model of an ancient village. Undine couldn't resist the elephant, and it broke all our boxes one after another with its unwieldy weight, and, I think, when we finally arrived in England, two of its legs stuck stiffly out of the shattered hat-box. As we progressed round the world, we gradually threw away all our clothes to make room for odd curios, till ivory, china, bronze and brass were mixed up inextricably with a few dilapidated silks and muslins!

One morning, early, we went to see the Sultan's palace, and I felt we had really stepped into *The Arabian Nights' Entertainments*. First, we passed a guard of slaves with curly, black pigtails, sugar-loaf hats, and tall scarlet spears. Then we saw the red-splashed wall against which all suspected traitors are beheaded, I gather without being given much time to prove their innocence. Next, after crossing several court-yards, we came upon a guard of nobles, mostly asleep on fat, yellow bolsters; they had wonderful jewelled ivory swords stuck in their scarlet sashes, and blue cloth coats above embroidered sarongs with long trains. Into the inner courts no native may penetrate unless he is excessively *décolleté*— as our guide explained triumphantly in French—the men to the coloured sash, which marks their waists and their rank, and the women to a slightly higher line!

Farther on, we found the harem guard of old, grey-haired women, also with exquisite krisses stuck through the folds of their embroidered belts. We saw the Sultan's clothes being brought from the bath in a scarlet lacquer chest carried on the shoulders of old women under gorgeous gold umbrellas. Outside the marble and gold audience hall, we found a circle of Ministers, smoking very long, thin pipes and sitting on beautiful Persian rugs, round an old carved well out of which every moment I expected to see arise the genii of the enchanted palace. The Sultan has sixty fighting cocks, each one with a separate attendant. Except when they are taken out for exercise, these cocks sit in cages on the top of poles thirty to fifty feet high, as it is supposed to give them bold hearts and great courage to live high up in the air.

Our last effort in Java was not very successful, for we motored endless miles from Sourabaya to Tosari to see the Bromo Crater, which erupts regularly every twenty minutes. We spent two very cold nights in a little wooden hotel shivering under all the blankets, coats, and hearth-rugs we could collect, and came down from the inhospitable mountains having seen nothing at all, as thick mist had enshrouded us the whole time. After that we went to Sumatra, where there are more delightful white towns with dainty gardens and excellent hotels, but, unlike Java, civilization is confined to within a fifty-mile radius of the coast. In the interior are endless forests and high mountain ranges with blue Toba Lake hanging dizzily between earth and heaven. When they have nothing better to do, the fierce Achenese come down from the north of the island and harry the peaceful Dutch settlers.

We motored whole days through tobacco and tapioca plantations and through the grey teak forests, where lurk a small species of tiger and crowds of chattering monkeys, and we inspected Battok villages, where all the houses have steep, thatched roofs with immense eaves and are decorated with clay oxen heads with real horns. All the labour in Sumatra is Tamal or Malayan, for the native Battok will not work; he prefers to live in comfort in the hills. When Medan, with its absurd new mosque and its blindly racing eccas, each pony trying to out-trot or out-gallop its neighbour, palled upon us, we went aboard a Dutch tramp steamer and amused ourselves all the evening, as it was a neutral boat, trying to signal to the cautious British steamers, slinking swiftly through the straits with all lights veiled, but they scornfully ignored our efforts at conversation.

1919

Between Two Armies in China

From Chapters xv and xvi of
Unconducted Wanderers (1919)

Southern China

CANTON, STRANGEST CITY in all the world, held us with her lure of wealth and pain, mystery and colour. Once across the canal, which separates the foreign concession, with its neat green lawns and white square houses, from the teeming, age-old native town crushed in between grey crumbling walls, one leaves behind the matter-of-fact atmosphere of the twentieth century, and plunges into scenes that can have changed very little since the days of the Tartar siege.

Down from the wide arcades one steps through a tall gateway into a maze of narrow cobbled streets lined with silent shuttered houses. A Chinese house always has an air of aloof reserve, because it has no windows, and generally a little wall is built across the door, a few feet away from it, to keep out the evil spirits, which can only move in a straight line, and are unable, therefore, to twist round behind the protecting wall!

Canton streets are so narrow that only one sedan-chair can pass through at a time, and even then, in the busy markets, one's elbows brush bundles of embroidered shoes or strings of fat roasted duck. Above one's head the dark eaves of the houses almost meet, strips of gay-coloured silk shut out the sun. Carved and gilded dragons adorn the projecting beams of the houses. Scarlet lacquer vies with golden scrolls in profuse adornment of the shops, which are all open to the mellow gloom, and hung with great orange lanterns.

Every shop looks like a richly-carved temple, and when one does come suddenly upon a great shrine, guarded by rows of great stone beasts, one is almost disappointed because art can do no more. All the wealth of colour and design has been lavished in the long streets of the silk stores and the jade-merchants, in the market of the singing birds, and even in that dim alley, where the coffin-makers hammer all day at the vast ungainly tree-trunks that the Chinamen buy long before their deaths, and guard jealously in their houses.

Within the great walls of the old city several millions lead their crowded lives, every type of human being jostles his way through the maze of streets: rich merchants sway giddily in cushioned chairs above a pulsating, shouting sea of humanity; fragile pink and white dolls totter on tiny feet leaning on the arm of a silk-clad amah; the golden-robed lama from Thibet pushes aside the beggar, whose sores gleam through indescribable tatters; the pale scholar lifts his long silk coat-tails out of the mire, and the neat black-robed house-wife, with dangling jade ear-rings, is elbowed by clamorous coolies monotonously calling, "Hoya, hoya!" as they trot through the dense crowds swinging their burdens from stout poles.

All the spices of the world mingle with the smell of oil and hot humanity; all the colour of the world flows down from the open shop fronts in store of oranges and golden shaddock, in wealth of gorgeous embroidery, in fantastic shapes of jade and crystal, even in massed scarlet cakes and saffron macaroni; all the disease and suffering of the world looks out from under the matted hair of lepers, or from the kohl-darkened eyes of child-women.

It is strange how one can sometimes see the spirits of cities. Bangkok is a dancing girl, shaking a chime of golden bells from her fluttering skirts, dropping perfume from her henna-stained finger-tips; Macao is haunted by the click of high heels, the gleam of dark eyes and a tortoiseshell comb under a dark mantilla, a wistful spirit dragging tired feet through silent deserted streets; but the genius of Canton is something primaeval, fierce and grasping, hiding raw wounds under gorgeous silk, clutching at knowledge and wealth behind a veil that is never lifted.

There are temples, of course, amazingly dirty and quite uncared for; there are flower-boats heaped with scented trophies from the country; there is a broad river bearing the traffic of a nation towards the sea; there are canals crowded with heavy junks and painted house-boats; there are tall pagodas on lonely hills, but these things are not Canton. Only in long, footsore pilgrimages through the teeming bazaars can one come in touch even for a minute with the spirit of the walled city, changeless—because for the celestial race time exists not and fate is unalterable.

When we had worn out the soles of our shoes on the cobbles, and when our rooms were overflowing with tapestry and ivory, bronze animals with fatuous smiles and serene, but exceedingly heavy, Buddhas, we decided to go up country and try to get overland to Hankow and the beginning of the Pekin railway. Undine cheerfully pointed out to me that we should have to circumvent several armies and a great many brigands. I replied by reading to her delightful extracts from various local newspapers, which gave hair-raising accounts of atrocities committed in most of the villages through which we intended to pass. Then we interviewed the consul, who firmly refused us a passport, after which we extracted promises from various people to rescue or ransom us, and then with a very little, very necessary luggage, chiefly filled with the weighty silver coinage of the interior, we slipped away to the station to find that all trains had been commandeered by the troops.

However, a goods train full of ammunition was about to make its slow progress north, so we piled ourselves uncomfortably into the most solid-looking van, in company with forty bare-limbed coolies and some toy soldiers in charge of a much roped-up prisoner, who looked miserably uncertain as to his fate. For ten hours we crouched on the floor with rain dripping through the roof down our backs, and then, when dusk was producing eerie shadows in the corners and the coolies were gulping their evening rice, there was a sudden commotion. The train roared and rattled to a standstill, the soldiers grasped their rifles and flung themselves to the doors, a Chinese girl threw herself shrieking on to the floor, the coolies huddled in a frightened heap, and Undine remarked sleepily: "What! Brigands so soon! How very trying!"

I expected shots to fly through the wall in a minute, and was looking for the cleanest place on the floor—a Chinese soldier always shoots from the hip, and the bullets fly skyward, so as long as one lies flat, one is moderately safe—when it turned out that the cause of all the turmoil was the escape of the prisoner, who had quietly slipped off the van while his guards were eating. I am glad to say he was not recaptured in spite of a prolonged search, as he would certainly have been shot to pieces before our eyes.

At Shui-Chow, the rail-head, we emerged stiff and grimy, and a hospitable wolfram-buyer took us to his Chinese house, which was adorned with an enormous Union Jack nailed on the wall. The town was full of little grey soldiers who were billeted in all the temples, overflowed into the narrow streets, and even camped on the broad city wall, overlooking the river. A few wounded were straggling in with tales of defeat. All the men were being forcibly recruited by order of the magistrate, and one saw them drilling in sullen-looking squads in every available corner. Blue-bloused countrywomen were tottering along carrying great boxes of ammunition. Maxim guns were being trained across the river, but the two high hills which entirely commanded the town were left utterly unguarded. I believe the magistrate had actually asked for suggestions for the defence of the town from the wolfram-buyer, and had been told that the army ought to go out and fight in the open.

"But surely it would get hurt!" gasped the astounded magistrate.

At the time I thought that was the general point of view of the Southern army, but later on I changed my mind. The Chinese soldier goes to the front in a large, floppy straw hat, with a fan, an umbrella, and very often a woman coolie to carry his luggage, but apparently he fights when he gets there!

We spent two days in the grey house with a little decorated courtyard in its centre, on to which opened all the rooms, sleeping on polished wooden couches, and eating river fish and rice, while we tried to get a boat to go up the North River. The troops had commandeered everything, but by dint of much bribery we induced the owner of a long, low salt-boat to attempt the journey. We crept away through the empty streets at night, avoiding the brilliantly-lit gambling houses, where all the soldiers were playing fan-tan, and, feeling like conspirators in a Drury Lane melodrama, we reached our boat, which was moored beyond the city wall. We paddled away in the darkness and picked up our carefully selected crew some miles out in the country. Thereafter, for three days, we were poled and towed up the very rapid stream by a mob of howling, yelling coolies, who gurgled and gasped like souls in torment as they flung themselves on the bending poles. When asked to restrain their vocal efforts, they replied that they must let the breath out somehow or they would burst!

I shall always remember waking up the first morning under the low, curved roof of the boat—behind me was a little painted shrine, in front of which were burning some joss-sticks, and in front I had an uninterrupted view of Undine's golden hair spread over a bag of rice and an enormous bundle of red blankets which I took to be the wolfram-buyer! A screen of plaited reed shut off the front bit of the boat, so, in search of our retinue, which consisted of one thin and hollow cook-boy, and one fat, jelly-like interpreter, I cautiously crept out on hands and knees and crawled along the foot-board outside the boat. To my amazement, when I reached the front I discovered endless bundles of grimy rags, from which protruded various unkempt heads, and, of course, in the most comfortable corner the fat interpreter, with my only cushion under his head. Indignantly demanding the reason for the crowd, I was told that they were refugees whose only hope of getting back to their homes in the country was under our protection. As it appeared that, in addition to this, their only means of living was on *our* rice, I made a bargain that they must work their passage—consequently strange beings appeared at the poles for short periods, and then dropped off into mid-river and waded home.

At Lok Cheung, loveliest of Kwantung towns, with towering pagodas and carved belfries leaning right over the swirling brown river, we made our first halt to renew provisions. We bought chickens and oranges and lots of funny little sponge-cakes like Japanese castera, and wherever we went we were followed by a wondering crowd of women and children, who were extremely interested in our skirts and gloves—they lifted up the former and shouted with mirth at the size of our feet, while pointing to their own tiny crushed stumps. Certainly our heavy brogues were a ludicrous contrast to the dainty embroidered slippers under the swathed bands that support the swollen ankles. Mrs 4-inch foot can run pathetically on her heels, while Mrs 3-inch can only totter uncertainly. Luckily, the young girls have almost given up the habit, and, of course, the ruddy-cheeked peasant women who labour in the rice-fields go barefoot.

There were very few soldiers at Lok Cheung, so we easily got a small boat to continue up the river—cramped quarters these, for the roof was very low and not solid enough for one to perch bamboo-chairs on top, so we had to sit tailor-wise all day long, and at night there was always much dispute for the outside edge where a little air penetrated the reed screens! As we went on, the river narrowed till it became a brawling, mountain stream, with dangerous rapids through which even our large crew had great difficulty in poling us. Sometimes we had a dozen coolies on the tow ropes and nearly as many punting—yet a hundred times destruction on a sharp projecting rock was only saved by a hair's breadth. Once we passed the shattered remnants of two large boats, which could only just have upset, as their disconsolate crew were still drying themselves on the bank.

As the river narrowed, the great cliffs towered above us on either side, and the only traffic consisted of small fishing-boats full of cormorants. It is interesting to see them working at night with torch flames throwing weird shadows over rock and water—the light attracts a shoal of fish—the big black birds plunge down regardless of the strings which attach them to the boat, and each comes up with a flash of silver in his beak, unable however to swallow the dinner for which he has dived as a tight rubber ring is fixed round his throat.

We spent most of our time on board making a wonderful Union Jack, but, unfortunately, we could not remember where the white went, so we had to leave it out altogether, and personally I thought it looked remarkably like the battle flag of the Southern army! However, it inspired the retinue with much courage and pride, and we flew it from the mast till we reached Ping-Shek, where such crowds welcomed and followed us that it was almost impossible to move. Gaily dressed babies were held up to look at us, their solemn little faces framed in embroidered skull-caps with dangling amulets.

Women who were the proud possessors of sons followed us into the outhouse behind a grain merchant's shop, where we proposed to spend the night, but the despised mothers of girls were ruthlessly refused admittance. I remember in another village, when I admired a girl-baby, the sullen-looking mother pushed her into my arms and said, "Keep her, keep her, I don't want her." In the big towns superfluous girls are sold to become dancing and singing girls. The desire of every Chinese woman's life is to bear a son—thus she may hope one day to attain the honoured position of mother-in-law.

That was an awful night at Ping-Shek. We tried to get a bath, but the largest receptacle the merchant could produce was a shallow tub which leaked badly. However, Undine boldly dragged it on to the balcony above the river, but, while she was still struggling to find a moderately clean place to stand on, a dozen coolies insisted on coming into the outhouse to cook their rice. The jellyfish interpreter, scenting trouble, disappeared from view, and the cook-boy argued only half-heartedly with the angry mob, so the vision of baths had to fade into the dim and distant future. We slept on narrow boards raised on trestles, but, as John Chinaman retires to rest noisily at midnight and rises with equal clamour at 4 AM, sleep is reduced to a minimum. Besides, all the perfumes of Araby would not have sweetened the atmosphere of that shed. We traced three different odours to a dead and decaying cat in one corner, to several barrels of ancient, putrid fish in another, and to various completely open drains, but many other elusive smells wandered around at their own sweet will.

Morning brought torrents of rain. Nevertheless, after a couple of hours wasted in bargaining and weighing loads, we started off across country in Sedan chairs borne shoulder-high by ferocious-looking coolies, who put one down with a thump whenever they got tired or cross, flatly refusing to progress another step. For three days we meandered slowly across country in this fashion, chiefly through a desolate hilly region with a few grey, gloomy villages, stone built, slate-roofed, curly-eaved, generally adorned with some strips of scarlet paper exorcising the spirits of evil. We lived entirely on eggs and rice, and slept on the floor of any peasant's hovel that we came across. Sometimes one could get a bundle of straw or some trestles and boards, sometimes a charcoal fire, whose smoke nearly blinded one, as there was no chimney, and every door and window was firmly barricaded, as the country was full of deserters and small bands of brigands who lived by looting. A few weeks previously they had captured an American engineer and two missionaries and were still holding them up to ransom. I don't know which the country people feared most—the brigands or the army. They are the same thing really, for when a particularly savage band of robbers defies authority the magistrate bribes them to enlist as soldiers.

Chin-Chow

CHIN-CHOW, OUR DESTINATION on the Sian river, was in a panic. We came one morning into deserted shuttered streets, and had difficulty in finding an inn at all. Finally we turned two horn-spectacled scholars out of an upper room, looking over the river to a nine-storied pagoda throned high above the town, and modestly furnished with two beds made of boards and covered with thin straw mats. There we fed gorgeously on strange green soup in which floated all sorts of edibles, from macaroni to snails and fishes' fins, while we watched the hospital boats poling up the river, flying lots of small white flags.

The streets were full of wounded, who lay even upon the temple steps. Flags of the various generals hung in front of the biggest houses. The town had been looted for food and all the shops were shut. Tales of disaster were in the air and rumours of a battle three miles off. Every boat and every chair had been seized for the troops. The last magistrate had fled, because the Southern General had sent in a sudden demand for 30,000 dollars to pay his troops, and his successor of three days was preparing to follow his example, after having beheaded five men in the main street and forgotten to remove the debris.

Some very gallant American missionaries had turned their school, just outside the town, into a hospital, and were struggling with a couple of hundred wounded where they had beds for fifty. They worked in peril of their lives, for the Southerners had massacred the Northern wounded after a recent success, and the North had vowed revenge on the first hospital it captured. The doctor took us all over the hospital where the toy soldiers lay with their rifles under their heads and looks of sullen, mute endurance. Some of them had walked in miles with appalling abdominal wounds, and yet there were very few deaths. The instant a patient was *in extremis* the orderlies hustled him out into the veranda for fear of his spirit haunting the house. Nearly always, a Chinese is put in the coffin before he is dead, and the instant the last breath is gone the lid is shut down, so that the spirit may not escape and haunt the family.

Sometimes, when this precaution is not taken search has to be made for the spirit with wailing and calling. I've heard these cries at night by the river bank after a battle, and it is the most weird, unearthly sound—a long, rising "Kii-ii-rie" that makes one shiver and forget one lives in an electric-lighted, steam-heated age! Often they take the clothes of the dead person and go out searching for his spirit; if they see a little gust of wind whirling some dust into the air, or a dead leaf blown suddenly against a wall, they fling the clothes on top of it and believe they have caught the wandering ghost. One day in Chin-Chow we watched the funeral of a soldier. The immense coffin—a complete tree trunk, painted scarlet at the ends—was borne by some thirty mourners, who danced and shouted, jerked and bumped their burden, waved rattles, and let off fireworks—all this noise to frighten away evil spirits. Theirs is a religion of fear, it seems.

The Confucian code of ethics is little known among the peasants and only a very degraded form of Buddhism is practised. The propitiation of a multitude of spirits and the veneration of their ancestors alone occupies their minds. I was reading an old book of Chinese law once, and I discovered that the penalty for striking an elder brother was strangling; for a woman who struck her husband it was beheading; for killing a husband or father it was "slow death," which I presume means the death by a thousand cuts. A story that illustrates the extent to which the Chinese carry their veneration of their parents is told in the life of the Emperor Li'. He succeeded to the throne as a child, and his mother, the Empress-Regent, during her son's absence from the capital, killed his half-brother, the child of the former Emperor's favourite, and had the woman herself so tortured and maimed that she resembled nothing human, and could only drag herself on the ground. The boy Emperor, returning to his palace, saw the pitiful spectacle, and exclaimed impulsively, "My mother has done wrong!" All the contemporary historians recount this episode, and *all* of them blame, *not* the Empress for her cruelty, but the Emperor for criticizing his mother.

We utterly failed to get a boat at Chin-Chow, and, as our cook seemed to be in great danger of being beheaded—he was a native of Kwantung, a rival province—we decided to walk down the river bank to some smaller village, so set out accordingly with large stores of rice, some chickens, a few bandages borrowed from the kindly Samaritans, a beautiful Red Cross flag, hastily pinned together in the mission veranda, and a very frightened retinue. The cook-boy was green and livid in patches, for which he could hardly be blamed, as we'd all seen several of his country-folk tied to convenient posts awaiting the advent of the great red sword which would end all their fears. The interpreter, who always reminded me of a plump penguin with his tight white trousers tied with ribbons round his slim ankles and his long grey silk coat with flapping tails, refused to stir out of a curtained chair. Undine was feeling extraordinarily ill, as we'd had to drink river water all the way up country, and one might meet anything in that river from a humped cow to a soldier's corpse, or from a dead mule to a mountain gun. I myself was feeling far from courageous—I don't think one can be brave on bad eggs and hard rice!

However, we finally discovered a decrepit boat hidden away in a cave and, after long arguing in the burning sun, we prevailed upon an ancient, toothless crew to pole us slowly down the stream towards the Southern lines. Peace at last! We rigged up a shelter, as this was an open boat, and drifted down with the current through wonderful purple gorges, where precipice upon precipice towered high on either side, shutting out the sun, and the river flowed still and deep in perpetual shadow. Strange rock houses were hewn out of the solid face of the cliffs, and perilous temples, dragon-guarded, leaned sheer over the perpendicular mountain-side—a wild and rugged country, but exquisite in the dawn, when the first pale light broke through the sapphire mists and the mighty rocks looked like columns in dim palace aisles.

At Wai-ya-ping we came upon the ambulance fleet moored in serried ranks under the shadow of a vast cliff. They challenged us, but we floated swiftly past, and our two amazing flags probably saved us from a volley. Several times we landed to try to get fruit or firewood, but always the villages were deserted, save for some ancient crone who insisted that the fighting was very near. This so terrified the cook that he forgot even to feed the chickens, and food became scarce. However, at Yum-Shing our progress was very effectively stopped by an admirably workmanlike barrier of boats and rafts drawn right across the river and manned with many soldiers with modern rifles and large stores of ammunition. We applied bribery, threats, persuasion; all in vain. There was no way to pass that barrier.

Nothing daunted, Undine insisted on seeing the officer in charge, who supplied her with much green tea, but listened unmoved to her most subtle arguments. She assured him we were so used to war in Europe that we felt lost without the sound of guns. I gather she left him under the impression that there was daily battle in Hyde Park, and that one dodged every kind of projectile as one shopped in Bond Street. All he replied was:

"You get killed in Europe—no trouble. Perhaps you get shot here—very much money cost!"

She returned gloomily to the boat, where the wolfram-buyer and I were distributing excellent Egyptian cigarettes to the puzzled soldiery. The subsequent council of war was interrupted by commotion on the bridge of boats, where stretcher-bearers could be seen hurrying to and fro.

"Of course they're evacuating their wounded," I said, and watched with interest the procession of the halt and the lame.

"I believe they're coming here," said Undine in a small awed voice.

We looked at each other in mute horror.

"The flag! That Red Cross flag!"

I turned to tear it down, but too late—the vanguard was upon us. With much bowing, smiling, and chin-chinning a limping figure was hoisted on to the deck, who cheerfully pointed to a most horribly swollen foot, smeared over with some black oily substance, which seems to be the only dressing they use. We did our best. We struggled with sores and broken bones, and inflamed, fortnight-old wounds. The only things we firmly refused to touch were the awful skin diseases. Our stock in trade consisted of Pear's soap, cold cream, and the precious bandages that we were treasuring for our own need. Bullets we had to leave in their hidden resting-places, as the warriors had a great dislike of being hurt: the smaller the wound the more noise they made.

"I wonder now how much damage we've done with the best intentions!" I said ruefully as the last sufferer was dragged away.

"I only hope we shall get away from here before any of them die," added Undine.

They have no idea of cleanliness. They wanted us to wash our hands every two minutes—vague memory of some sojourn in a mission hospital, I suppose—but they didn't like having the wound cleaned at all.

The oddest episode happened at night when, just as we thought of curling into our rugs for a few hours' sleep, a little procession of soldiers arrived with swinging scarlet lanterns. By signs they made us understand that there were wounded in the town who needed our assistance. The wolfram-buyer and the interpreter were interviewing some reluctant general, so, while I guarded our few belongings, Undine was carried ashore by two sturdy war-riors and disappeared with a flutter of torches up the high steps leading into the single narrow street. There, apparently, a guard of honour awaited her with several hospital flags, and more musical comedy lanterns. The whole company marched briskly along to a dilapidated court, where she and her two original guides plunged into one of those labyrinthine Chinese houses that go back and back in a series of filthy passages and squalid smoke-filled, airless rooms, with here and there a small court piled with rubbish.

On an amazingly dirty bed were lying two badly wounded sol-diers, whose tattered dressings had never been removed since they were first put on on the battlefield. Undine's description of the reeking atmosphere, the circle of bayonets behind her, the suspicious, sullen faces of the family, and the appalling state of the wounded, made me glad that I had elected to stay in mid-river with only a mourner's wail, or some clashing dispute on the bridge of boats, where the guards were gambling, to break the silence of the night.

We got up with the dawn next day, and tried to get an interview with the officer Undine had seen the previous day, but were told that he had gone "to look at the battle" and, as we also learned that there were two more barricades of boats farther down the river, we decided to try our fortunes on land. We managed to impress some trembling coolies with such a magnified sense of our importance that they consented to carry our modest luggage, and once more we set forth through trampled rice-fields and woods full of pale dog-roses. We passed a telegraph section putting up a field telegraph, a couple of mountain batteries with trains of sturdy mules and some officers returning from the front in Sedan chairs, with orderlies carrying their huge swords in embroidered scarlet scabbards behind them. Our idea was to get through both the Northern and Southern armies and strike the river farther north, if possible beyond Heng-Sha, which unfortunate town was captured almost every week by a different army, while, between whiles, brigands pillaged it and held up fat merchants to ransom.

We were challenged at the first outpost, but swept through, waving English passports, French motor licenses with large red seals—any document that looked official and important! The guard started after us, and even the prisoners tied to the posts of a cattle-shed evinced a mild interest, but the attempt to stop us was only half-hearted. Our triumph, however, was short-lived, for, after traversing a peaceful, sunlit stretch of country, we turned into a wood and almost fell over a line of little grey soldiers kneeling with rifles ready to fire across the low-lying fields in front, while several machine-guns protruded wicked-looking nozzles from the undergrowth close by. For one moment the army did nothing but gape, and Undine and I had actually passed through the line before they recovered their senses. Then they rushed after us and arrested us, and I imagine the officers argued as to what was to be done with us while we stood forlornly by our chairs, Undine firmly clutching the Red Cross Flag, and the coolies huddled into little heaps round our luggage. Finally, we were sent back to headquarters surrounded by an armed guard, in company with a batch of prisoners who had to be dragged along, howling.

It was a most unpleasant march. I know *I* felt every moment that a bullet would find a resting-place in my back. The wolfram-buyer stormed in fluent Kwantungese, but as the soldiers were Hunan men nobody understood him. Undine read a novel, chiefly upside down, and the interpreter looked as if he were dying of heart disease. We were taken to a sort of barracks square, where the prisoners were instantly pushed into a very dark shed—then there was a pause, and our guard looked at us doubtfully, so we very firmly stalked out in the direction of the general's quarters. Various excited officers tried to stop us; but, feeling desperate, hungry, dirty, and extraordinarily tired, we didn't much care what happened to us, so we went on rapidly. The general had rather a nice house, with a garden full of mulberry-trees. We all sat on the veranda and drank strong green tea till our brains reeled, while we tried to persuade blandly impassive Orientals that it was essential for us to get through to Chang-Sha.

They repeatedly urged us to stay in the village till the war was over, and it was only with great difficulty that we persuaded the general to give us a pass, even to go back! The North is supported by the foreign powers, so the South is extremely anti-foreign; perhaps they looked upon us as spies. Late that night, having had nothing to eat since dawn, we regained the river to find that soldiers were occupying all the boats. However, for once the jellyfish interpreter bestirred himself, and about 4 AM we found ourselves poling slowly up-stream, the crew consisting of an old woman, a toothless septuagenarian, and a small boy tastefully attired in a blue sash and one straw sandal.

Then began our 300-miles retreat. The South had had several successes, so the country was clear of Northern troops, but there was a steady stream of refugees hurrying like ants in all directions. Delicately painted girls in pale silk coats, clutching most of their household possessions on their knees, looked timorously from

Sedan chairs; portly merchants in purple silk waded through rain and mud; strings of wounded ambled along on small, shaggy ponies—and always it rained as if the skies had burst. For a week we struggled on with little rest, fearing to find the north river impassable. When we did arrive back at Ping-Shek, only one boatman would face the torrent, and he did it only because his wife's greed exceeded his own fears. I cannot imagine why we got down safely. The rapids were roaring whirlpools through which we dashed, swirling right across the river, sometimes turning completely round, the water pouring in torrents right over us, four men clinging for dear life to the rudder, the rest hammering equally feverishly at boards which continually broke loose under the strain. It was impossible to keep one's feet. One lay in the bottom of the boat, while every timber shuddered and cracked, and the wild howls of the boatmen rose piercingly above the crash of the turbulent water.

Ours was the only boat on the river—gone were fishermen and cormorants, slow-moving salt boats and family junks. Sometimes amazed peasants shouted to us from the banks as we whirled past, but the next jutting rock, the next sharp corner engaged our whole attention. In the smooth stream between the rapids the whole crew crouched down chin-chinning to the spirits. It took us six days and nights to go up that river. We came down in less than twelve hours, and were inside the grey walls of Shui-Chow before nightfall. Great masses of troops had moved in since our departure, and we watched them drilling briskly across the river. The cavalry ride ponies scarcely larger than Shetlands, and they look like little brown mice scampering about. A first-class ambulance station had been erected at the railroad, and all the horses were decorated with half a dozen red crosses all over them. Our train journey provided us with no excitement, which was lucky, as two days later the mail between Canton and Kowloon—the

British Concession on the mainland opposite Hong Kong—was attacked by several hundred brigands, and every carriage was ransacked. There were nearly two hundred fully-armed soldiers on the train, but it never occurred to them to fight!

Hong Kong appeared to us a sort of Nirvana of shower baths and French cooking. We had not had our clothes off for three weeks, we had not met a hot bath for so long that we'd almost forgotten the existence of such things; the number of eggs— mostly bad—that we'd eaten would horrify the food controller, and Undine's golden hair was like mouldy hay! We spent a cheerful week discussing what we were going to eat at every meal, and were further enlivened by news that the stern consul who had refused a Chinese passport for the Interior had grown several new grey hairs and wasted a good deal of Government money trying to trace us. His gratitude for our safe return not being unmixed with wrath, he had sent the minions of the law to arrest us on the Canton platform.

Now the up-country train generally arrives any time between five PM and midnight, but that particular day it chose to pant into the surprised station about four o'clock, so we were both eating buttered toast on board a big white river steamer when the representatives of law and order arrived on the platform. However, I believe they spent a very pleasant evening searching all the hotels in Canton, no doubt under the impression that they were looking for dangerous spies instead of two adventurous, travel-worn tourists.

Rumours afterwards reached us that we'd been arrested as we stepped on board an American liner, that we were found hiding in the Portuguese settlement of Macao, and that we were disguised as men! It seems easy to attain notoriety in China!

1921

The Secret of the Sahara: Kufara

From Chapters I and XIV of
The Secret of the Sahara: Kufara (1921)

We Enter on the
Great Adventure

THE GREAT ADVENTURE began at Jedabia, 190 kilometres from Benghazi as the crow flies. It is only a group of scattered sand houses, with the mysterious windowless walls of the East, flung down on a wide space of white rock and sand, yet it is the home of the great Senussi family. We arrived there on November 28, 1920, having come by divers methods across the stretch of stony desert which lies to the southwest of Benghazi, the capital of Cyrenaica. It is an almost deserted country of flat reddish sand, sprinkled with rocks and tufts of coarse grey grass which provides food for rare camel caravans and fuel for the Beduin fires. There are no made roads, but rough tracks link the scattered Italian forts, manned by companies of stalwart Eritreans and irregular Arab levies. To the south, the *altipiano* rises in a faint line of purple cliff which catches wonderful reflections in the setting sun. Otherwise the vista is intensely monotonous save for an occasional encampment of Auwaghir. Unlike the solid black "beit esh shar"[1] of the Syrian or Algerian nomad, their tents

---

1 Camel's hair tent.

are of the poorest description, made of patched sacking of various grey-brown shades; they are very low-pitched, so that even in the centre one cannot stand upright.

In the dry season, wherever there are wells, may be seen congregated flocks of sheep and goats and herds of camels numbering many thousands. After rain, however, so much water lies out on the rocky ground that the animals can drink wherever they like, so the country presents its most deserted appearance.

Benghazi is a little white town lying on the very edge of the Mediterranean breakers, unprotected by harbour or mole. Famine and disease considerably reduced its population during the War and the suqs[2] are almost deserted. An occasional donkey with scarlet tassels and a load of fresh dates passes down the Sidi Shabi where European stores and native booths stand side by side. A few camels come in from the country half buried beneath huge sacks of grain. In the evening there is a mustering of bearded merchants at the little café by the mosque, while contemptuous Askari in scarlet tarboushes and swinging capes stroll by, smoking Italian cigarettes, but the life of the town is confined to the European quarter containing the hotel and the Government offices.

The biggest of the white, Oriental-looking buildings is Government House, with a double line of great Moorish arches decorating its imposing façade. So different from the windowless dwellings of Jedabia with their discreet high-walled yards, yet it was there that I first saw Es Sayed Mohammed Idris bin es Sayed el Mahdi es Senussi, the man whose power is felt even beyond the boundaries of Libya and Cyrenaica. The Italians and the Senussi had ratified a few days before the provisional treaty of 1916 and there were great festas at Benghazi in honour of the newly made

---

2 Markets.

Emir, who was spending a few days in the capital on his way to Italy to visit the King.

There had been an official reception and down the broad steps moved the black mass of Italian uniforms splashed with the vivid blue of their gala sashes and the glint of their gay-ribboned medals. Foremost came the Governor, Senator de Martino, in the green and gold uniform of a Knight of Malta, and General Di Vita, with his splendid rows of decorations. Between them walked a figure which dominated the group and yet gave one the impression of being utterly remote from it. Robed all in white, in silken kaftan and trailing burnus,[3] the rich kufiya[4] flowing beneath a golden agal,[5] with no jewel or embroidery to mark his state, Sidi Idris came slowly forward leaning on a silver-handled stick. An Italian officer murmured in my ear, "Give him a longer beard and he would be the pictured Christ!" He was right. The ascetic leader of one of the greatest religious confraternities in the world had the strange, visionary eyes of the prophets of old. His long face had hollows under the cheek-bones. The lips were pale and the olive skin almost waxen. He looked out, under a broad brow, dreamily, far beyond the pageant prepared in his honour, to realms even more remote than his own untrodden deserts. Thus might the Nazarene have walked among the legionaries of Rome!

The following day I met the Emir at a dinner which Omar Pasha gave in his honour. Before the other guests arrived we conversed, I in faltering Egyptian Arabic, he in the classical language of the Hejaz. In the same flowing white robes he sat in a great chair at the head of the room and in a long line beside him sat the ekhwan[6] who were to accompany him to Italy. They were

---

3 Arab garment.

4 Arab head-dress.

5 The thick cords worn on the head above the *kufiya*.

6 Brothers. Used colloquially in Libya to mean "a brother."

a picturesque sight in their multi-coloured robes of ceremony. Prominent among them was the General Ali Basha el Abdya, a delightful bearded personage with a complete set of gold teeth, which touch of modernity contrasted oddly with his crimson kaftan and splendid dark burnus bordered with silver. Beside him sat the venerable Sharuf Basha el Ghariam, who had been the teacher of Sidi Idris and was now his most trusted councillor. His jerd[7] was a sombre brown, and the end of it covered his head over a close-fitting white ma-araka,[8] but his kaftan, with long embroidered sleeves, was vivid rose. He had a kindly, serious face and seemed much more interested in his surroundings than the others.

I stumbled over my words of formal greeting, expressed in the unaccustomed plural, wondering whether the man who looked so infinitely remote and uninterested would even listen to what I was saying. The brooding eyes softened suddenly and a smile that was veritable light flashed across his face. If graciousness be the token of royalty, then Sidi Idris is crowned by his smile! For such a look the Beduin prostrates himself to kiss the dust the holy feet have pressed! Thereafter we talked of my journey and he blessed me in his frail voice, smiling still and saying, "May Allah give you your wish!" I tried to tell him of my love of the desert, of how I was happiest when, from a narrow camp bed, I could look at the triangular patch of starlight beyond the flap of my tent. "I, too," he said, "cannot stay more than a month in one place. Then I must move, for I love the *scent* of the desert." It is true there is a *scent* in the desert, though there may be no flower or tree or blade of grass within miles. It is the essence of the untrodden, untarnished earth herself!

---

7 Native garment—a strip of woolen or silk stuff.

8 Skull cap.

We dined gorgeously on lambs roasted whole and stuffed with all sorts of good things—rice, raisins and almonds—and on strange, sticky sweetmeats that I loved and bowls of cinnamon-powdered junket and, best of all, the delicious thick Arab coffee, but the Emir ate little and spoke less. The Senussi law forbids drinking and smoking as also the use of gold for personal adornment, so after the meal glasses of sweet tea flavoured with mint leaves were handed round to the solemn ekhwan, who took no notice whatever of their fellow guests, consisting of the Governor, the general, the captain of the light cruiser which was to carry the Senussi to Italy, and myself. Omar Pasha made me sit beside the Emir, who suddenly turned to his venerable followers, "Come and salute this lady," he said, and instantly, with the unquestioning obedience of children, they clambered up from their low chairs and moved in a body towards me. "Aselamu Aleikum" they murmured gravely as they shook my hand without raising their eyes, but giving me the Moslem salutation to a Moslem!

Benghazi was *en fête* those days. There were so many ceremonies—a review, a great dinner in the Governor's palace in honour of Italy's new ally—so I did not see Sidi Idris again till the last night of his stay, when there was a general reception which brought streams of Arab notables as well as Europeans to witness the fireworks from the wide verandas of His Excellency's dwelling. I saw the Emir standing aloof from the chattering crowd, his ekhwan near him, and wondered what he thought of us all. Half the guests were of his own race and creed, yet not here was his real kingdom, but among the ten thousand Beduin who spring to horse or camel at his word, among the hundred thousand pilgrims who learn the law from his zawias![9] We stood together on a wind-swept balcony and looked down at

---

9 Colleges.

a wild dance of Abyssinian soldiers. A thousand black figures, each bearing a flaring torch, gyrated madly in the moonlight, yelling hoarse songs of victory and prowess. The three things a man may be justly proud of in Abyssinia are killing a lion, an elephant or his enemy! The fantastic dance we saw might celebrate one or other of these achievements. Gradually whirling into tempestuous circles, the soldiers flung their torches into flaming piles in the centre and their chaunt rose stronger on the wind. Sayed Idris was pleased: "You will see ceremonies like this in my country," he said, "but there will be no houses. You will not miss them."

The moment the last gun, announcing the Emir's departure for Italy, had been fired, Hassanein Bey and I climbed into the car most kindly lent by the Government. When he first consented to accompany me to the Libyan Desert, where his knowledge of the language, religion and customs was invaluable to me, Hassanein Bey assured me that he came for a rest cure. Later on he assumed so many characters that it was somewhat difficult to keep count. He was always the QMG of our little expedition and he used to produce macaroons at the most impossible moments from equally impossible places! He was a chaperon when elderly sheikhs demanded my hand in marriage, a fanatic of the most bitter type when it was necessary to impress the local mind, my Imam when we prayed in public, a child when he lost his only pair of primrose yellow slippers, a cook when we stole a bottle of Marsala from the last Italian fort and chased a thin hen till, in desperation, she laid an egg for our *zabaglione*! He also made the darkest plans for being a villain and murdering anyone who interfered with our affairs, and I nervously listened to tales of sudden disappearances in the Sahara.

However, on the day of our departure from Benghazi he was distinctly subdued, for, on looking at our piles of camp kit and my two very small suit-cases, I had suddenly noticed several exceedingly large and heavy leather bags. With horror I demanded if they were all absolutely necessary to his personal comfort. "Yes, really!" he assured me. "They are only actual necessities. As a matter of fact they are half empty. I thought they would be useful for putting things in." The words were hardly out of his mouth when one of the opulent-looking cases, slipping from the Arab servant's hand, burst open and deposited at my feet a large bottle of "Heure bleue" bath salts, several packets of salted almonds and a sticky mass of chocolates and marrons glacés, together with a pair of patent leather shoes and a resplendent Balliol blazer. Words failed me! "Necessities!" I stuttered as I marched towards the camion to see that the heaviest cases of provisions were not put on top of the rather fragile fanatis[10] intended for carrying water.

Ten minutes after leaving Benghazi the white town with its slender minarets had disappeared into the sand, and our camions crawled like great grey beetles over a sunlit waste, with here and there a line of camels black against the horizon. It was the season of sowing and the tribes were scattered far and wide, planting the barley that would suffice for their frugal life next year. Here and there, as we went farther inland, a stooping figure, in close-wound white jerd, pushed a plough drawn by a camel, while a friend guarded his labours, rifle slung across his back. Sometimes a rare traveller on gaily caparisoned mule, his coarse brown jerd flung over his head and hiding the scarlet sederiya[11] beneath, gave us grave greeting, "Marhaba!" "Bien venu!" We spent a night at Soluk, where the wells had attracted a great flock of sheep, black and brown, numbering about a thousand. The following day we rode the thirty kilometres to Ghemines on wiry Arab horses with

---

10 Tin water carriers.

11 A short shirt.

mouths like iron beneath the wicked curved bits, and high-pom-
melled saddles mounted on black sheepskins. Three irregulars of
the Auwaghir band accompanied us, generally galloping round us
in circles by way of showing off their horsemanship.

A small encampment of some half-dozen tents lay beside our
path, so we turned in to see if they would make us tea. At first they
refused because I was a Christian. Then a woman in striped red
and yellow barracan,[12] with a heavy necklace of carved silver, came
out to inspect us. "It is all right," she said to the others. "She is a
nice little thing and she has a Moslem with her"—this in appreciation of Hassanein Bey's white brocaded kufiya. They spread a scarlet camel's hair rug for us to sit on, but they were not really convinced of our good faith. My companion began asking the men if
they had made the pilgrimage to Mecca. "Not yet," said the oldest
wistfully. "What is written is written. If Allah wills it, I shall go."

We were rapidly making friends when a fierce-looking individual with a hard weather-beaten face and stern eyes appeared. He
carried tea and sugar, but bargained for them violently, thinking
we were both the scorned Nasrani.[13] When we told him we knew
Sayed Idris, he laughed in our faces. "Our lord Idris is travelling,"
he said. "Would you like to see a letter from him?" I asked. Awe
showed on all their faces, and their eyes followed Hassanein Bey's
every movement as he pulled out the somewhat crumpled enve-
lope from his pocket. They read the superscription reverently, and
then one by one kissed it with passionate earnestness and gravely
pressed it to their foreheads. They returned it in complete silence.
Without a word the atmosphere changed. The fanatic looked at us
with humble yearning. The old man's eyes were glazed. We knew
that we could have told these three men to get up and follow us to

12 A long cotton garment worn by the women.
13 Christian.

an unknown destination and they would have obeyed with unquestioning, ungrudging faith. "Sidi Idris has gone to visit the King of Italy," I said. "He has been made an Emir." They accepted the statement indifferently. How could a mere king confer honour on the man whom Allah himself had distinguished above all others living? As we remounted the old man kissed my hand with tender eyes, murmuring, "Inshallah ma temut illa Islam,"[14] and we galloped away amidst the wild "Ulla-la-een"[15] of the women and children.

Ghemines to Zuetina meant 120 kilometres in a camion over a very bad sandy track, but that night I slept in a tent for the first time for six months. There was a wonderful starry sky with a full moon, and a Senussi sheikh rode in to see us on a splendid grey horse with a scarlet saddle. The high pommels back and front and the wide stirrups were of silver, and the purple-tasselled bridle was heavily embossed with the same metal. Sayed Mohammed Hilal es Senussi is a cousin of Sidi Idris and a brother of the Sayed Ahmed es Sherif who fled to Turkey at the end of the War. A kindly, cheerful personage, he apparently had cut adrift from the stern rules of his order and found charm in a semi-European life. His language was so full of rhetorical flowers that I found it difficult to understand, but he lent me an excellent horse for the journey to Jedabia. He also requested me to deliver to his cousin, Sayed Rida, a poetic epistle which began, "Oh freshness of my eyes, may Allah bless your morning with peace and joy."

The sand dunes of Zuetina gave way to a flat, colourless waste tufted with grey brushwood. As we turned our horses' heads inland tiny jerboas scuttered into their holes at our approach, and occasionally a great hawk wheeled above our heads. Otherwise there was no sign of life save one solitary horseman in white

---

14 If God wills (or I hope) you will die a Moslem.

15 Women's cry of rejoicing.

jerd on a white horse and a boy sitting on a pile of stones playing an odd little tune on a wooden flute. Our grey Arab mounts
were tired when at last we mounted a low rise and saw before us
a fringe of patched Beduin tents. It was the first step on a long
journey. Everything was uncertain. There were so many difficulties to be surmounted, but we felt that now, at least, the last trace
of Europe lay behind us. We breathed more freely. We both loved
the desert and the dwellers therein, and we felt that they must
understand and respond to our sympathy. I turned to Hassanein
Bey as the sandy track ran between the blind mud walls that I had
seen in so many countries. "I feel as if I had left behind me the last
shred of civilisation. The simplicity of life is beginning to impreg-
nate me. I believe that old Beduin's blessing has bewitched me.
When we leave the desert I shall be a Moslem."

We sent to ask if Sayed Rida el Mahdi es Senussi, the brother
and wakil[16] of Sidi Idris, would receive us and we waited for an
answer at the edge of the suq, where grave, bearded men, with
the wistful eyes of those who look at far horizons, stood in white-
robed groups. A few camels lay beside piles of grain, but otherwise
the wide open spaces between the square walled-in yards, where
there were Arab houses, were deserted. The banner of the Senussi
family, a silver crescent and star on a black ground, floated over
two of the houses and the protesting roar of laden camels came
from one of the larger enclosures, for Sayed Safi ed Din, cousin
of Sidi Idris and brother of the banished Ahmed, was travelling
to the interior the following day with the whole of his family and
sixty beasts of burden.

A soldier of the Arab guard brought us news that the Sayed
would receive us at once and we dismounted in one of the windowless yards before the door of a big white house. We were ushered

---

16 Representative (steward or lieutenant-governor).

into the usual Arab reception room with a stiff row of crimson brocaded chairs and sofas round the walls and a table covered by a beautiful embroidered satin cloth in the centre. Sayed Rida came forward to meet us with a reflection of his brother's smile. One liked him at once. One appreciated instantly his warm kindliness and hospitality. Sidi Idris is a mystic imbued with the aloof dignity of another world, but his wakil is young, spontaneous and sympathetic, with a very simple, unaffected manner. He offered us immediately a house to live in while we were in Jedabia and put at our disposal a cook and two other servants. He made me talk Arabic to him and corrected my mistakes with his broadest smile. Sweet tea, flavoured with mint, appeared in delightful, painted glass cups, and I soon felt as if I had known our host for years. He was amused and interested in our divers journeys. He made plans to show us a falcon hunt. He wanted to give us instantly anything from horses to dates. In fact, I felt that I was in the presence of a magician who could wave his wand and produce the wish of my heart! In appearance Sayed Rida is large and imposing with a round, olive face and very dark eyes, soft as velvet, which crinkle up humorously as he smiles widely, showing strong white teeth. He wore a black jelabia[17] under his striped silk jerd, snowy white, and a rolled white turban above a red ma-araka. Arab hospitality is famous throughout the world, but we left the dignified presence of Sayed Rida feeling almost overwhelmed at his gracious welcome.

Our temporary home fascinated me. A solitary door pierced the mysterious expanse of yellow wall made of sun-dried blocks of sand of all sizes and shapes. One passed through a small roofed court to a wide sunlit yard whose high walls ensure the complete privacy of an Arab family. Hassanein Bey had a small room at one end and I a great high chamber, hung with texts from the Koran.

---

17 Wide native coat.

We were a kingdom to ourselves, for there was a well just under my window, charcoal in an outhouse and a large yard beyond where we could have housed camels and horses. As it was, we stored our simple outfit in it, for the evening was dry and fine. We knew from the beginning that we must travel light and that our final success might depend on our capability for riding fast and far. We might have to leave all our luggage by the way and, disguised as Beduin camel-drivers, slip away in the night into the uncharted land where none may follow.

Thus, besides our sacks of rice, tea and sugar—the two latter intended for gifts to Beduins who helped us on our journey— we had only a single fly tent, eleven feet by eight feet, which could be divided into two by means of a canvas curtain, a waterproof ground-sheet and a couple of beds which rolled into our immensely thick, wool-lined sleeping sacks, a small army canteen that was so heavy that we had grave doubts as to its eventual fate, a canvas washing basin and a shamadan case complete with vast supply of candles, for I foresaw burning much midnight wax over note-books and maps. We had reduced our provisions to the minimum which would support human life for four months, such as coffee, tins of army rations, slabs of chocolate, tins of cocoa and milk already mixed, bully beef, vegetables to avoid scurvy, and malted milk tablets, but the daily ration was absurdly small, for we trusted to supplement it with dates and rice.

By the light of Hassanein Bey's electric torch we picked our way back over flat white rock and sand to Sayed Rida's house to dine. This time we found our host accompanied by Sayed Safi ed Din, "the little warrior," as he is called among the tribes. He is a boy with a vivacious, pale face, a charming manner and a ready wit. He is intelligent and, far more than the others, he is interested in the ways of Europe. "I think we should get on well," he said, "for you are as curious about me as I am about you!"

The memory of that dinner will haunt me for a long time, for it consisted of twelve courses, of which eight were meat in one form or another. We began eating at seven-thirty and at ten-thirty the beautifully scented tea with sprigs of mint made its welcome appearance. During these three hours we ate soup, chicken, hashed mutton, slices of roast mutton, aubergines stuffed with sausage meat, fried chops, shoulder of mutton cooked in batter, ragout of mutton with vegetables, stuffed tomatoes, boiled mutton with marrow, savoury rice and sweet omelette. It can be easily imagined that the feast left us a little silent and comatose, but not so our host. He was literally brimming over with kindness and forethought. I was suffering at the time from a severely dislocated foot, which had not been improved by the long ride, and I was obliged to hobble in one shoe and a swollen native slipper by the aid of a stick. Sayed Rida slipped away for a minute in the middle of the meal and when we left the house, lo and behold, a horse was waiting for me outside the door! His kindliness was as simple and natural as his whole bearing. We asked him if he travelled much and he replied, "I have not time. I have so much work. You know it is just like planting a garden. Everything grows and grows till one's time is full!" This from the Emir's wakil, whose word was borne across half the deserts of the world, to Nigeria, to the Sudan, to the outposts of Morocco, to the doors of the "House of Allah" (Mecca).

I remember opening my shutters that night to a flood of moonlight as clear as the day. A faint myrrh-scented breeze, icy cold from the Sahara, came in, and I wondered whether it had blown over the unknown oasis we hoped to reach. We had had a long talk that evening of past difficulties and future plans. In Italy Kufara represents the goal of so many hopes, in Cyrenaica the ambition of so many daring young political officers, that it is difficult to realise that in England it is an unknown name. The sacred place of the Sahara, the far-off oasis, six hundred kilometres from Jalo, which in itself is seven days' rapid journey from the outskirts of civilisation, is spoken of with awe and longing in Benghazi. "I will tell you a great secret," said the Italian major who had spent a couple of days with Sidi Idris at Jaghabub, and had therefore penetrated many hundreds of kilometres farther into the interior than any of his compatriots, "Some day I want to go to Kufara. No one has ever been there except Rohlfs, forty years ago, and he saw nothing—nothing at all!"

Without going deeply into the story of the Senussi confraternity, it may be explained that their founder, Sidi Mohammed Ben Ali es Senussi, preached his doctrine of a pure and ascetic Islam from Morocco to Mecca, but his teachings met with their greatest success in Cyrenaica, where the Beduin had almost lapsed from the faith of their fathers. Rapidly his zawia spread along the coast, and his authority was acknowledged by the Sultan of Wadai, who made him responsible for the caravans traversing the great deserts of Wadai, the Fezzan and Lake Chad. Thus the stern beliefs of the Senussi spread with every caravan that went into the interior. Mohammed Ben Ali, so holy that he never unveiled his face to his disciples, so honoured that his followers prostrated themselves to kiss his footprints, died at Jaghabub in 1850 and left to his son, Mohammed el Mahdi, the leadership of one of the greatest and fiercest religious confraternities in the world. Their laws were harsh—for even smelling of smoke a man might lose his right hand! Their hatred of the infidel was fanatical. They ousted the Zouia and Tebu from their ancient homes in Kebabo and established impregnably their holy of holies in this oasis which nature herself had protected by surrounding it with a belt of mighty dunes and two hundred and fifty miles of waterless desert.

Kufara, the Kebabo of old, lies some six hundred kilometres south, faintly south-east, of Jalo. It is the heart of the Eastern

Sahara and the centre of its trade, for the only big caravan route from the Sudan and Wadai to the north passes through it, yet the journey is so difficult that none but the strongest caravans can attempt it. From the well at Buttafal, a day's journey south of Jalo, seven hard, waterless days bring the traveller to Zieghen, where there is a well, but no fodder or oasis. After that he must continue another five days, two of which are through dunes, before he reach Hawari, the outskirts of the Kufara group, sometimes considered by the Arabs to be a separate oasis because it is divided from the main group by a chain of mountains. This is the main route and the easiest. It continues to Wadai.

To the west of this track lie three other oases. The first, Taiserbo, is also seven days' waterless journey from Buttafal and it is rarely approached, for it has neither civil, religious, nor commercial importance, but its Tebu ruins might make it of interest historically. Some hundred and fifty kilometres beyond in a south-westerly direction is Buseima, which is famous for its dates, for which caravans sometimes visit it, and still farther south lies Ribiana, to all description a lawless spot from which come the marauding bands which make the neighbourhood of Buseima exceedingly dangerous.

Of course, all this information was acquired at a later date. When I arrived at Jedabia I knew less than nothing of Libyan geography. I did not know that the principal villages in Kufara were Jof, the seat of government, and Taj, the holy of holies of the Senussi faith. I did not know that mountains and lakes, fields of tamarisk and acacia, peaches, grapes and figs were to be found in this Garden of Eden lost amid the impenetrable sands, between the Dakhla Desert to the east, untraversed by Europeans, and to the west the trackless waste stretching to Uau Szerir at the edge of Tripolitania, to which remote prison some of the unfortunate survivors of the Miani column were sent as prisoners. To me,

Kufara was almost a mirage. It represented the secret which the Sahara had rigidly guarded for so long against Christian eyes. The tragic story of Rohlfs' ill-fated expedition fired my enthusiasm to reach this centre of the world's most fanatical confraternity, the unknown, mysterious country untrod by foot of stranger, be he Christian or Moslem.

Having regard to the amazing difficulties of the journey and the almost maniacal hatred with which strangers are regarded, it is natural that, with one possible exception, no European should ever have been able to reach the sacred cluster of zawias and morabits[18] at Taj. A French prisoner spent some time in Kufara during the war; he was sent there from Uau Szerir by order of Sayed Ahmed. Over forty years ago a German explorer made a very gallant attempt to solve the mystery of the far-off oasis. In 1879 the Kaiser Wilhelm I sent a scientific expedition to Libya consisting of four men—Rohlfs, Steeker, Eckhart and Hubner. It was backed by the whole power of Turkey. It carried magnificent presents from the Emperor. It was laden with cases of silver and gold. Hostages were held at Benghazi, while Rohlfs led his party to the southern deserts. He left Jalo on July 5 with a hundred camels and a large escort of Zouias mounted on horses, including several sheikhs, the principal of whom was Bu Guettin. He accomplished the amazing feat of reaching Taiserbo in four and a half days, by riding nearly twenty hours out of the twenty-four. In his most interesting book on his North African travels, which has unfortunately not been translated into English, he suggests that Taiserbo may have been the site of the original Tebu sultanate, as he saw ruins which might possibly be those of a castle or stronghold at Diranjedi. He continued his southern course by way of Buseima, till he reached Hawawiri, where he was persuaded by

---

18 Tombs of holy people.

a friendly sheikh, Korayim Abd Rabu, to camp in an outlying palm grove to avoid any friction with the villagers, who refused to allow the Nasrani to enter their country.

The plucky Teuton describes the gathering outside his tent and the long discussion as to whether he and his companions should be murdered or not. The day following, August 14, they were induced by Bu Guettin and the treacherous Zouias, who were fanatically opposed to the presence of strangers and greedy to share the spoils of so rich a caravan, to leave Hawawiri and, skirting the oasis, to isolate themselves in Boema, the loneliest and most deserted spot in the whole group. Rohlfs apparently agreed to this plan because the neighbourhood of any of the main villages was dangerous. He had to oppose the combined hatred of the ekhwan and pupils of the zawias, religious fanatics, the villagers who jealously guarded the privacy of their country and the passing caravans of pilgrims and merchants. After being held a prisoner for nearly a month in this lonely camp, in daily fear for his life, he was helped to escape by his original friend, Korayim, who took him by night, with his three companions, to his son-in-law's camp, somewhere in the neighbourhood of Zuruk. That very night the German's camp was attacked and looted. Every single note-book, map, drawing and scientific instrument was destroyed, so Rohlfs was unable to attempt much description even of his journey up to Hawawiri.

In the book which he calls "Kufra" he devotes a chapter to his perils and battles in that inhospitable oasis, but, after his rescue by Korayim, whose son we met at Taj, his narrative becomes very disjointed. He was moved to another place before being allowed to leave the oasis. He himself thinks it was Jof, but from his description of the journey this seems impossible. He spent another fortnight under the surveillance of Korayim—he tells us that he was not allowed to move without a guard of twenty rifles—during which he seems to have confronted every form of extortion and threat with calm and intrepidity. On September 27 he left the oasis with Korayim, who took him all the way to Benghazi, where, unfortunately, the sheikh died. Consequently there is a legend that Rohlfs poisoned him. With experience of the greed of our own escort, I came to the conclusion that the grateful German probably gave him too much of his own cherished stores and the Arab over-ate!

After this ill-fated expedition no alien presence cast a shadow on the sanctity and isolation of Kufara till Sayed Ahmed sent his prisoner there. Many attempts were made from Siwa to pierce the first barrier of dunes, but in vain. The secrets which Rohlfs had so nearly solved remained wrapped in the mirage of the great deserts and Kufara was still a legend more than a fact.

The amicable relations at present existing between Italy and the Senussi, and the genuine friendship of Senator de Martino and Sayed Idris made it easy for us to reach Jedabia as the guests of the former's most hospitable Government, but thenceforth it was left us to fend for ourselves. We could not take our kindly hosts of Benghazi into our confidence, as they would have been aghast at the idea of a young woman venturing alone into a territory as yet unexplored. The agreement that had just been signed with Sidi Idris gave them control of the whole of Cyrenaica, thus assuring a future of great prosperity to the colony, but it left the great Libyan desert from Aujela to Jaghabub, with Kufara still another six hundred kilometres to the south, in the hands of Sayed Idris as an independent ruler under Italian protection.

A most humorous complication added immensely to our difficulties. Hassanein Bey, having been secretary to the Italo-British Mission which arranged the treaty of 1916 with the Senussi, was promptly suspected of the darkest Pan-Islamic designs. For a week at Benghazi we lived in a state of suspense. Intrigue was in the air and everyone suspected the motives of everyone else. If a camion broke down, we decided that we were not to be allowed to reach Jedabia. If Hassanein spoke to a Beduin, using the Moslem salutation, the eyes of our so-called interpreter would almost pop out of his head with interest and dismay. Relays of kindly individuals took the utmost interest in our history, plans, ideas and belongings. We were "pumped" until we could not think of anything more to say; and we, in turn "pumped" every hospitable and amiable individual who politely and indifferently asked us our destination! At times we must have worn such strained and agonised expressions that I wonder we were not suspected of Bolshevism at the very least. The most amusing part of the business was afforded by the spies who constantly surrounded us and who were so thrilled with their own importance that I used to have daily fights with Hassanein Bey to prevent him playing delightful little comedies to excite them still more.

However, once Jedabia was reached we felt happier. The open desert lay before us and the lure of the great tracks south! Somewhere far beyond the pale mauve line of the horizon lay the secret of the Sahara, the oasis which had become the goal of every explorer, from the enthusiastic coastguard officers who dreamed of forcing a trotting hajin[19] through the sands, to the governments whose camions and light-car patrols had failed to pierce the waterless drifts. The masked Tuaregs, those lawless riders who threaten the lumbering south-bound caravans, bring strange tales of a white race, blue-eyed, fair-haired, whose women live unveiled with their men. Legend has attributed its home to the mysterious oasis whose position varies according to the whims of the mapmaker. "Inshallah" I breathed to the stars and the winds!

---

19 Riding camel.

The Elusive Dunes

O N FEBRUARY 2 we started north at 6.30 AM after a violent argument as to the best way of saving the camels. I wanted to follow the summer plan, start an hour before sunset, walk all night and camp two hours after dawn. One can do much longer marches this way, but the Beduins were reluctant to face the cold of the night. On the other hand, Mohammed was desperately afraid of another sandstorm, which would inevitably delay us. He therefore wanted to walk at least 15 hours a day. It is an unfortunate fact that a camel does 13 hours, at a pace of 4 kilometres, infinitely easier than 10 hours at 5. He is capable of plodding along evenly without halting for an indefinite time, but the slower he goes the longer he will last. Mohammed was a bad camel-man. Frightened of the desperately long route in front of him, which had to be traversed in 12 days, he was anxious to push on at first in order to have something up his sleeve; yet the loads, chiefly fodder and water, would grow lighter every day. I refused, therefore, to do more than 12 or 13 hours a day, especially as our camels would not feed properly when it was dark and cold. The best way of travelling is to start at 5 AM, barrak for a few hours at midday, feed the camels as the afternoon grows cooler and walk late into the night. But it means a double loading and we had not enough men or energy for that, so our beasts had to accustom themselves to feeding by starlight night and morning.

That first day we had a cool wind, so we all walked cheerfully across the unbroken stretches of monotonous fawn sand. The world had become a level disk again, infinitely flat, its smoothness polished by the glaring sun till the mirage broke the edges, which seemed but a few yards away. I asked old Suleiman how he knew the way. "You put Jedi[1] over your left eye and walk a long way— thus. Then you turn a little toward the kibla[2] and walk still more and then, if Allah wills, you arrive." It was not exactly a reassuring answer after Abdullah's vagaries, so I asked him where Jedi was at the moment. "I don't know," he replied with engaging frankness. "Where is she?" I showed him by the compass and he trudged on perfectly placidly, nibbling a date from the little store he kept tied up in a corner of his tattered jerd.

When the sunset had painted our narrow world flame-red and, one by one, the stars had come out to show how infinitely remote is "that inverted bowl we call the sky," Mohammed pleaded for an extra spurt. "Let us just put that star out," he urged, pointing to the brightest point in the west. Having noticed, however, that all the camels were stumbling and swinging out of the line, I thought a race with the evening star would be a mistake, so I insisted on bar-raking. We made no zariba,[3] leaving the loads ready coupled for the morning. We had taken very little hattab[4] from the Mehemsa[5] because of the weight, so our fire was of the smallest description and we should have been asleep in an hour, but for a prolonged

1 The Pole star.
2 The kibla is turned towards the ka-aba at Mecca.
3 Improvised stockade constructed of thorny bushes—Ed.
4 Mounds covered with sticks and leafless bushes.
5 Feeding ground.

dispute between Mohammed and Suleiman as to the necessity of agaling[6] the camels. "They will not move, my son," said Suleiman. "They are tired, like me, and I am an old man." "Old, too, in experience," replied our polite retainer, "but make my heart at peace by agaling them." And he related a lurid story of how 70 camels had stampeded midway on the Zieghen route. They all reached Jalo safely, but some of the men, unexpectedly left to carry their food and water, died on the march. Suleiman was already rolled like a dormouse between two hawias,[7] so he appealed to me for support. "Know you the saying of the Prophet, Uncle Suleiman," I asked, "how a man came to him and asked whether he should agal his camel or put his trust in Allah? 'First place the agal on the camel and then your trust in Allah,' was the reply."

Various grunts and roars, mingled with my sleep, told me that the guide had been impressed by my theological learning and it seemed only a few minutes later that I woke to the sound of Yusuf's voice, "Allah make you strong! Are you ready for rice?" Protesting that it must still be the middle of the night, I poked my head out of the flea-bag, dislodging a shower of sand from its folds, and a few yards away was one of the odd, vivid little pictures that flash suddenly into one's life and that one never forgets. A crackling, scented fire, criminally large in the circumstances, threw a wavering golden circle in the midst of flat, shadowed sand, interminable, bourneless. Against the brilliant stars a tall, white-robed figure was silhouetted, hands raised to heaven, white hood framing the stern, dark-featured face, intoning the dawn prayers. "Allahu Akhbar!" rang out with undaunted faith, with undimmed courage, to the one Guide whom the Beduin trusts to lead his labouring caravans through desert and dune to the desired oasis. Beside

---

6 Tying a camel's legs wth a rope.

7 Baggage saddles.

the glowing brush-wood, Suleiman, bent double over a huge cauldron, monotonously pounded the morning's "asida,"[8] his long pestle moving to the rhythm of his quavering chant, while Amar, huddled under his coarse jerd, stirred red sauce flavoured with filfil.[9] Yusuf's plump face was set in immobile discontent against the flames, as muffled in every conceivable garment and wrap, he methodically fed the fire, twig by snapping twig. White robes, a fire and the paling stars, with a circle of camels looming formless and dark in the background. That was my picture and then Yusuf's cross voice spoiled it. "The girba[10] water is very bad," he said. "The rice will be black!" "Maleish! I shall not see it!" I said, shivering; but a few minutes later we *tasted* it when the plump one, sleepy-eyed, shuffled across with a grimy frying-pan. He had sand on his nose and forehead to show that he had said his morning prayers, but, whereas the rest of the retinue devoutly bowed their heads to the earth three times a day at least, I always suspected Yusuf of calmly dabbing a little shingle on his face as he went along.

The hard-boiled eggs gave out that day, so we had to drown the taste of the girba rice with sardines. Our midday meal now consisted of dates and a handful of "bucksumat," for we had been given a couple of bags of these hard, unleavened biscuits, slightly sweetened and flavoured with carraway seeds, by the kindly ekhwan of Taj. In the evening we shared a tin of corned beef, but, alas! our great support of the Taiserbo journey had failed us, for the dates we had brought from Hawari were too fresh and they stung our mouths, blistering our gums and reducing us to agonies of thirst. The water allowance was too small to allow of our drinking except in the morning and the evening, so we had reluctantly

8 Sticky mass of damp flour flavoured with onions and oil.

9 Red pepper.

10 Dried goatskin water carrier.

to discard our dates. Yusuf insisted on eating one only each day, because there is an Arab proverb, "A date by the way or a young girl smiling makes a fortunate journey."

We started at 6.30 AM on February 3 and walked till 7 PM, when the whole party, men and camels alike, sat down and groaned. It had been absolutely torrid, without a breath of wind. The girbas began to look distinctly thin and the clank of the water in the fanatis showed that a good deal had evaporated. Unfortunately, it had been very cold after the sandstorm the evening before our departure from the Zakar well and the camels had not drunk properly. Yusuf had made gloomy prognostications most of the day and when we came to a mound of sand, which had drifted over a few old hawias thrown away by a former caravan, he poked them viciously. "How many of our own shall we throw in this way?" he asked of fate.

There is no logic in desert weather. After midday heat we had a very cold night. I remember I ate my chilly dinner with my gloves on and was not surprised to find there was frost, when a sudden storm of shouts and roars brought me rapidly out of my flea-bag and I fell over the thermometer in the dark. The camels apparently had gone wildly mad, for in spite of their agals they were all hobbling and hopping wildly round making immense noise, which the retinue were exceeding in their anxiety to drive the beasts away from our neatly arranged girbas, protected, as usual at night, by a hedge of baggage saddles.

February 4 saw us away by 6.15, a good effort chiefly due to a loading race between Amar and Yusuf against the guide and Mohammed. I think the former couple won, but all the loads were a little wobbly that day. A black duck flew low across our path, heading north. "It has gone into the upside-down country," said Suleiman, pointing ahead; and there, on the far horizon we saw pale dunes and ridges, clear-cut, with violet shadows below peak and cliff. They looked but a few hours' march away and we were all immensely happy, though we knew they were more than a day's journey away.

Again it was very hot, but Yusuf, who always enjoyed a burning sun, took it upon himself to cheer up the whole party. When a camel lay down and groaned, he carefully made a row of toy "asidas" in the sand, modelling the little hole at the top for a sauce with infinite trouble. "These are for him to eat, then he will be strong again," he said smiling. When Suleiman complained of his eyesight the plump one cried: "I will ride ahead and see the way." And, mounting his stick, he gambolled round, imitating every trick and gesture of horsemanship with perfect art. Finally, when the rest of us were so oppressed by the heat that we only wondered what we could take off next, we saw Yusuf solemnly fill the skirt of his shirt with sand and begin sowing it like grain right and left. "What on earth are you doing, you man?" exclaimed Mohammed. "The next traveller will find patch of green grain and will be happy," he said placidly. Nevertheless, that night, when the elusive dunes had failed to materialise even as shadows on the horizon, anxiety spread. Hassanein balanced himself perilously upright on the back of the Tebu beast, but could report nothing in sight, so consoled himself by re-mending his yellow shoes.

All the afternoon there had been disputes as to whether we should go east or west of certain invisible dunes, and the retinue disagreed violently as to how soon we ought to see these landmarks or in what direction they were. Therefore, I was not surprised when I heard a bitter argument behind me. Reproaches were being hurled at Suleiman, who replied that he was old and could not see: "He has lost the____" wailed Mohammed. "We must stop. We cannot go on." Yusuf joined in. "Is he sure he has lost it? Think, you man! Let him think, I tell you!" Expostulation and suggestion followed in loud chaos. I had coped with one such dispute on the morning when there should have been a ridge to the left and there wasn't! I determined that Hassanein should struggle with this. Slightly deaf, he was nodding over his shoe—making far ahead on the grey camel. I rushed up to him crossly. "Get down at once," I urged, seizing the beast ruthlessly by the neck and feeling angrier than ever at the sight of Hassanein's mildly surprised and protesting face, as he desperately clutched his boots and the nearest supporting rope in preparation to being forcibly barraked! "Pull yourself together! Suleiman has lost the way. They are all fighting desperately. If it's an important landmark he's missed we had better wait till the morning. For heaven's sake hurry!"

One anguished glance at the angry group in the rear, who were all pointing backwards, was sufficient to make Hassanein swing off without question. I watched him literally propel himself into the argument, heard "Wallahi!" furiously repeated, saw hands flung skywards and then, surprised, saw him extricate himself from Mohammed's detaining hands and walk slowly to his camel, methodically picking up the possessions had ruthlessly scattered at my peremptory request. "Well, what is it? What has he lost?" I shouted impatiently. Hassanein waited till he was quite near and then he gave me a withering look and said very slowly, each word enunciated separately: "It—is—a—small—leather—bag—which—the—kaimakaan[11]—gave—him—to—sell—in—Jag-habub. Suleiman—has—left it behind!"

On February 5 we broke camp at 6.30, singularly indifferent to coffee mysteriously mixed with candle-grease and rice, hairy with girba fur, in our anxiety to see the morning mirage. This time the dunes looked even nearer. One could see the wavy furrows along the ridges and every separate golden hillock, yet an hour later everything had vanished and the flat, fawn disk stretched

---

11 Governor.

drab and monotonous, on every side. Suleiman was confident, however, that we should sleep in the dunes that night. Yusuf was cheerfully certain that, as we not yet seen the Mazul ridge to the west, we should not "see land" for another day. When Beduins are travelling across a big, trackless desert, they always speak of any known country as "the land." It is rather like a long sea voyage with the guide as pilot. He keeps the caravan's head turned in the right direction by the stars and waits to pick up a familiar landmark before making directly for his oasis. At 10 AM the old guide uttered something nearly resembling a shriek and threw himself on Yusuf's neck. "I see the Mazul!" he claimed, "and it is near, very near." Leaving the pale line of distant hillocks to our left, we headed directly north towards other dunes which began to appear, a faint blur on the horizon. The two little nagas[12] edged away to the west all day in the most determined way. Yusuf said they knew that their mothers, from whom we had separated them at Taj, were now travelling on the Zieghen-Jalo route and instinct was driving them towards the soldier-slaves' caravan.

The plump one's character always appeared to greater advantage in really hard times. When things were going easily his scowl was a marvel of discontented endurance. His eyes shut into little slits and his voice became a plaintive whine. When big difficulties arose, when camels were failing and everybody was overtired, Yusuf cheered up the whole caravan. His absurd little songs trickled out hour after hour, he told long fairy stories about giants and princesses, he made elaborate jokes which we daily received with new interest. Thus, if anyone lagged behind they were always greeted when they rejoined the caravan as if after a long absence, upon which they replied that they had come from Jedabia or Jalo in two or three days, were congratulated on their walk, and asked

---

12 Female camels.

minutely for news concerning every person in the place. This particular game never wearied and we all grew most inventive at the expense of the good folk at Jedabia.

One would think that in a thirteen hours' walk each day one would find time for much conversation, but the desert breeds reserve. It is so big that one's own plans and projects seem too little to be talked about. Also, there is so much time to say anything that one continually puts it off and ends by never saying it at all. We used to walk for hours without a word, till Yusuf broke the silence by some reflection on his approaching marriage or the sickness that he saw in some camel's eye. By this time I had learned how to make myself understood in Libya. The nouns are nearly all different, but after one had learnt a list of those one gets on very nicely with but two verbs. To express any more or less peaceful occupation like travelling, stopping, loading, unloading, letting fall, starting, etc., *ad infinitum*, one employs the word "shil." If one wishes to imply any more or offensive action, like fighting, attacking, climbing hurriedly, eating, burning, becoming angry, "akal" seems to be elastic enough to express it.

We finally arrived at the dunes nearly two hours before sunset, luckily hitting two very big dunes that were well-known landmarks. Yusuf wanted to turn in behind them. Suleiman insisted on going to the right, which brought us into a wide, flat stretch some 12 kilometres long. We barraked at the end of it in a rising wind, which soon put out our little folding lantern, so that we lost everything, including the tin opener, in the dark. It was rather a miserable night, for the hattab we had brought from the Mehemsa was exhausted and our efforts to make tea over a little fire of "leaf" torn from one of the hawias were not very successful.

The water from the girba we opened that night was really bad. Its colour and taste alike were extraordinary, so we regretfully decided to use it only for cooking. Suleiman looked at it with interest. "We have enough water, Hamdulillah!" he said. "In any case I can live for a week without drinking." When we questioned him as to this amazing statement he told us that Sidi el Mahdi habitually sent out caravans to explore the country round Kufara. Suleiman, an old man and a boy, had formed one of these parties, and they had wandered as far afield as Merg, thirteen days south-east of their starting-point, when one dark night their camels were stolen by a band of brigands. Presumably something happened to the girbas and provisions, for in the morning the the exploring party found themselves with enough water and dates for a day and a half and they were six days' journey from the nearest well, the Oweinat. However, the three started off to walk to it, actually carrying their rifles. The old man got ill after one day and insisted on being left behind. After two days his erstwhile companions discarded their rifles. After three, Suleiman got fever and lay down to die, but the boy went on and arrived safely at the well. Our guide unexpectedly recovered from his fever after twenty-four hours and started off again, walking only at night and lying down all day. He arrived at Oweinat on the seventh day so exhausted and so parched with thirst that he could not get the liquid down his throat, so he lay in the water in the well for a whole day and was then able to drink. Luckily a caravan had thrown away some dates, and with a small store of these and the little water he could carry, Suleiman calmly walked on to Kufara, another week's journey! The old man who had been left to die on the road arrived a day later with *his rifle*. The feat seems inconceivable, but Yusuf vouched for the truth of the story and Amar told how he had drunk only once in 72 hours when the water in the girba went bad. Then Mohammed, not to be outdone in endurance, related how he had travelled from Jalo to Jaghabub in four days and four nights, without sleeping, eating as the camels went along, because the girbas were all leaking and he was afraid of running short of water.

By this time we felt that our own little effort to draw a new red line across a survey map was very small and insignificant and that we should certainly be able to walk to Jaghabub carrying a fanatis and a tin of corned beef if necessary! We were much less confident of it next morning, however, when all the camels turned up their noses at the date food offered them and deliberately ran away. There was nowhere for them to run to among the dunes, so we got them back after a laborious half-hour, but I felt that the word "agal" and not Kufara would be written across my heart in future! There was no fire that morning, and uncooked soaked rice is not appetising. I remember I was tying the remains of my stockings round my feet when I heard a gloomy voice say: "We ate the last box of sardines last night because you lost the beef-tin-opener in the sand and the rice is coal black. I wish you would not be so miserly with the fanatis water!" I didn't pay much attention as I hadn't any more stockings. Evidently the primrose and scarlet boots which I had bought for four mejidies (sixteen shillings) at Jof were not suited for walking, for I had been wearing two pairs of woollen stockings one over the other and now they all hung in shreds round my feet. However, I did look up when the plaintive tones continued. "I've found one sardine. He must have fallen out when you upset the canteen in the sand." With horror I saw a soddened, dark mass and on the top of it a minute yellow block shaped like a fish, but I did not like to be discouraging. "Are you sure that there is a sardine inside that sand?" I asked diffidently. Hassanein was offended. "Will you carve him or shall I?" he asked majestically.

On February 6 we plunged right into the dunes. On the whole they ran north to south in great wavy ridges which would be impossible for camels to cross. In between were wide stretches of rolling ground, rising gradually to lower dunes through which Suleimian confidently picked his way. The little old man was very calm. "I have never been this route before, but if I keep Jedi in my left eye we shall arrive, Insha-allah!" he said, and when Yusuf complained violently that there was no hattab—the retinue had eaten raw flour and gravy that morning—he answered simply, "Allah will bring provisions." A few minutes later we came upon a camel skeleton, a most welcome sight, for it proved that we were on the right track; inside the ribs were some large slabs of dried dung. Mohammed pulled this out triumphantly. "A fire! A fire! Hamdulillah!" And therefore everyone was cheerful till Amar brought the news that Yusuf was ill. We had seen the plump one lie down some way in the rear, but thought he was only resting for half an hour, a thing we all did in turns, only the difference between the nature of East and West showed at these moments, for whereas the Beduins slept peacefully in the rear and then ran after the camels, I used to toil on ahead and lay myself across the path of the caravan, so that I must wake at its approach. It appeared that Yusuf had fallen down and then lost consciousness for about an hour; it was very lucky that he managed to catch up the caravan at all. We mounted him on the Tebu camel, which was the strongest of the caravan but was already showing signs of thirst, and toiled on.

It was much harder walking in the dunes, for the sand was soft and deep in patches, but the great curly ridges, golden as Irish butter, which Yusuf always looked at affectionately, because they reminded him of his beloved "asida," were friendly spirits after the dreary disk of the preceding four days. It was always a thrilling moment when one mounted a high gherd,[13] for there was the possibility of a view. Logically one could expect to see only waving yellow crests, a sunlit expanse of sand valley and mountain in every direction, but the impossible might always happen. One might espy a caravan or an oasis—or at least some hattab!

---

13 Dune.

For this reason we always hastened ahead up the big rises to look down on wind-tossed ranges, and towards the evening we were rewarded for our energy by the appearance of little black specks in one of the hollows. "Hattab," said Suleiman laconically and Yusuf recovered at the word—or perhaps it was the quinine which we had given him earlier in the day! We raced down to the brittle stalks of twisted coarse-grained wood that meant fires and hot food that night, and everyone began to talk of what they would eat!

Just after sunset we came to an almost perpendicular dune which the camels refused to descend. We had to dig a sloping trough down it and push the beasts into it one by one. Everyone was tired and the camels were incredibly stupid. The young nagas simply rolled down, flinging their loads in front of them, at which Mohammed lost his temper and made matters worse by violently beating the animals, still hesitating at the top. They stumbled forward in a huddled mass, and I saw the girbas threatened. Luckily the Tebu beast was carrying most of them. He plunged solidly down on his great splay feet and I had just enough energy left to seize his head-rope and drag him out of the chaos. We barraked before our short-sighted guide could lead us over another such precipice and, because it was a joy to be wasteful of anything on that journey, we made no fewer than three fires and recklessly poured everything we could find into the frying-pan together—rice and corned beef and tinned turnips—so that we ate a hot, very hot, meal. We even drank our one cup of tea hot, debating the while whether coffee were not preferable, for, though it made one thirsty, it somewhat hid the taste of the girba water.

Everything by now tasted slightly of wax, for, in the hot days, all the candles had melted in the canteen. It is certainly possible to clean pots and pans beautifully with sand, but it needs a great deal of energy to do it and I defy anyone to have any superfluous

energy after loading and feeding camels before a twelve to thirteen hours' march, unloading and feeding the tired and smelly
beasts at the end of it, agaling them while they persistently tried
to escape, preparing some sort of meal and then, worst of all, oh!
intolerably worst, the sand-rash that tortured our nights! Let no
one who dreams of a poetic, Swinburnian desert come to Libya!
We had not washed anything but our hands since leaving Hawari
thirteen days before and not even these since the Zakar well; since
then we had had a sandstorm which had filled every pore with
minute grit, so that by day the irritation was just bearable, but at
night, in the warmth and the restricted space of the flea-bag, it
was a torture beyond belief. I used to feel that never, so long as I
lived, would I be able to bear seeing water spilled or wasted.

Fate had been cruel to us in one respect, for the day at the
Zakar well, when we had dreamed of sandy baths in the canteen
lid behind a friendly palm tree, she had sent us the first of our two
sandstorms, so washing had been confined to a teacup for our fingers. One lay at night, sleepless and burning, and looked up at
the aloof peace of the stars and wondered vindictively how one
could get even with the desert for this last trick of hers. Yet, in the
cold, still dawn, the desperate tiredness vanished and one made
a huge, unnecessary fire to breakfast by and ate black rice with
immense relish. Yusuf was very proud of his skill as a cook, so we
did not like to tell him of all the foreign bodies we found in our
food—bits of leaf and straw from the baggage saddles, grit, hair,
pebbles and sand—it was the Libyan sauce and I think Hassanein
suffered much in silence, for it was his first desert journey and he
still hankered after cleanliness. I used to find him desperately and
secretly rubbing a plate with a corner of his muffler or his best silk
handkerchief and, whenever he was late for breakfast, I knew it
was because he had been unwise enough to look at his cup or fork
before using them!

On our second day in the dunes the flat spaces grew rarer, so that we climbed up and down ridges most of the time. The camels began to show signs of wear. One of the nagas trailed her head most of the time. The big blond beast had to be relieved of his load. They were all very smelly, which is the first sign of thirst. Luckily, we found patches of green hattab, the prickly, juiceless bush of the Mehemsa, scattered under the dunes and the animals raced to it, fighting for the freshest tufts. Amar got fever and had to be allowed to ride, while I was so tired that I found a way of festooning myself over the pegs of the baggage saddles, my knees wound round one and my neck round another. In this extraordinarily uncomfortable position I actually dozed, while Yusuf wandered beside me doubtfully. "You are very long," he said politely. "I think you will fall." And he tried to double up a dangling foot much as if it was a piece of baggage slipping.

I could not understand the presence of green bushes till I found my pillow that night wet with a heavy dew. Then I realised that we had left the southern lands behind us and next day, February 8, there were little clouds in the sky, just specks of fluffy white, but we had become used to the molten blue that roofs the red country of Kufara and her encircling wastes. That was for me the worst day. The little camels persistently threw their loads, ill-balanced because the fodder had become so much lighter. There was a cold east wind which blistered one's skin on one side, while the sun scorched it on the other. The camels would not keep together, but strayed off to each patch of green. The dunes seemed steeper than ever and the sand softer and heavier. No one was sure of the way. Even Suleiman was a little depressed at not picking up any of the landmarks he had known on previous journeys. He insisted on keeping his course due north, though we knew Jaghabub lay north-east, and his only explanation was that it was easier to approach the place from the west. Logically, I thought it would be easier to strike east, so that if one went past Jaghabub one would at least reach Siwa. To the west lay only the seven days' waterless stretch to Jalo.

However, Suleiman was immovable and we plodded wearily on, placing one foot in front of the other with desperate firmness and flinging ourselves flat on our faces for a few minutes' blessed sleep whenever the camels lingered to feed. I remember wondering, as I dragged myself up after one of these short respites, how many separate and distinct aches one's body could feel at the same moment. I was getting quite interested in the problem when Hassanein's bronzed face—it seemed to have grown hollow these last few days—appeared beside me. He was painfully shuffling on blistered feet after a twelve hours' walk the previous day. "When we get to Cairo everyone will say, 'What fun you must have had!'" he said drearily. Even this idea could not make me speak. I had discovered it was easier to walk with my eyes shut and so, mutely, I shuffled after the guide, dragging my stick till I dropped it and was too tired to pick it up again.

Yes, it was a bad day, but it ended at last with a few patches of black pebbles, sure sign that we were nearing the northern edge of the dunes. Even the sand rash, combined with a most remarkable tasting dish produced by Hassanein's efforts to clean the frying-pan, could not keep me awake that night and I slept soundly till Yusuf's plaintive voice, saying all in one breath, "Allah-make-you-strong-the-fire-is-ready-for-the-rice!" roused me to a starry world and an exceedingly damp one, but I imagine these very heavy dews helped the thirsty camels considerably, so I didn't regret a wet barracan which twisted itself reluctantly round everything but me!

February 9 was memorable, for on climbing the high dune under which we had camped we saw a long, faint ridge, blue on the north-east horizon. "Land at last!" exclaimed Mohammed. "It must be the mountain between Jaghabub and Siwa!" Even this reassuring suggestion would not turn our guide from his northerly course, but signs that we were leaving the great desert abounded. So far the only living things had been large, unpleasant beetles, mottled black and fawn creatures, some nearly four inches long, which looked like scattered stones till they suddenly raised themselves on long legs and scuttled away. That morning, however, we saw many black and grey birds and at last, when the green patches of hattab had developed into large brown-like shrubs and neat little dwarf trees, leafless and but two or three feet high, we came across gazelle traces. We also found two complete skulls with the tapering horns in perfect condition. The country was changing noticeably. The previous day there had been a few patches of the Jaghabub grey stone among the sand, the sight of which filled the retinue with delight. On February 9 great blocks of it appeared in fantastic masses rising suddenly from dune and hollow. We noticed scattered pieces of fossilised wood, some of which appeared to have been part of the trunks of big trees. Stretches of what looked like black pebbles shimmered dark beyond the farthest ridge.

Finally, Mohammed, mounting an immense curly backed sand peak at noon, tore off his turban, tied it round his staff and, waving it bannerwise above his head, shouted wildly, "I see my country! The land is near!" The camels were the only indifferent beings in the caravan. They were too tired to quicken the pace, which had dropped to two miles an hour during the last day or two. They had got very thin, with dull eyes, but luckily there was a slight breeze to relieve the intense heat which scorched us whenever we stopped for grazing in a hollow. There were streaks of white cloud in the pale sky and I imagined a breath of salt flavoured the northern breeze, so that suddenly I was desperately home-sick for the great free desert, lawless and boundless, that we were leaving. Ahead were the comfortable lands where the nomads camp in their tattered "nuggas"[14] and the Beduins pasture their herds, the Gebel Akhbar and Cyrenaica, the welcome of the tent-dwellers for all caravans who have travelled the "big routes."

Somewhere, "east of us," said the compass, "north of us," said Suleiman, lay the last outpost of the wilderness, if not the birthplace, at least the training ground of Senussi-ism, but the lure of space dragged one's mind back. The claw of the desert was tearing away the peace that should lie at a journey's end. I do not think I ever felt mentally flatter than when, just before 2 AM, we passed through the last little hollow where green and gold were mixed and the mighty belt of dunes lay behind us. In front was a most desolate country of grey slate and streaks of white chalky sand and pebbles, with here and there a dull madder gherd or stony cliff. A faint thrill of interest was given to the moment by the fact that none of the retinue knew where we were, but as I was determined that east we should now go, whatever they said, it did not much matter.

Suleiman climbed one dune and said we were between the hatias[15] of Bu Alia and Bu Salama on the Jalo road. Mohammed climbed another and said that both these places were to the east of us. Yusuf lay down firmly on a soft spot and said that all known country was still to the north and he was going to sleep till the guide found his head again.

The happy-go-lucky Beduin spirit had completely got possession of us, so no one was particularly surprised when, after an hour on the course insisted on by the compass and myself, we picked up a definite trail with some slabs of stones stuck upright as landmarks. As a matter of fact we had struck the Jalo-Jaghabub route, rather more than a day's journey west of the latter place, but at

---

14 A Beduin tent.

15 A depression containing brushwood.

the time nobody was certain as to our exact position. Amar, however, announced that undoubtedly Bu Alia lay behind us, and no
sooner had the whole retinue agreed on that one point than the
beginning of the hatia of that name became visible a few hundred
yards ahead! "Hamdulillah! We shall camp to-night in our own
country!" exclaimed Mohammed, and hurried on the caravan in
spite of Yusuf's expostulations. Gazelle tracks were now plentiful
and we tried to track down four in the hope of getting a shot, but
Suleiman was nearly dead-beat. "The last word is in your hands,"
he said, "but I am an old man and very tired. Let us barrak here."

The hatia was really a wadi stretching about 5 kilometres
north to south, with a breadth of 4 kilometres. The whole space
between the white shale and sand banks was filled with mounds
and shrubs of hattab, mostly green, while here and there massive
blocks of greyish sandstone stuck up in strange shapes. As one
wandered slowly through the low bushes far away to the north a
long purplish ridge with a mound at the end shaped exactly like
the dome of a mosque caught the first red of the sunset. "That is
the gherd of the qubba,"[16] exclaimed Yusuf, his round tired face
lighting up, "and look, in front of us is the Gara of Sidi el Mahdi!"
At the farthest end of the hatia was an immense block of red
sandstone flung up by the hands of some forgotten giant upon
a mighty base of polished white, so that it looked like a primeval
altar to the gods of earth and sky. Here the Mahdi used to halt his
immense caravans on the Jalo journey and under the shadow of
the rough natural sanctuary pray for a prosperous venture or give
thanks for a safe return.

Even Suleiman spoke no more of barraking. Without a word
spoken, everyone felt that the Maghrib prayers must be said
where the spirit of the Mahdi would surely welcome travellers

---

16 A domed holy tomb.

from the far-off oasis, whose red and amber he had changed to
wealth of grain and fruit and flowers. The weary camels were hurried from their indifferent nibbling among the dry shrubs. When
the full glory of the golden west lit up the strange altar, balanced
between heaven and earth, and the faint silver crescent of a new
moon glowed pale amidst the flame, we came round the corner of
the rock and saw the simplest kibla that ever the faithful turned
towards the Ka-aba. It was but three grey, rough boulders, with
a circle of stones to mark the shape of an imaginary mosque, yet
it was holy ground and we left our worn shoes outside, before
we bowed our faces to the desert sands. What prayers the stern
Mohammed mixed with his, "In the name of Allah compassion-
ate and merciful," I know not. What simple thanksgivings were
murmured by our weather-beaten guide, if the young zawia student, Amar, grasped the perils from which he had been protected,
if Yusuf's mind realised for one fleeting moment that there was
something beyond his comfortable practicality, I cannot guess,
but I know that never in my life have I offered more wholehearted gratitude to the Power that, called by many different
names in many different cities, is omnipotent in the deserts!

1922

An Attempted Pilgrimage to Mecca

From Chapters XXV–XXVII of
Adventure: Being a Gipsy Salad—
Some Incidents, Excitements and Impressions
of Twelve Highly-Seasoned Years (1928)

An Adventure that Failed

AT ONE TIME it was the ambition of my life to see Mecca. I had been living for some months in the African desert among the simplest and most fervent of Moslems. Nightly round the campfires, daily on the torrid marches, I had heard these men speak of the House of Allah and the pilgrimage they hoped to do.

I had seen beggars wandering across the Sahara, barefooted, penniless, sick, but sustained during a three or four years' trail by the dream of Mecca. I had seen old men grow young at the thought of it, and the swords of warriors unsheathed with the cry: "Next year, Allah, I come!"

Inspired by something of the same passion, I determined to attempt the pilgrimage, believing that the mosque at Mecca must be as great a revelation of faith as St. Peter's on a Roman Easter or the Cenotaph on Armistice Day.

At that time the pilgrimage, which varies ten days in our year, happened to be in August, which, of course, is the hottest month in the Red Sea. I started at a moment's notice and, owing to the intense damp heat, was unable to find any paint that would stay on my skin. As I had just come out of a hospital after an operation, I had not time to burn my usual brown. This, added to the fact that, though my face with its flat cheek-bones passes muster, I am much too tall and thin for the class of native easiest to represent, made success precarious from the start.

A confederate secured me an Egyptian passport and the Sitt Khadija—the name which had brought me good fortune on several former journeys—was reborn in a darkened railway carriage somewhere between Ismailia and Suez on the hottest of July nights. An Englishwoman walked into the carriage in an embroidered French frock, high-heeled shoes, and a hat that was only simple to the uninitiated masculine eye.

An Egyptian woman came out of it. In the shapeless black habbara and heel-less slippers she seemed to have lost at least 4 inches of height, and the only things that could be seen above her strip of white "burwa" were the painted eyes of the East. If they were grey, they were so heavily kohled that they looked as dark as the formidable brows above them. With beads and straw fan firmly gripped in black-gloved fingers, she shuffled along the Suez platform in the wake of a porter carrying one of those nameless yellow suit-cases whose special mission in life seems to be to resemble every other piece of luggage that was ever conceived. Unused to walking, the Moslem woman moved across a wide sandy square with the uncertain, swaying gait peculiar to dwellers in the harem.

Arrived at a very modest hotel, she timidly asked for a room in a high-pitched voice, and was conducted to a shuttered apartment whose temperature struck her like a blow.

"Allah bless your sleeping," muttered the retreating Arab, and Khadija hanem was left alone to wonder if there was anything in the world more complicated than a pilgrim passport.

I was wakened from doubtful appreciation of the hardest of hard pillows by a thunderous knocking at the door and the impatient voice of my confederate shouting: "Are you ready? Are you ready—we must go to the town for the Hedjaz visa to your passport."

With some *froideur* I pointed out that it was only 6.30 AM, but, nevertheless, half an hour later we were speeding over the causeway from Portofia to Suez. The visa proved to be merely another formal decoration of my already ornamental passport, but once more in the car, my confederate turned to me gloomily: "You must have a bath," he said.

I merely gaped, so he explained further: "They will wash you at the disinfecting station and you will be inoculated for cholera."

"Oh, no, I won't," said I with considerable firmness, gingerly moving my already thrice inoculated and vaccinated arms. My companion's emphatic reply was cut short by our arrival at the gates of the wharf, where some policemen asked us our business and misdirected us to the quarantine building.

There I was put in charge of a worn-looking female reminiscent of station waiting-rooms. Impressed by my thick silk habbara, she shuffled through a large bare room where several women were waiting and unlocked what appeared to be a private apartment. There was nothing in it but a bench and a tap. Noticing the latter, I thought this was the moment to try a bribe. It was eminently successful. "You look very clean," she said, and the tap was turned on by way of camouflage, while we sat comfortably on the bench and discussed life in general. The faded lady was Italian and spoke even worse Arabic than mine. She took for granted that I was a Turk and our intimate conversation was only interrupted by the surreptitious entrance of an official who beckoned me out.

Thereafter we bustled from place to place with a crowd of nerve-racked pilgrims, all determined that they *had* lost their luggage, or *would* lose the boat. Courteous officialdom finally came to the rescue, saved me from a further dose of microbes—though my picturesque handmaiden, Bahia, was wrathfully forced to submit—and ushered us on board the small Khedivial steamer that was to take the last batch of Egyptian pilgrims south to Jedda.

I found that, owing to the amazing distaste of even wealthy Egyptians to paying a first-class fare, I had a small six-feet-square cabin to myself and actually on the cool side of the ship. "Cool," of course, is a comparative term, for the heat at midday was stupendous, and Bahia and I presented the appearance of those who had freshly bathed.

My handmaiden, who to the end believed that I was the much-maligned sister of a wealthy Cairene, was of Bedouin origin and must have had a chequered career, according to the stories of her life with which she regaled me at the most tropical moments. They were not moral, but they were enlightening, and I determined to keep a strict eye on the lady. She was shapeless as to the figure encased in an ill-fitting sage-green galabia, with a sapphire and rose handkerchief adorning—one cannot say "covering"—two immensely long plaits of straight dark hair. This splendour was covered in public with a black meliya; but Bahia, like all women of her class, was careless of veiling and displayed her big brown eyes, kohl-rimmed, and her beautifully shaped mouth marred by blue tattoo marks, with indifference. When I first saw her she had handkerchiefs bandaged right up her forearms, but, in the privacy of my cabin, she unrolled them and displayed rows of heavy gold bangles, at least half a score on each arm. Some of them were made of English sovereigns linked into a chain. She explained that most of them belonged to a fellow-passenger who had lent them to her because she herself was frightened of thieves. I said I was, too, and would she kindly give them back as soon as possible.

We were on board a couple of hours before the boat started, so we bought fruit from the wharf, an immense quantity of grapes, and a water-melon twenty inches in diameter. I thought it would last us a week, but I had reckoned without Bahia's appetite and the fact that water-melon undoubtedly grows on one. We ate it at intervals all through the day, when we were not occupied in unsticking ourselves. As the heat increased, we stuck to the paint of everything—seats, walls, and berth rails, and it took a good, hard wrench to separate the nameless suit-case from an equally yellow trunk, which contained our cooking apparatus, our prayer-carpet, and our pilgrim clothes.

When the last perspiring pilgrim had scuttled aboard and the last unwieldy bundle had been hauled after him, a muezzin loudly intoned the call to prayer, and pilgrims on board joined with their friends on the shore in the afternoon prayer. Amidst sustained chanting in monotonous cadence, broken by weeping on the wharf from those who, apparently, would have liked to come but could not, we drifted away, but not till Suez had faded to the north did the rhythmic chant refrain from praising Allah and his Prophet.

Thereafter the day was monotonous, save when I suddenly came face to face with a sheikh whom I had met at Siwa on my return from Kufara. He could not possibly have recognized the blurred, bistred eyes between stiff black and white, yet my heart missed a beat at the sound of his grave "Salaam aleikum" as he passed me. The next interest was provided by Bahia, who would insist on smoking. Having warned her that it was "haram" (forbidden), and everything else I could think of, I left her to her fate. It came swiftly. We had been sitting with two or three other women on the lower deck, amidst a mess of melon-seeds and fig-skins. A loquacious dame had been discoursing on the virtues of her only son, while trying to find out exactly how much money we all had, in order that she might attach herself to the most suitable party. Not wishing to be selected as a companion for her journey from Jedda to Mecca, I was just retiring to my cabin when a stern-faced desert Arab passed, his face hard and lined beneath his ma-araka—"Moslems do not smoke," he said harshly to Bahia, and waited immobile till she dropped her cigarette overboard. I had expected swift storm of protest, but there came from the culprit only an unintelligible murmur.

In order to be ready for the sunset prayers, we decided to bathe early; but, to my horror, I found that one had no chance of using the bathroom alone. Brown skin, white skin, black skin, limbs young and svelte, unspoiled as yet by harem or by peasants' labour, limbs gnarled and unwieldy as the branches of old trees, disported themselves in swift turn under a cold, salt douche, but soap was at a premium and my scented tablet returned to me very thin and worn.

As night approached, a frenzy of prayer and song arose on all sides. I managed to discover an empty square foot or two on the upper deck, of which I took almost forcible possession, with the aid of a Fayum sheikh who felt the heat as much as I did. From this post of vantage, I watched the devotions of the crowd. It was an interesting sight, for 600 pilgrims were crowded on the little steamer. Every inch of deck was occupied by crouching human beings surrounded by every shape and form of luggage, most of it bulky. Nobody had room to stretch themselves out straight, but certainly nobody seemed to mind. The utmost good temper reigned and everyone made way for his fellows. On the first-class deck, whole families, or groups of students, or clusters of elderly grey-beards occupied the same carpet within a sort of wall of piled luggage, wherein the women brewed coffee and made sweet lemonade, alternately chewing dry biscuits—of which every pilgrim seemed to have a basketful—and sucking bitter limes.

Below, the crowd was much greater and they must have slept in a sitting posture, cross-legged, for there was no room to move. All, of course, were Egyptians, but the difference of type was marked. There were fat, pale merchants from the cities and grey-bearded blacks from the South. Tattooed Bedouin women, brown and lean, rubbed shoulders with unwieldy, untidy dames who looked as if they had never walked an inch in their lives. There were keen, quiet old Arabs, whose far-seeing eyes already visualized "the House of Allah," of which they had dreamed all their lives, the sheikh in his spotless robe and the beggar wondering if his poor hoarded silver would suffice. The young men, plump and pale, intoned quick passages from sacred books, each one attempting to read quicker and louder than his fellows. Their elders muttered over the polished sibhas (beads) which slipped monotonously through their fingers.

From all sides rose songs in praise of the Prophet, or loudly repeated sentences, such as: "Here I come, Prophet of God," or "This very month, if Allah wills, in the mountain of Arafat I shall be." Sometimes a circle of fanatics would spring to their feet, and one of them would shout "Allah, Allah," all bending forward violently with each mention of the name, till the spokesman's frenzy exhausted him, when the next one would take up the cry till his voice or his strength flagged, and so on round the circle. The Bedouins improvised their own rhymes of praise and prayer, and these, sung in drawling nasal tones, were often loudly applauded. Whenever the riot of sound died for a few minutes, some elderly man would rise and intone slowly and magnificently the "Shehada" with its triumphant "There is no God but God."

By ten, however, everybody was apparently asleep, curled into the smallest possible space, and there was silence till a muezzin woke the pilgrims for the dawn prayers.

I remember I spent most of the morning crouching on the lower deck, far aft, behind the wheel. It was rather a cool spot and I had been asked to share her carpet by a woman from a Cairo village. She was with a party of four men, so I asked her why there were not more peasant women on board, and received the startling reply: "They fear the English."

"But why? Is there any danger from the English?" I asked apprehensively.

"Nobody knows," she replied. "But of what use are the English now?"

Feeling it was scarcely the time for propaganda, I changed the conversation, and we made a quite new-tasting coffee underneath the wheel. "It has much spice in it," said my hostess, "therefore it does not dry up the body."

She told me my Egyptian paper money would be useless in the Hedjaz, where I would receive only a quarter of its value; borrowed a pair of white cotton stockings, as she had forgotten to bring any for the "Ihram," (pilgrim garb) and finally asked me: "Are you going to visit the Prophet after you have seen the house of Allah?" I replied that I would like to go to Medina if I had enough money. "It is very expensive, I fear," she answered; "but it is all well arranged and the prices are fixed. Would you like to travel with us, as you have no man?"

Again I was struck by the general spirit of helpfulness which prevailed. The poorer pilgrims bring with them sufficient food for the whole journey, chiefly dry cake, nuts, biscuits, coffee, tea and sugar, with quantities of immense, pink-fleshed water-melons, and they are only too anxious to share it with anyone less well provided. Of course an act of charity on the pilgrimage is doubly blest and no one need fear to ask for alms or help.

After we had discussed our family history at length—mine was rapidly becoming exceedingly complicated—the Siwa sheikh and two followers came aft and were entertained by our neighbours on the left, one of whom apparently was the only Hanbali (one of the four Sunni sects) on board, which led to a discussion on the merits of the various muftis at Mecca. The Siwa man cut it short by announcing that they were all Senussi in his town. I decided I had better make his acquaintance, so carelessly upset a bag of biscuits over his side of the luggage bales, against which I was leaning. By the time the last one was retrieved, he had offered me the dates for which his land is famous, and I felt our friendship was established.

A very cheerful friendliness prevails among all classes on the pilgrimage, and also a certain laxity. Even the upper-class women are careless with their veils, and talk with men almost on equal terms. It is an extraordinary mixture of picnic and religious festival. The "Haj-el-Beit"[1] may have represented an almost impossible ideal, handed on by the father whose savings had not quite reached the requisite amount, to the hardworking son who sees a vision realized when he leaves the quay at Suez; but it is also the greatest "outing" of the Moslem's life and he is determined to enjoy it.

The two great subjects of conversation were how (on returning) we could smuggle the holy water of Zem-Zem well, a certain cure for all sickness, through the impious quarantine, which persisted in considering it infectious and confiscating it, and how to outwit the nimble thief who makes a fat living out of the pilgrimage. Concerning the latter, tales waxed thrilling and wild, till Bahia warned me never to let a camel-man help me off my steed lest his cunning fingers should be feeling for hidden coin.

---

1 Pilgrimage to the house of (God).

Being the Account of an Attempted Pilgrimage to Mecca

O N THE THIRD day we all donned the Ihram or pilgrim garb, which necessitated very thorough ablutions beforehand. My enthusiastic servant woke me at 6 AM, just as I was dozing off after a night of literal torture—the heat had been so intense in the stuffy cabin, that I could not bear to lie down—but we did not manage to enter the bathroom till nearly noon. Every single one of the 600 pilgrims had to have a bath and, as rows of sweating humans crowded round the doors, fragments of conversation were amusing. "The English sell the water. It is not good to make money out of poor pilgrims!" and the captain's north-country voice shouting: "You must stop those folk using so much water. Ten tons yesterday and ten tons to-day; soon we shan't have enough to drink."

The necessary ablutions consist of a bath, washing the head, cutting the nails, and shaving all hair from the body. When Bahia and I finally forced our way into the bathroom, we found everyone frantically scrubbing each other's backs in an effort to be friendly and helpful. Then there was much consultation as to how to put on the Ihram. The men's garments were of extreme simplicity, for they consisted simply of two sheets or rough bath towels, one wound round like a kilt and the other slung across the shoulders. In the case of the fat and the portly, there was always a considerable hiatus which afforded some amusement to their friends, but the sheeted men looked rather well, because their draperies were long and one end could be flung in graceful folds, toga-wise, over the shoulders. The women wore a straight white galabia made of coarse thick calico, like a very cheap nightdress. Over a close-fitting white handkerchief which hid all the hair, they donned a flowing transparent scarf which could be arranged to hide as much of the face as one wished and, over all, a "meliya"—merely a large bed-sheet. This last item was the difficulty, and it very soon got draggled.

The pilgrim crowd has sometimes been described as reminiscent of a Turkish bath. Certainly individual instances are distinctly humorous, but, taken generally, the mass of snowy-robed figures, tense, eager, lit with a common purpose, the men bareheaded under the intolerant sun, the women shrouded and spotless as white Carmelite nuns, is an imposing sight.

All through the hot afternoon we crouched in our few square feet of deck, waiting anxiously for the siren blast that would announce our entry into "Haramein"—the sacred territory. As we were all feeling particularly clean and immaculate, we amused ourselves by criticizing Europeans, and I remember we decided that the English were a very dirty race. When at 6 PM the longed-for blast thrilled the ship to sudden life, it was drowned in the great wave of sound that burst from 600 throats. Few knew quite what they were shouting, but everybody shouted something. The Imams formed circles of their followers all over the decks, and blared forth the prayers of their sects and confraternities. Ancient "ulema," with shaven heads and horn spectacles, read aloud page after page from well-thumbed books, while the ignorant gathered round them for instruction. The simpler pilgrims contented themselves with crying repeatedly: "I am here, I am here, oh Allah, I am here!" A couple of long-haired dervishes flung their tortured bodies from side to side, shouting a repetitive prayer till foam frothed from their mouths and their upturned eyes showed fixed and glassy.

Everybody tried to explain most enthusiastically to his neighbour the complete rites of the pilgrimage. Consequently, after the first hour, we gathered so much information that we were obliged to go and sit at the feet of a noted Alim to have it all sorted out. "Tell me, oh my Father," I asked, "what is sin and what is not sin?" The old man had done the pilgrimage five times, so he was fluent. "For the 'Omrah,'" he said, "you must use no scent and no kohl and you must not take off the Ihram for four days and four nights, neither must you bathe nor comb your hair." He paused and the full horrors of it sank into my mind—not to bathe or to change one's stiff, hot clothes for ninety-six hours in a climate where everything was literally soaked in less than one hour! The prohibition of kohl also worried me, for without their dark fantastic rings, my eyes were a very English grey.

"If thou lettest one single hair be seen, pull it out and give a sheep to the poor." This was a triumph for me, for I was most discreet with regard to my curly locks, but Bahia's black plaits straggled recklessly wild.

"If a paring of thy nail falls, or an eyelash, kill a sheep for the poor, and if thou seest a flea upon thyself catch it and do likewise." After this last remark we were so depressed that we left the ancient sage.

"Insha-allah, sheep are not expensive in Mecca!" muttered Bahia anxiously.

If it were possible for the weather to grow hotter, I think it did so on the fourth day, for I could bear the cabin no longer: so, for comfort and support, I sought the company of a Suez family who had done the pilgrimage half a dozen times. One of the women broke to me the horrible fact that henceforth it was a sin (literally "haram") to cover one's face. She pulled at my stiff transparent veil till she had arranged it like a nun's coif, close wound from chin to brow, but leaving one's features most unfortunately visible. Then, of course, came the inevitable questions—my father was an Egyptian, my mother Turkish, I said, and raved about Stamboul, from memory of Pierre Loti and Claude Farère. We talked for some time in well-turned religious phrases and they taught me some of the special Hadj prayers. "But have you put on pilgrim garb for the 'Omrah' or the 'Hadj,'" they asked—the latter means at least thirteen days without a bath, so I chose the former.

"And what is your sect?"

"I am a Malki."

They looked puzzled. "But the Turks are all Hanafi," they said, and I saw that I was irretrievably relegated to the Ottoman Empire, which struck me as odd, as I have never entered its bournes and my knowledge of the language is negligible.

However, an old sheikh came to the rescue.

"I have always wanted my son to marry a Turk," he said, inspecting me closely. "When we return to Egypt—with safety, Inshaallah, you shall be his bride."

The idea evidently pleased him, for he returned to the subject several times and, having asked my age, name, full family history, and whether I could cook, he announced that he would approach my brother (a wholly fictitious individual) on the subject. At that moment one of the sailors passed and threw me an English phrase—I wondered if he guessed.

On the evening of the fourth day we anchored in the open road-stead outside Jedda and thereafter commenced a period of forty hours which can only be described by one word—hell. As soon as the boat stopped, there was uproar, as every pilgrim started shouting questions at his neighbour and, with a brief interval, during which a doctor rushed on board and looked at the ship's papers, it continued all night and rose to a babel of inarticulate yells shortly after dawn, when a crowd of feluccas gathered round the boat and everyone tried to get into the same one at once. Some three hours were spent in lowering the luggage, arranging it, rearranging it, and wedging the unfortunate passengers on it and between it—very often underneath it.

A felucca should hold comfortably twenty or twenty-five people. Ours contained fifty-seven, with immense quantities of inconveniently-shaped luggage, and we drifted forth into a dead calm sea without a breath of wind. Consequently, we spent four of the hottest hours of the August day crouched, cramped and dripping, in our intolerably stiff and sticky clothes, on the least sharp-cornered luggage we could find. As a matter of fact there was little choice, because we were so wedged in that nobody could possibly move without upsetting the perilous positions of half a dozen neighbours. After the first hour or two, women began to collapse from the heat, but there was nowhere to put them. I squeezed myself into a still smaller corner to allow one sufferer to curl up with head on my knee, but my holland umbrella I would not give up. Umbrellas are permitted to women and forbidden to men, but many of the latter use them to protect their bare or shaven heads. Just when I wondered whether I could endure much longer and whether the woman in my lap was already dead, for her groans had suddenly ceased, a mountainous female who literally bulged over us from behind, chose this opportune moment to remark: "You are not in the least like a Turk, I believe you are English or French."

Luckily, everybody was so hot and tired that her comment aroused no interest. I exploded into a shower of completely meaningless Turkish words—verbs and nouns strung together, helped out with Japanese and Spanish. She was one of the few Pashawat ladies on board, and she knew that this was no Latin or Saxon tongue, so she quailed a little and merely demanded the "Fatha." I was able to satisfy her that I was a Moslem and, when she began to waver about my nationality, I laughed at her till she gave in; but the remaining two hours I spent in that human sardine box were filled with agonized prayers that there might be nobody on board who spoke Turkish.

Fortunately, practically all the pilgrims were of the poorer classes, many of them Fellaheen, and nothing further happened save that three more women and one man collapsed, and when, about 2 PM, we finally accomplished the few hundred yards between our steamer and the quarantine island, they all had to be carried ashore and laid limply in the coolest spots.

I think our felucca must have been somewhat more heavily laden than the rest, for we were the last to arrive and, therefore, all places were taken in the long barn-like structures that shelter the unfortunate pilgrims for twenty-four hours. The island, Gezira, is perhaps 200 yards square and, of course, there is no water on it. All water has to be brought from the mainland and stored in cisterns. It is doled out in small rations to the pilgrims, but it is often insufficient and the wise bring their own zemzimayas full. As a matter of fact there is not much hardship for the ordinary pilgrim, as he is never desirous of privacy and probably finds no fault with the long bare shed which he shares with fifty or sixty others, but it is very hard indeed for the better class hadji. If he arrives late, he may not even find a place in one of the rooms, and he will have to spread his mat on the shore, or sit on the jetty where he will have the shelter of a roof.

Bahia and I found that there was no place left in the shade. Every room was crowded and every corner on beach or wharf remote from the sun already had its occupants, while a free fight was going on round the water cistern. However, luck favoured us, and I finally discovered a rather dusty passage between a room labelled "bureau" and a sort of guard-room. Here we spread our very nice carpet and on it deposited the one thing we had had the physical energy to lift from the boat to the jetty, and carry all over the island in search of rest—a basket of food.

A passing soldier, seeing our parched expressions, mercifully offered us some of his water, and we found we could buy dates, olives and bread from a store on the island. We had barely laid down to sleep, hot, dirty and exhausted, pillowless and cross, when we were joined by the ponderous lady, mighty of stature, with coal-black brows and flabby cheeks. The passage positively shook as she marched up it, followed by her ridiculously small slave, about eight years old. The latter's name was Amma, but I christened her "the Afrit," because she was the most fiendish child I have ever known. The PL[1] had been even less fortunate than we, so she settled herself firmly beside us and her amazingly raucous voice spoilt all chance of sleep. Towards evening, however, the soldier (Mohammed) took pity on us, and allowed us to spread our carpet in a corner of the guard-room, while the PL found shelter with a family in one of the smaller rooms. Mohammed also made relays of tea for us, and we felt altogether happier until a rumour started that some of the people suffering from heat-stroke had got typhoid or cholera. The idea of being quarantined for any lengthy period on that island was terrible, and, for the first time in my life, I realized the awful feeling of utter helplessness—the useless, rebellious despair of the masses against even beneficent officialdom.

---

1 Ponderous Lady.

We were visited by many pilgrims who came to hear if we had any further news, and a rather pretty woman offered me a tube of attar of roses in exchange for some water. When various other cases of heatstroke (or whatever it was) had been discovered, we felt sleep was the only thing left.

I have spent many uncomfortable nights in my life—I once sat up for thirty-six hours in a second-class Chinese troop-train in Cochin China, I got quite used to polished wood opium couches with no pillow; and I remember a weary night spent on a singularly hard table in a mosquito-infested hut on a Samoan volcano; but I have never spent more acutely miserable hours of darkness than those in the Gezira. I made a pillow of my shoes, while Bahia curled her portly, dripping form much nearer me than I liked, and the soldier and his two sons arranged themselves on the window sills.

After half an hour the Egyptian doctor arrived and was noisily ushered upstairs, after which "the Afrit" came in no fewer than eight times to look for some mysterious object of which she apparently did not know the name. The last time the soldier's patience gave way and, as there was no key with which to lock her out, he retired with his mat to the passage. Then the nocturnal chanting began, and wave after wave of sound beat against our walls. One particular cry, a wild, reiterated "Zoh!" "Zoh!" is like the roar of lions in the desert.

I lay awake listening to the majesty of prayer, its fury and its fanaticism apparent in the still darkness, till about 1 AM, when the PL thundered in with elephantine tread and flung herself on the shaking floor.

A couple of hours later she woke to have a dispute with "the Afrit" and, complaining loudly of the heat, stumbled out again, sending her attendant imp back to fetch the things she had left behind. By that time my spirit was broken and I welcomed the dawn and a slice of pink-fleshed melon and sour bread, which was all that Bahia's appetite had left of our provisions. About 6 AM, it was suggested unanimously that I should visit the doctor, whose footsteps could be heard above, and find out our fate. Of course it was unwise, but I stumped cheerfully upstairs knowing that I was gaining a tremendous reputation for courage among the watching pilgrims. Several elderly sheikhs summoned up sufficient energy to follow me and we were welcomed by a delightful young Egyptian, who calmed our fears by assuring us that we could depart at 7.30 AM. After which the men talked politics and I listened with interest in the background till the usual question came: "You are Turkish, ya hanem, I am sure you talk French or English."

"Only French," I replied sadly, and thereafter we had the most charming conversation about our mutual acquaintances in Stamboul and Cairo. Luckily we had so many in the latter place that I was able to be a little vague about the former. I was enjoying myself very much when the young doctor exclaimed: "But of course I will introduce you to a nice Turkish family in Jedda. I will take you straight to their house and you will feel at home and be able to talk Turkish with them."

If only he could have guessed how little I should feel at home— but worse was to come. "The Emir Zeid is in Jedda. His mother is Turkish, so I must tell him about you—you must meet."

"Oh, thank you very much," said I feebly, wondering in how many different countries I had met Emir Zeid and his famous brother, and whether he could possibly fail to recognize me, and what his feeling would be if asked to talk Turkish to me.

I kept my head sufficiently to say I thought I would rather meet all these friends after I returned from Mecca, having given up the pilgrim garb.

"But you are the cleanest person I have seen," said the doctor, surprised, and departed to glance hastily round the island, before ordering everyone aboard the waiting feluccas. This time there was a faint breeze, which strengthened as we tacked in and out of the reefs near Jedda, so we managed to endure the four and a half hours more or less happily, in spite of a violent dispute between Bahia and the boatmen over a coin representing the value of about threepence. All those not completely incapacitated joined in on one side or the other, till the boatman, with an oath, flung the nickel at my handmaiden with the remark that he could not conceive how a good Moslem like Khadija hanem could employ a Christian servant. This, however, was felt to be too great an insult, and the whole boat protested till the boatman gave way and, making a sudden perilous run along the edge of his craft, seized Bahia's head in both hands and imprinted a warm kiss on her forehead. Just as we were in the middle of one of our repetitive songs, there was a terrific bump and we stuck fast at the entrance to the inner roadstead. Thereafter the hell in which we had been living for the last thirty-six hours increased considerably.

One by one the overcrowded feluccas stuck in the shallow water and, under a noontide sun, we sweltered till flat-bottomed craft came out to rescue us—infinitely slowly. As all the pilgrims leaped into them at once, hauling after them as much baggage as possible, and dragging the sick helplessly between them, the larger craft overturned and several pilgrims, including myself, were flung into the water. This would not have mattered very much because it was only about three feet deep, but we got wedged down between the sides of two of the smaller craft, and, for a horrible moment, I thought I should be drowned in an ignominious scrimmage.

Mercifully, someone caught my arm from above, and, with a jerk that nearly wrenched it from its socket, hauled me up into the felucca, where Bahia was screeching wildly without attempting to do anything.

For a moment, I could not understand why, even in the turmoil of the moment, people were looking at me curiously. Then

I discovered that most of my clothing was gone. Veil, sheet and scarf were lost in the harbour and my curly hair waved above a hot, pink face, and a severely plain calico galabia! At this terrible instant I found myself gazing across a heaving mass of pilgrims at the portly occupant of a Sherifian boat, which had come up to see the cause of the disturbance. I remember thinking even then that the official's face showed more surprise than was justified; but various women were pulling me about, offering me portions of their attire, so the incident made little impression at the moment.

Even the little feluccas stuck once or twice on their way in, and we were laboriously pushed off by nude bronze figures splashing in the shallows. Finally, our particular craft ran solidly aground a few yards beyond the end of the jetty, and we were dragged by enthusiastic pilgrims from boat to boat till at last we stood on the quay.

Behind a scarlet curtain, an English doctor was doing quick work with a hypodermic syringe, but this I felt I could not bear, so I pushed myself in between two pilgrims unknown to me and, when my turn came, I said swiftly: "English, been inoculated for four diseases already." I do not know whether English quarantine doctors at Jedda are in the habit of being thus addressed by grey-eyed pilgrims, but this one showed remarkable presence of mind and swiftness of invention, so that I passed on plus a yellow sphere of disinfectant on my arm, but minus a second dose of cholera mixture.

The rest of the quay was divided into little pens, through which we were driven like sheep. I rather think the guardian of the first one demanded proof of inoculation, whereon he smeared an indelible pencil across my wrist, while in the second we were requested to pay a somewhat exorbitant fare for the last bit of our slow passages.

The Pilgrimage Continued

A T LAST, HOT, tired, desperately hungry and thirsty, we passed out of a gate and out of the nightmare. Somebody said, "here are the mutowifeen," and we found ourselves in another pen between a double row of well-dressed intelligent-looking Arabs, one or two of them with short swords in bright embroidered belts. The most imposing personage near the gate, with gold sword and splendid kufiya, was the head mutowif, and if any pilgrim had not already chosen his temporary guide, philosopher and friend, he was asked his nationality by this individual and doled out to the correct mutowif.

As a matter of fact the mutowifs themselves live in Mecca, but they have wakils in Jedda who meet the pilgrim boats and take charge of those whose countries they respectively represent. I was very fortunate in having an introduction to one of the best-known guides—Bakr Hanowi—so, as soon as I called out this name a couple of pale, thin individuals rose from somewhere in the double line of chairs and took possession of us in the most comforting manner. They shepherded us out on to a large wharf where half a dozen sellers of bright-coloured liquids bore down upon us with most inviting looking drinks. Their taste was not quite equal to their appearance, but I drank one glass of each colour, with the idea that if one was going to get cholera one might as well do it thoroughly. The wakil, Abdulla, spread our carpet beside a convenient pillar, took away our passports, which we had been wearing hung round our necks in flat tin cases, and left us to wait the arrival of our luggage, still stranded in the heavy feluccas. We were immediately surrounded by sweetmeat-sellers who offered us all kinds of sticky delicacies on trays, but they were not as prettily coloured as the drinks, so I waved them away. The ponderous lady soon joined us with a few other pilgrims, all bewailing their lost luggage and the hated "needle." I believe the most ignorant considered this was a truly English method of getting rid of superfluous Egyptians. I assured them (with infinitely more truth than most of my statements contained) that "it had not hurt me in the least."

As there was no sign of the luggage, Abdulla suggested we should go up to his house and return later; but Bahia was feeling ill and refused to move from the shade and comparative cool of the wharf, so I left her with some of our friends and the wakil, and started off alone into a white blaze of heat that upset all my preconceived ideas of the tropics, even those of Livingstone and the Zambezi in June. Nevertheless I found Jedda attractive, especially when we turned out of the dusty main street, with semi-European shops and the mosque with a slender white madna, into delicious shady by-ways, where the tall, irregular houses leaned together so that their latticed balconies of carved wood seemed to be whispering harem secrets above the heads of the rare passers-by.

Everywhere were preparations for the pilgrimage—lines of girbas hanging on a wall, a row of shug-dufs, clumsy and unwieldy, waiting for hire, and, blocking every side street, the slender, shaven Hedjazi camels which take the pilgrims to Mecca—yet there were no crowds. Even the covered suqs through which we passed, were almost deserted, save for the sleepy merchants lazily flicking flies off their meat and fruits, or asleep on their piled carpets, or for a few sturdy Bedawi in coarse blue galabias, with curved knives in scarlet sashes and tasselled kufiyas swinging over long plaited hair. To me it is the old houses of Jedda which are its chief charm, not the suqs, which cannot compare with those of Fez or Damascus.

Bakr Hanowi's dwelling was typical of its kind—infinitely high, grey and secretive, with its closed balconies built out in tiers above the very narrow street. Abdulla led me up dark flights of stairs into the cool rooms stretching right across the house, so that the breeze blew through them. On one side, the open balcony of dark carved wood looked into a little yard with pots of mauve flowers hung above it, and, on the other, an immense divan was built out above the street with delicious latticed panels, making the room dim and shadowy, but allowing one to peep through the fretted carving at the pilgrims below. There was nothing in either room except the carpets which covered the floor, and the wide, hard divans with their rows of stiff, solid bolsters; but I have rarely felt more thankful than when I curled myself into a corner of the largest one, and peered down from my projecting seat on to the dusty porters who were squabbling over a few qurush in the toy street below me.

The lady of the house came to visit me—a pale, frail woman, grey and worn, with lovely slender feet, whose toes were hennaed and whose ankles were encircled by heavy silver bands.

She wore tight-fitting white trousers and a thin white galabia with a transparent scarf wound over her head, and she looked so clean she made my stiff calico garment feel dirtier than ever. The appalling state of dirt one must get into if one follows the rule strictly, is perhaps the worst hardship of the pilgrimage. My hostess had a soft sweet voice and she talked to me sadly about the way the pilgrims from Egypt were decreasing in numbers. "This year only three thousand have come and few of them are people of good class. It is the Gezira that they are afraid of, and the English do not like the pilgrimage. They have made many severe rules so as to stop it. Besides, there is war between the Egyptians and the English, isn't there?"

I assured her we had led a very peaceful life in Alexandria, but my words had little effect.

The Egyptian pilgrims are more frightened of, than averse to, the English, but they apparently spread some odd stories in Jedda. We came by the last Egyptian boat, so we got the full flavour of them.

Bahia arrived with the luggage about 4 o'clock, in a state of complete collapse from heat and possibly too many sweetmeats. She developed fever and had to be nursed seriously for twenty-four hours, during which time she lay limply on a divan and I had to cope with many visitors alone.

The day of our arrival I was so tired, having eaten nothing since the melon at dawn, that I discouraged as much as possible the flow of curious pilgrims who came to ask our news and tell us theirs, and devoted most of my attention to securing food. Generally, pilgrims buy their own supplies in the suqs and cook them; but Bahia could not move and my culinary skill is not great. There-fore Abdulla arranged for a cook-shop to send in a meal and, just as the dark came on and the first mosquitoes began biting, there arrived a small boy almost invisible under the big tray he carried. The feast was somewhat reminiscent of Kufara days, for there were the same numerous dishes of vegetables and oddments of meat buried in rich sauces, and flanked with piles of savoury rice and flat hot cakes of bread. Unfortunately, the Jedda water is bad and scarce, because it is brought in from wells outside the town by camel loads, and sold to the people for 4 or 5 qurush a tinful. There is a government condensing machine, but the pilgrims do not get the benefit of its water. The night we arrived, Abdulla's brother developed fever, which became so bad the next day that the gentle lady with the silver anklets left us alone except for a few short visits.

Abdulla woke me at 5 AM, and we went to the suq to buy necessities for our journey to Mecca. There was plenty of meat of a somewhat inferior quality, grapes, figs, bananas and melons sent all the way from Taif by camel and, therefore, very expensive, dates, but practically no vegetables.

India, Egypt and Persia, apparently, all contribute their goods to a town which has no special industries of its own, and European stores may be bought at about double their usual prices. The one thing in which Jedda appears to specialize is strange non-alcoholic drinks of startling hues, such as sherbets, syrups, lemonades, etc. Returning laden with parcels, shuffling in heel-less pilgrim sandals and trying to keep my sheet from slipping off altogether, I could not resist a shop where the bottles were all colours of the rainbow, so Abdulla and I split a rich purple drink and consequently dripped more than usual as we toiled up his uneven stairs.

"Bahia is a little better," announced one, Fadda, the blackest slave girl I have ever seen, whom I had left in charge, so I determined to spend the morning writing in my delightful balcony corner; but my peace was rudely destroyed by the sudden appearance of two richly-garbed and imposing individuals in silken kaftans and white turbans swathed round plaited straw caps or brimless hats. I have not the least idea who they were, but it was quite evident that they were deeply suspicious of me. While sitting one on each side of me on a big divan, they politely and smilingly plied me with intimate questions. I think they thought I was a Greek impostor. One of them had a disagreeable face and I disliked him at once, but the other had a friendly smile and I felt we might get on quite well if I knew who he was. When I had told him the name of my Egyptian father and husband and my

Turkish mother, with other details of my life, he suddenly asked me if I had been in America. I replied no, but that I knew Paris well and, in order to change the conversation, I added that I had seen the Emir Feisul there, upon which the nice one smiled his widest and said that the Emir was beloved in whatever country be visited. I thought this might not be strictly true of Paris, but I had already found that his name worked magic in Arabia. We discovered his photograph in a corner of the smaller room and subsequently a friendly conversation waxed round the merits of the Sherif's third son. However, my uninvited guests departed obviously suspicious, and I wondered what their next step would be. I spent a miserable morning thinking of the unveiled appearance I had presented at the quay, and trying to remember the name of the official who had looked at me most suspiciously from the Sherifian boat. It was not till the afternoon that I remembered it was Abdul Melek, the Sherifian wazir in Cairo, whom I ought to have known as well as my own brother, considering the many times we had met. If only my veil and sheet (meliya) had not been torn off in the free fight among the feluccas, all might have been well. At the time I had paid little attention to it, because the arm by which I had been roughly hauled out from a wedged position half under water between two feluccas was badly wrenched, and several of the women were in worse condition than myself. However, all these memories now came to torment me, and Bahia must have found me an unenthusiastic companion as we bought stores, arranged a camel string for Medina, and visited certain notables to whom I had letters of introduction.

Nothing more happened that day, and I made all arrangements to start for Mecca the following afternoon. We bought a shugduf, a most amazing construction in which two people balance perilously on a couple of wide bed-like trays slung on either side of the camel, with the luggage piled in the middle. It has a lattice roof and sides, covered with a carpet, so that the whole thing resembles a sort of clumsy tent; but, unless both travellers are equal in weight, and unless they both get in and out at exactly the same moment, the whole shug-duf overbalances. We wandered through the suqs in search of provisions and bought dates, melons and bread, with olives and onions for Bahia, who had odd tastes, and clay jars to keep the water cool, and a sheep each to give to the poor in order to ensure a successful pilgrimage. Then we returned to our house and watched the crowd of pilgrims all preparing for the journey.

We were lodged in one of the streets in the Egyptian pilgrim quarters. Consequently all our friends of the boat could be heard shouting and screaming in various directions. I should not have conceived it possible that even 600 throats could have made such a noise, and the babel only increased with the darkness. The richer pilgrims hire a couple or more rooms, as we had done, but the poorer merely pay a few qurush for floor-space in an immensely long hall, and do most of their cooking in the street or on any flat available roof. Most of that night we had a stream of visitors, including the ponderous lady with her attendant "Afrit." I remember that, while conversing pleasantly about the exorbitant prices of the country, I caught forty-three bugs crawling up my ankle. Sleep was an impossibility in any case, because of the mosquitoes who do not content themselves with humming. They have a particularly vicious squeal, and after that second night there was not a single unbitten space on my anatomy. On the contrary, in most places, the bites were superimposed one upon another.

We rose with the sun to see the departure of my Medina camels. I had to send them on ahead, as this particular year there was to be no regular pilgrim traffic between the two holy cities, and all the camels in Mecca would be needed to bring back the ordinary pilgrims. I had some difficulty in persuading Mirzuk el

Ourdi, a well-known Bedouin, to undertake this journey, as there was much fighting between the Ateibah tribes, the latter of whom show leanings towards the Ikhwanism of Nejd. However, a gold watch and a tactful bribe decided him to brave the perils of the Eastern track—the famous Darb esh Sharkia. The Egyptian caravan was not due to start till late afternoon, when it would ride all through the night to Bahari, the half-way halting-place on the way to Mecca, but Abdulla went to fetch his charges' passports in the morning.

Then the blow fell. All were returned except ours, and no reason was given for this omission. All Abdulla would say was that it was the will of Allah, but his whole manner had changed. Instead of almost cringing politeness, he became frankly threatening, and I expected we should be turned out of the house. Bahia wanted to sit down and weep, but I remembered the name of a friend's friend, an Egyptian who lived in Jedda, and I determined to invoke his aid. Nobody knew where he lived, so, for three hours, we trudged wearily from street to suq, from house to house. Veiled and muffled as I was, the heat was intolerable, and pilgrim sandals are not conducive to comfort. Very soon I had huge blisters on my soles, but I was determined not to give in. As we were pilgrims, we met with courtesy everywhere and, at one very large house where we hoped our quest would have ended, we were invited in by a pretty girl in the lightest of attire. She wore only a little transparent muslin corselet and a length of striped cotton stuff, rose and blue, wound round her slender hips. She made us "fadhl" in a great airy room, and slaves brought us cups of unpleasant scented tea with sweet sticky biscuits.

We escaped as soon as possible to resume our quest, and I could not help being struck by the varied charms of old Jedda. Quite unexpectedly one would turn a corner and find oneself in an open square, or wide street, with a tapering white madna at one corner and odd little booths of carved woodwork in the shadow. The main population appears to spend its time asleep on string bedsteads before the doors of their houses, but the women are among the most discreet in the world of Islam, for one sees nothing at all of their faces. The white, transparent indoor dress is tucked up round the waist, and the long white tight-fitting trousers stuffed into soft primrose-yellow leather boots. It is a formidable garment, whose top edge is stiffly starched to stand erect above the head and support the meliya's folds, and, with only the tiniest slit for the eyes, it falls wide and embroidered to the knees, making a sort of apron which can be occasionally glimpsed when the blue silk striped meluja, edged with silver or gold, sways open an inch or two. Some of the women have tiny gilt bells sewn into the edges of this upper garment, so that it tinkles as they move.

My friend's friend was finally discovered, just as life had become a flaming river of heat which dripped from brow to heel, and, with swift generosity, he put himself entirely at our service. "But it is to the English you must go, Khadija hanem—I know an officer here. He arranges all the Egyptian passports. I will take you to him and he will help you at once."

In vain I protested that I was shy, that I was exhausted, that I was not used to talking to men. My new-found ally was, as yet, cool and therefore enthusiastic, and I found myself shuffling along beside him, almost weeping from my blistered feet, out beyond the suqs to a strange, clean quarter of the town where England occupies a large white house with a wide view of hill and sea. Thereafter I seriously began to wonder whether I was dreaming. After a short wait in a breezy hall, where a Sikh gave me the first good water I'd tasted in Jedda, my Egyptian friend beckoned me upstairs into an office replete with every kind of punkah and fan.

"I have told him. He will help, but he does not speak good Arabic. Have you no few words of English?"

I regretted deeply that I had not, but said hopefully that we all spoke French in the Alexandrian harems.

A hot, bored, somewhat shy officer greeted me with stilted, courteous phrases, upon which I became so loquacious that he turned helplessly to my companion. I apologized and proffered my story in French, my countryman replying in a most exotic language, with many gesticulations to help him out. However, he promised to write to the Minister of Foreign Affairs and secure the passports and, in a state of complete bewilderment, I left. On the stairs the dreamlike feeling increased, for Colonel Lawrence passed me, demure and neat and very hot under his yellow kufiya. He glanced disgustedly at my dirty white and made a disparaging remark to his unknown companion, who replied: "She has rather fine eyes, but probably she's got skin disease under that veil. They all have."

In the hall we met my old friend Haddad Pasha, mopping his brow, and the sudden frantic desire to laugh and laugh, with which I had been struggling for the last half-hour, overcame me. I kicked off a sandal and choking, coughing, blindly groped for it till my friend had stumped upstairs.

The whole town was full of camels as we returned by dim, twisting by-ways, under old arches and through covered passages, where Bedouin drivers with scarlet kufiyas and coarse sacking abbas, smoked long-stemmed shishas and discussed the prospects of the pilgrimage. The different quarters of the town might have been different countries, for each was devoted to pilgrims of special boats. Thus just below us were Javanese, and farther away Indians. That year no pilgrims came from Syria or Turkey, and the cross-country routes were closed, but 40,000 Javanese had come from Islam's new nurseries, where yearly she is gaining ground in the Far East, and 4,000 Indians. Two boat-loads of Persians, Shias of course, were expected that day, but the great mass of pilgrims had already gone on ahead. The Mahmal was arriving and would visit the tomb of our Mother Eve the following day with cere-mony and music, before going on to Mecca.

As we were assured by the sympathetic Egyptian that we should most certainly receive our passports next morning, we were able to watch, unmoved, the departure of our fellow-Egyptians. The loading of their camels took nearly seven hours, during which the deafening babel never ceased for a single instant, so that even Bahia breathed a sigh of relief when the end of the camel string, roped head to tail, lurched out of our narrow alley with final shouts and roars of expostulation, encouragement and good wishes. Our peace was short-lived. Abdulla and Mohammed ner-vously, but quite definitely, refused to be seen in the streets with us, or to perform any other service for such doubtful characters as we had become. This attitude, however, merely roused the sympa-thies of some of the neighbours with whom we had fraternized, and shortly the Egyptian quarter was divided, but the larger por-tion was in our favour. In every country where the masses suffer silently at the hands of officialdom, it is enough to murmur the words "Hakooma-siassa" (government-politics) with a significant gesture, to become a popular martyr. Many people came to ask me not to "anger myself sick," and my Egyptian relations became more and more powerful with Bahia's righteous indignation.

The mosquitoes took their nightly meal, and about 5 AM, with a most sympathetic escort, we made the obligatory visit to the tomb of our Mother Eve, who, by the way, was considerably more than two hundred feet long. On the way we met some of the Egyptian officers escorting the Mahmal, and the oddity of the pilgrim garb struck one forcibly when one saw these smart, mod-ern young men riding well-groomed polo-ponies, yet clad only in bath towels! Mother Eve seemed a long way off that morning, though she is only just outside the town. One of my blisters had burst, which rather marred my enthusiasm for walking all round the sort of trench where Mother Eve is buried, with a little qubba about the middle of her anatomy and a chapel at each end.

Crowds of pilgrims were doing the visit, but we got near enough to touch the bars of the first chapel and repeat the suitable prayers after one of the guardians, who perform this office for a small fee. Beggars of all ages swarmed on every side, for the pilgrims are generous, but they were contented with minute coins, as was also the incalculably filthy crone who took our shoes at the entrance to the qubba. Here we paid the guardian to make a special exhortation that Bahia's next child might be a boy and, having kissed the tomb and pressed our foreheads to the rail on all four sides, my hand-maiden forcibly wrenched some hairs from my head and tied them round a bar. "You will now have many sons," she said gravely, "perhaps thirteen."

When we returned to Bakr Hanawi's house, I found a letter, in execrable French, stating that the Minister of F.A. had been on the point of returning our passports, when he had heard that Abdul Melk had reported the matter to King Hussein.

This really settled the matter, for the king, who, like Abdul Melek, knew me personally, was the last man to allow a Christian on the pilgrimage; but I determined to make a final effort. I went to see the Sherif Mohammed and, by dint of quite shameless bribing, procured an introduction for Khadija hanem, to the Emir Zeid. The Sherifian family are generally easy of access to pilgrims, but an international conference was occupying all their leisure moments, so I had to wait till next day before a black soldier from the famous Bedouin guard led me up to a cool, wind-swept room overlooking the sea, where I was shortly met by the Sherif's youngest son in a brown abaya and golden kufiya. I had almost touched Lawrence as he went out of the house and his unrecognizing stare made me confident that Zeid would not know me; but the East is more used to camouflage than the West, and, before I had said three sentences, I found my confession forestalled.

Unfortunately, the king had departed that morning for Mecca, but his son promised to write to him at once and ask for a special permit. He also made me the most valued gift that Jedda can produce—a camel-load of water, which considerably cheered my remaining days in the town, in spite of the fact that the Sherif proved unrelenting and permission was refused one Khadija-daughter-of-Abdulla Fahmi to make the pilgrimage. She had, however, the doubtful satisfaction of being lionized by a large section of Jedda, who came to the conclusion that it was all a political arrangement of the English to stop a lady closely connected, through her well-known brother, with the Egyptian government, from coming into contact with the powers that be in Mecca.

"The English have good hearts," said one learned sheikh, "but their politics are bad."

Shortly after came the news of the Emir Feisul's unanimous election to the Mesopotamian throne and, in the wave of enthusiastic satisfaction with which all Jedda acknowledged the triumph of her most popular prince, the wrongs of the Sitt Khadija were forgotten.

1923

Odyssey in Yemen and Asir

From Chapters X–XII of
Adventure: Being a Gipsy Salad—
Some Incidents, Excitements and Impressions
of Twelve Highly-Seasoned Years (1928)

The Odyssey of a Sambukh

MOST PEOPLE ASSURE me that it is impossible to pick out any particular moment as the best or worst in their lives, but I know without any shadow of doubt what was the worst physical ordeal of my heaped-up, though often incomplete, experiences. Not for all the gold of Ephesus would I repeat that fourteen-day journey in a leaking, wind-racked and most unsavoury dhow, symbol of perpetual motion and such violent nausea that one of the Arab sailors remarked to me; "Had I thy middle, I should throw myself and it into the sea!"

When, after eighteen months of intermittent negotiations, Sayed Mustapha el Idrisi finally invited me to visit Asir, I was warned by an Arab that, in all probability, his cousin, the late Emir, had little to do with the invitation. "No foreigners are allowed in that country," he said; "it is for Moslems only. Be assured that if you land at Hodeidah you will be received courteously, entertained with the utmost hospitality, and dismissed before you have set foot outside the town."

Determined not to miss the chance of learning more about an almost unknown country which was then the Naboth's vineyard of King Hussein, Ibn Saoud and the Imam Yehya, I decided to give Hodeidah a wide berth and attempt to sail direct to Jizan, 150 miles farther north, and the winter head-quarters of the Idrisi, by means of a sambukh from the African coast. With this object in view, I went to Port Sudan and set about looking for a dhow— cautiously, because I was not certain how my scheme would be regarded by a paternal Government which strongly objects to wasting departmental time over such "unfortunate incidents" as a subject or two getting lost, stolen or strayed.

The first few days were disappointing. Not only were there no available sambukhs, but the local sailors insisted that they had never heard of Jizan.

One raïs (captain) doubtfully offered to land me at Lith, in the Hedjaz, but volunteered the information that we should probably be captured by the Dhuwwi Hassan, who, with their neighbours, the Dhuwwi Barakat, the tribe which butchered the unfortunate survivors of the *Emden*, are notorious pirates.

Other headmen produced more and more unpleasant stories of slave traffic along the Arabian coast, till, after I had been five days in Port Sudan, an old man sailed in, in a sambukh full of salt, and it appeared that not only had he once been to Jizan, some forty-five years ago, but that, for £70 Egyptian, he was willing to go there again.

"I will not go near the Italian land," he said, "for there are bad men and robbers in those parts, and there are two places from which the slave dhows come, where no man is safe, but, if you will let me keep out at sea the whole way, I will take you in safety, Insha-allah," and he spoke of the infamous Zaraniq tribe, whose territory is south of Hodeidah, but who creep up the Idrisi coast and out to the Farisan Isles in search of prey; and of the Zubeid, who make a fat living by looting sambukhs.

My spirits fell at the idea of weeks in an open boat in the middle of the Red Sea, with a temperature of 92 deg. Fahr. in the shade; but the old man was adamant, and the bargain was finally struck with the aid of the kindly harbour-master, Captain Higgs. Explaining to me, with a twinkle which belied his caution, that his spirit of adventure had been killed by years of routine, he threw himself with zest into the conspiracy which was to allow a certain dhow, apparently as devoid of passengers as of cargo, to slip away unsuspected in the middle of the night.

An Egyptian, Kamel Effendi Fahmi, an intimate friend of Sayed Mustapha, had kindly agreed to accompany me, and we crept on board in starlight while a swarm of cat-like creatures, nude except for a loincloth, hustled our luggage after us. The raïs, distinguished by his red turban, murmured comfort as we acquired our first bruises, and warnings with regard to the inadvisability of showing a light. Captain Higgs wished us luck in a voice which was almost as suitable for a conspirator as my hollow whispers. Then, with the first streak of dawn, our craft was gliding out of harbour, and, as I remembered bitterly afterwards, that was the last bit of gliding she did on the journey.

For the benefit of those who are fortunate enough never to have travelled in a dhow, I must explain that the *Khadra* was an open boat, between 30 and 40 feet long and perhaps 10 feet wide, with a depth of some 5 feet in the middle. Her crew of eight lived on a small decked-in space some 9 feet by 7 feet, which they shared with the rudder, while Kamel Fahmi and I camped under a piece of canvas below. Now, at this season, a very strong south or southeast wind blows up the Red Sea (the "Azzieb"). As the crow flies, it is 350 miles from Port Sudan to Jizan, but this adverse wind generally prolongs the journey and forces sailing-craft to hug the coast as long as possible. As we had insufficient ballast, none being obtainable in a hurry at Port Sudan, the *Khadra* stood right out of the water, and the least ripple swayed her, while anything in the nature of a swell reduced her to the consistency of a cork.

She did not roll or pitch in the ordinary sense of the word. She wallowed in great, heaving circles. She lurched up again with a sickening spin, to crash back with a loving attempt to absorb as much of the ocean as possible into her empty interior.

Moreover, the Odyssey of a sambukh is expressed in smells. Subtle and unmistakable, superimposed one upon another, yet losing none of their original force, there drifted round me the stench of every cargo the *Khadra* had ever carried. At one time she must have been laden with dried fish—I could almost see the bones sticking out of shadowy corners. I recognized the sickly smell of salt, the fetid odour of wet doura, and the muskiness of long-forgotten coffee. The thin cat, which crept about and licked all our provisions, had not completely dispatched her victims— some must have slunk beyond her reach and rotted in the interstices of the boards—but beyond and above all this *soufflé* of smell was a pervading reek of stale seaweed from the rocks which had been hastily torn from the reef to take the place of sand ballast.

Idly, while I thought of the *Khadra's* past as apparent to my nose, I had been watching a thin dark line which trickled across a corner of my bedding. Finally I put out a finger to examine the mystery. Twenty-two little, round, brown ones were making for home under my pillow, but the twenty-third was fat and squelchy. I waited for no more, made for the air and the dizzy swing of the rudder platform, where in future I camped day and night with compass and charts, a mattress, and some tins of sausages, which were easy to heat on the box of charcoal fixed in the middle of the restricted deck. Round this lived and slept, prayed, ate and smoked the curiously mixed crew.

There was Saeed, the son of the raïs, a startlingly black person, born of a Sudani mother, who never left the rudder unless "abu salama" (porpoises) were sighted, when he would rush to the bows, with a spear ready to throw if any incautious fish rolled within reach. The brothers Hamad were light brown Hedjazis with curling hair and beards, who were never seen without their long pipes, and they had a small kinsman, Ali, who looked like one of Andrea del Sarto's angel children till suddenly he shaved his curls, and from a boy of twelve turned into a stunted youth of twenty. There was Salim, the slave, and Mohammed, who never spoke during the day, but at night, having cleaned the last grain of rice from the deepest crack in the common platter, used to tell amazing stories of fishermen and jinns, to which the last and smallest member of the crew, the little black Ahmed, listened with eyes almost as large as his preternaturally enormous mouth.

The first sunset found us anchored within the reef a little north of the islets of Tella Kebir and Tella Szerir. With a north-east wind, changing to east, we had come 69 miles down the coast, but the two following days the wind was from the south, and we lay helplessly rolling in company of two other sambukhs. Saeed caught us fish in the shallow water, and it was while watching his skill with the round, lead-weighted net, which he flung ahead of him whenever he saw a patch of silver, that the idea came to me of camping on the patch of sand to which I had paddled in the huri—a 12-foot canoe about 18 inches wide, scooped out of a single piece of wood.

The islet was full of curious holes, and it was very damp, but at least, it was motionless. One glance at the swinging *Khadra* decided me. "Fetch my kit," I told Mohammed. He waved his hands and murmured "Bish-Bish." Saeed joined him and shouted the same word, but as I did not understand what it meant, I ignored them, and rolling myself up under a bit of scrub prepared to wait. Perhaps I slept for a few minutes; in any case I lay very still, and when I opened my eyes I thought I was in the middle of one of those horrible nightmares from which one cannot awake, though one knows they are unreal. The island had turned yellow.

Moreover, it was moving—a fantastic, heaped-up, writhing move-ment. Everything moved, and everywhere bits of yellow heaved up above the rest and scuttled hither and thither. In fact, from every hole which made the surface of the islet like a sponge had come crabs—fat, long-legged, yellow crabs. As soon as I stirred, there was chaos. Pink, bulgy crabs emerged from under the yel-low ones, and with startling rapidity the whole mass scuttled to the sea or helter-skelter into the holes. At one moment there was a seething stretch of long legs working furiously, of unpleasant bodies piled one upon another. The next there were a few bubbles in the sand and some yellow patches rapidly disappearing under the waves—but I no longer wanted to camp on that patch of sand.

By 1 AM on that night (November 12) the wind had swung round to the east, and the raïs was shouting: "We start; let us start"; and then, to a neighbouring dhow: "Ya Masri—oh, Egyp-tian—Start!" With a chanted "Alù, Allah! Alù, Allah!" ("The sails, oh God!") we slipped from the protection of the reef and beat out to sea against the wind, to discover if the elements were more favourable away from the coast; but were driven in again, 39 miles to the south, and anchored outside Akik, beside a flat island decorated with the remains of two recent wrecks, which provided us with fish for our dinner. It was fortunate that we were capable of eating it, for the wind had been strong that day and as we bore down full speed, carrying a large amount of canvas, on the narrow opening into the reef the sails stuck for a second. We missed the passage, and the raïs flung the rudder round a fraction too late. There was a faint jarring grind, and water seemed to leap at me as I crouched in the stern. Then, amidst a pandemonium of shouting, I was hurled across the charcoal box on to a water-bar-rel, while heavy chests slid after me, but luckily, by the time I had picked myself up, drenched and bruised, the *Khadra* had recov-ered her balance. She had knocked a hole in her starboard side, and, henceforth, Ali spent much of his time baling out most evil-smelling water. I understand, too, that a portion of sha-ab (coral reef) adhered to us until the boat was dragged ashore at Jizan and subjected to a week's overhauling.

On November 13 we started at 3 AM, but only achieved 13 miles in a choppy sea before anchoring off Ras Abid, and the following day we experienced our first really bad weather. We made good pace in the morning, but the wind strengthened towards evening to an easterly gale, and white crests seemed to embrace the labouring *Khadra*.

Apart from being permanently seasick, by this time I felt as if my spine were being crashed through the top of my head with each downward lurch, so, when the raïs put in to the Eritrean coast and anchored in shallow water, where there was no reef and no protection from the wind, I insisted on going ashore. It was no easy task in such a sea, but choosing the moment when the huri swung up on the crest of a wave, I dropped into it and was landed, completely soaked, but still clutching a blanket and a pan of charcoal. We had come 44 miles and were within sight of a post of native askari, marked on the chart as "Stone House," but called by the Arabs, "Taqlein." As we had no papers and no desire to be asked our business, Saeed and I hid our fire in a hollow among the sand mounds, and crawled to and from the huri with the utmost caution; but I slept like a log in spite of wet garments, and was furious to be awakened shortly after midnight with the announcement that the wind had gone down and the raïs wanted to start.

This time we sailed for thirty-four hours, for, though we picked up the light of Difnein (62 miles) after sunset on November 15, there was so little breeze that we did not reach the island till 11 AM on the 16th.

After the indescribable filth of the sambukh, the crystal-clear water in the shelter of rocks and scrub tempted us to bathe, so we camped for the night, and only started beating south towards Harmil the following morning.

That day the raïs's sense of direction left him, and when, after sunset, we anchored near a group of islets with a curious coral formation in the shape of a giant T sticking out of the reef, he confessed he did not know where we were. Generally, though he liked to hear that his landmarks appeared on the chart (often by different names) he scorned my compass. "At sea we look at the sun and the stars," said Saeed, "and near the reef we pray."

On the morning of the 18th there was much argument, after which the crew decided, but without much spontaneity, that we were at Kad-hu. As this is charted a single island, and as we could already see several different islets, I insisted on treating the nearest as Tanam, 28 miles from Difnein. On this supposition I took a bearing on Harmil from the chart, and kept the boat to this course, amidst half-hearted expostulations, which faded away altogether when we passed land which resembled the Wusta and Isratu groups.

"Allah Akbar! Allah Karim!" exclaimed the raïs, when Harmil duly appeared in the afternoon after a certain amount of suspense caused by unidentified rocks; but he said nothing about my compass. As we came into the bay, a mass of wreckage drifted past us, with several bales which looked like carpets and native clothing, but the sea was too bad to tempt the greed of the crew. The wind was blowing up for its usual evening gale, so I decided to sleep ashore, as the wide flat sweep of Harmil gave little shelter to the sambukh. With infinite labour we put up a tent on the soft ground, but the noise of straining rope and canvas only ceased when, at dawn—by which time everything was inches deep in sand—the whole thing collapsed on my head.

After that the wind began to go down, and since Saeed had spent several hours "plumbing" the worst deficiencies in our reef-battered craft, at 2.30 PM (November 19) we started on the longest lap of our journey, steering for Sorso in the Farisan Islands, in a strong south-south-east wind. As soon as we left Harmil we came into a heavy, white-crested swell, but we travelled well, and the men grew more cheerful. Elated by my success at finding Harmil, I urged them to steer north of east to avoid the main bulk of Farisan, of whose regard for strangers the raïs expressed himself so doubtful that he had produced four rifles, and urged me to follow suit with my revolvers. Saeed smiled and said nothing, for he had recovered his sense of direction. All that night we sailed, and the next day; after which everyone began to worry as to where on earth we were going. "Wallahi! I do not like this work," said Abdul Kheir; "it is dangerous to go into the reef at night. We must stay at sea."

But naturally I could not agree with him. The sight of anything as solid as a reef would be Paradise for me, besides which I was very anxious about Kamel Fahmi, who by this time was seriously ill.

Our drinking water was practically exhausted, but this did not affect the Arabs, who, on long dhow journeys when they follow the winds from Persia to Bombay, or Aden to Zanzibar, are in the habit of diluting their fresh water with salt, so that by the end of the second month they are drinking the sea waves neat.

For food, we were reduced to the fish we could catch with a trawling line. I remember that particular day produced a monster, a fabulous cross between a conger eel and a shark. When the combined efforts of the crew had hauled the brute on board, its struggles nearly upset us. Pursued by half a dozen knives—personally I thought nothing but dynamite or first-class exorcism would finish the mythological creature—it flopped off the rudder platform on to Kamel Fahmi, who lay semi-conscious below. The breath must have been nearly knocked out of his body and he woke with a gulp, felt the swirl of bilge water over his feet and the slither of scales on his face, so decided that he was already dead and at the bottom of the sea! It took considerable argument and some physical force to convince him that we had not been shipwrecked; but after that no one had much time to talk, for the *Khadra* was leaking like a sponge. It was only by baling in relays that we kept her afloat, and, hourly, water gained on us.

Fortunately, just before 2 AM on the 21st, by which time the crew were trying to wedge what was left of their rags into the starboard rent, not only land, but mountains, loomed in front of us. There was hardly any swell, so we anchored some way out, and, with a muttered "God is great," Saeed dropped the rudder and in two minutes was asleep at my feet, while the old raïs shook his head. "Only Allah knows where we are!" he muttered disconsolately, as he lay down and drew an incredibly dirty quilt over his face.

The crew slept in turns till the sky was aflame and the land red-gold with that peculiar glow of desert Arabia, between the blue of mountain and sea. A few palms broke the line of sand, and a couple of smaller hills stood between the distant escarpment and the shore. One of these we identified as Jebel Rakab el Kudain on the coast of Asir, some 60 miles northeast of the island for which we had been steering. "You wanted to go to the north, ya Sitt!" cackled the raïs, and I had to join in the hearty laugh at my expense.

An unexpected current and the heavy swell had swept us right out of our course, and round the northern limit of the Farisan group, so that, though we had travelled 120 miles in the 39½ hours since leaving Harmil, we were still 60 or 70 miles from Jizan, which now lay south-east of us.

All that day we crept down the coast, half-waterlogged, but tacking clumsily back and forth against a south wind, yet the long promontory of Ras Turfa never seemed to grow any nearer. There were other sambukhs about, pearl fishers perhaps, for this is one of the principal trades of Jizan, but we kept away from them as much as possible and anchored at sunset, just off the sandy neck which guards the Khor Abu-s-Saba.

While the stars were still bright we were off again, tacking round the headland and along the narrow strip of Ferafer Island. The south wind still held, but we saw the "Gebel" of Jizan at 7.30 AM and crept slowly closer all the morning till we could see the shape of the rocks jutting out in a spur from the flat "sabakha" on either side. The white sails were slipping in one by one, and gradually we could make out the dark mass of houses north of the old Turkish fort, crowned with the Idrisi's guns. At last, just after 2 PM, the *Khadra* found her way into the reef and anchored in the double line of sambukhs under the shelter of the cliff. "Allah is generous," said the raïs, as he started changing his loin-cloth for a garment which looked like a night-shirt.

We had been fourteen days on board, and taking our journey point to point, had done 469 miles.

"Never again," I said to Kamel Fahmi, who had miraculously recovered at sight of land, as I crawled under the awning to change into native dress.

Guests of a Hermit Emir

JIZAN WAS THE starting-point of a journey by car, camel and donkey through southern Asir and the flat strip of Yemen which lies between mountains and sea. I had hoped to go up into the highlands where Ibn Saoud was then raiding his enemy King Hussein, but that thrilling project did not materialize. However, some account of what is still approximately unknown country may fitly find place among these impressions of adventure.

It was no easy matter landing at Jizan, muffled in the folds of an Egyptian habbara over a long tight-sleeved dress of magenta silk embroidered with gold, for I could hardly see through the double thickness of my veil and my heelless slippers always fell off at the critical moment, while the sun beat fiercely on my head, inadequately protected by the thin silk covering. The water is so shallow that even the canoes cannot go right inshore, so I finished my journey on a sort of rope tray, borne shoulder high by four swollen-muscled porters accustomed to carrying out 500-lb. loads of skins, coffee and flour to the waiting sambukhs. Deposited suddenly at the feet of an exceedingly good-looking young Arab in an azure robe, whom I afterwards found out was Sayed el Abed, cousin of the Idrisi, I could think of absolutely nothing to say; but, fortunately, all the sheikhs who came down to meet me were so embarrassed at being in the presence of a woman that my silence passed unnoticed. We shuffled up through the sand to the guest-house of the Sayeds, a curious building, half-fortress, half-dwelling, which proved to contain some comfortable rooms, furnished with hard divans covered with carpets and rows of stiff bolsters.

Here, after a ceremonious visit from Sayed es Senussi, the late Idrisi's vicegerant at Jizan, we were given a mighty meal, consisting of a sheep stuffed with almonds, raisins, rice, hard-boiled eggs, and all sorts of spice, and flanked with dates which had come by sea from Basrah, bitter limes, and olives served on oyster shells, bowls of curdled milk, and sweet sticky pastes, pink-fleshed water-melons, whole chickens and reddish-black millet bread. The repast was served by soldiers of the Idrisi's own guard, which numbers 500 picked men from Sabya and Abu Arish. When they stacked their rifles in a corner of the room, they looked rather like dancing girls, with their bunches of neat, well-oiled ringlets under a silver fillet, fine long features and well-cut mouths, whose curves were as feminine as their lithe boneless bodies. They wore kilts (futahs) of striped Yemeni cloths and little boleros of mauve or primrose linen, which were most picturesque, but somewhat out of keeping with their immense cartridge belts and the curved silver swords attached to them.

Asir is an ascetic and primitive country, where life is divided between work, prayer, eating and sleeping. The day begins with the dawn and ends three hours after sunset, when a drum is beaten loudly round the town as a sign for people to keep inside their own walls. The ladies never leave their houses, where they occupy a single inferior apartment isolated from the building, which generally contains two rooms almost as high as they are long. In the street you see only servant girls scurrying along to the bazaars in crimson tobhs (straight dresses) with black veils, red bordered, over their heads.

Portly merchants, with huge turbans of saffron, rose and orange, ride by on minute grey donkeys, almost lost amidst the riders' drapery. Fuzzy-headed Bedouin, naked to the waist, their bodies gleaming with oil, drive strings of camels laden with firewood at 4d. a load. Here are fish merchants with their silvery wares spread out on leaf platters. Here is a pearl seller with his precious grains tied in a scrap of scarlet muslin. A few yards down the narrow alley, roofed with mats, you may buy a basket of custard apples for a farthing, or hammered-silver belts that tinkle with a score of bells, or a tiny piece of raw black amber, which, as everyone knows, is the very best charm against the evil eye. A little farther on small boys in golden yellow, with daggers almost as big as themselves, will sell you anything from a camel at £4 to a chicken at 1½d. Life is cheap in Asir and luxury is forbidden. There are no cafés and no dancers, smoking is a punishable offence, and gold so sinful a thing that the Idrisi will not even have it in his house. For this reason my gift of a gold watch and seals was somewhat unfortunate, but the Emir's tact was equal to the occasion.

It had been arranged that I should pass as Kamel Fahmi's sister, as no European woman had ever been seen in the country; but even my strictly Moslem dress and behaviour did not prevent crowds following us as we wandered through the markets, with a rising murmur, "These are not of the sons of Adam."

Fortunately, my companion was a great personal friend of the Idrisi family, so, after two days at Jizan, the Emir commanded his presence at Sabya, the summer capital, 25 miles away. A Ford car was put at our disposal, and a Turkish chauffeur, obviously under the impression that it was a tank, for he avoided nothing smaller than a sandhill, and did his best to wreck our nerves with his precipitous dashes through scrub, rock and wadi. In order to do honour to Fahmi, who had rendered his family signal services in Egypt, the Idrisi sent a guard of fifty horsemen to meet the car half-way to the capital, and these careered wildly around, showing off their horsemanship at the expense of their steeds, mostly half-broken stallions bred from Nejd stock.

Sabya, with some 20,000 inhabitants, lies between two small tabular hills called Gebel Aquar, where emeralds are supposed to be found. It is divided into two parts. The old town, at the foot of Aquar el Yemeni, consists chiefly of the same pointed huts (areesh) as Jizan; but in the new "city" the Idrisi was completing quite an imposing stone-built palace, surrounded by the houses of his ministers and the chief merchants.

The Hermit of Arabia—so called because he used to shut himself up for months, though business of State could only be conducted when he descended to his liwan, and because he preferred a life of philosophical, religious and judicial study to the political power which had been thrust upon him by circumstances—was an imposing figure, very tall and dignified, with the dark skin inherited from his negroid grandmother rather than his Indian mother. Disinterested, just, sincere, and fabulously generous, he had a great reputation amongst the Bedouin, who considered that "Allah always helped the Imam,"[1] and looked upon him as the peacemaker of Arabia and the court of appeal against Ibn Saoud, King Hussein and the Imam Yehya of Sana. He had a critical appreciation of British administration, and often, in discussing some injudicious action of postwar years, he said: "At heart the English are sound. These are only small things."

---

1 "Imam" means a religious leader and, in this case, refers to the Idrisi and not to Imam Yehya.

In spite of this admiration for our powers of organizing, the Idrisi appeared to have a great antipathy to foreigners, and would neither allow them to enter his country nor meet them, unless in the case of a very rare official visit, which, if he could not depute to his cousin, he received as near the edge of the waves as possible. This may have been due to a strain of mystic reserve in his character, or to the belief that his country had not yet reached the state where it could benefit by association with Europe.

Outside the towns, the people are wild and savage—primitive creatures, half-nude, with shocks of coarse hair, distrustful and suspicious, almost pagan, believing in a hundred superstitions, and wearing as amulets polished black stones which must surely be relics of the pre-Islamic stone worship which existed in ancient Yemen. I have often seen the Asir Bedouins say the Moslem prayers with their backs to Mecca and their faces turned to the sun.

When I was in Asir, the Idrisi had made a treaty with Ibn Saoud, by which his eastern frontiers were guaranteed, while he supplied famine-haunted Riyadh with thousands of live stock—sheep, goats and cattle. With King Hussein, who then reigned on the north, he preserved friendly relations—at least outwardly—though the Sherif of Mecca, whose ambition was not limited either by common sense or honesty, continually subsidized the rebellious Hassan ibn Aidh against him. On the south he was involved in a mild and not very dangerous warfare with Imam Yehya, chiefly because all the tribes of the Tehama as far south as Taiz wished to come under his rule.

It was a remarkable fact that the Idrisi had never fought for anything for himself. It was the demand of the people that made him gradually extend his sway until the little state, where his family had been but one among many more important religious houses, had become the key to the problem of Western Arabia. Only the

Idrisi had remained unchanged, and, if any of his ministers tried to involve him in too complicated politics, he would shut himself up in Sabya and deliver lectures on the Koran and the sayings of the Prophet. His only human weakness was a penchant for green tea and scent; his only pleasure listening to the astounding voice of his Imam echoing (I had almost written "bellowing") over roof and wall in a recitation of the Koran, which lasted from soon after midnight till dawn.

I must confess, however, that his obstinacy equalled his intelligence, and he was looked upon as the most learned man in Arabia, having taken the highest degrees which the famous el Azhar can bestow. Not all the eloquence of Kamel Fahmi, who argued with him for seven hours on end, while Sayed es Senussi, the Qadi, the Commander-in-Chief, and the Minister of the Interior sat mute and anxious, could induce him to allow us to go north. "The best of my country lies to the south," he repeated.

I sought to comfort my disappointment with his gift of a small silver box filled with pearls.

There are no roads in Asir, and the traveller who would go beyond the immediate neighbourhood of Sabya and Jizan, or the flat strip of sabakha which orders the coast, must resign himself to the use of donkeys, or a particularly small and thin breed of baggage camel. As soon as we left Miklaf el Yemen, the central province of the 270-mile by 80-mile strip over which the Idrisi exercised effective control, we were offered the choice of all the steeds of the neighbourhood.

"Ala kaifik—at your pleasure," said Jusuf, the plump wakil with incredibly long eyelashes, who had been appointed to accompany us, trying to look as if he could conjure up all the horses of Araby for our use.

"We will go as far as possible in the car," said I firmly, "and then we will take mules."

"Taht amrik—under your orders" answered Jusuf mournfully, making a mental calculation of the number of mules in the country. I think there were perhaps six!

Thus it came about that the fierce-looking Turk, who always took both hands off the wheel to gesticulate whenever a particularly large obstacle loomed in front, drove us to Madai, the largest village of the Masareka tribe. We went through a land of mirage, where laden camels turned into rocks, trees took to themselves legs, and straw-hatted women looked like islands in the middle of a lake.

Gradually the flat desert, with its mounds covered with rough grass and scrub, gave way to stretches of cultivation, doura, dukn and sem-sem, with tamarisk and mimosa in the wadi beds, and feathery tamarind trees, under whose shade goatherds slept in the noon heat. We saw gazelles and numbers of vultures and kites, but met nobody till the conical huts of Madai appeared amidst fields of grain, where blue-robed women toiled with sickle and hoe. "Man is born to fight, woman to work," said one of my companions. "Man carries the gun, woman the tools and the child," added another. I said I thought she was overloaded, and turned my attention to the crowd of wild figures who had rushed out to meet us brandishing staves and rifles. Jusuf was a trifle pale. "Wallahi! Traveling is not a pursuit for wise men," he said, and leaned out to impart the news of our great station and our close friendship with "his holiness the ruler."

His eloquence produced immediate effect, and we were taken to the cluster of huts belonging to Sayed Omar el Barr, a Government official, who received us warmly and put his whole dwelling at our disposal. It was very cool in the "areesh," which were lined with clay a couple of feet thick and furnished with a few rope couches. There was a hearth made of mud, with holes shaped to fit the various vessels, and the walls were decorated with rows of woven grass mats, platters, bowls, hats and other domestic objects. A woman brought me coffee in a clay jar. "I have never seen anyone so clean," she said, looking wonderingly at my skin, which I had dyed a beautiful olive colour by the aid of some bottles from Clarkson's. Embarrassed, I took a great gulp of coffee and nearly choked. It was indescribably nauseous, made of husks, raw ginger, cardamom and cinnamon. "Isn't it good?" asked a slave, seeing my anguished expression.

"Oh yes, yes!" I gasped, and added truthfully, "I've never found its equal anywhere."

It was at Madai that I saw the curious custom of ordeal by water. A young hillman was accused of murder. His tribe ordained that he must undergo the test of the water-bowl and the red-hot spoon. A sheikh who had the necessary powers was summoned. The headmen and their families gathered round a brushwood fire.

The old "fikki," or wise man, filled a little gourd and set it beside him. Then he prayed that the water, the purest element in the desert, might reveal if blood-guilt stained the district. There was a breathless silence. The gourd is supposed to move slowly round the circle and stop in front of the murderer. I suppose it is on the same principle as table-turning, or any other form of levitation. I have seen some tables jump about in quite inexplicable fashion, and I saw that bowl move! I can't explain either phenomenon. The gourd slid slowly over the sand, completed the circle and returned to the wise man. The first part of the ordeal was safely over. Water had found no pollution among those present.

The fikki turned to heat his spoon and the sheikh beside me murmured that the accused had fever. "His tongue is as dry as the sand. It will assuredly stick to the metal," he insisted.

When the young man approached the fire, it was obvious that his temperature was abnormal. The wise man felt his hand. It was like sacking dried in a mangle. There was no moisture about his body. Still, he professed himself ready for the ordeal.

"Is there none of thy family to stand proxy for thee?" asked the fikki.

Instantly a woman burst into the circle. Before anyone could protest, she rinsed her mouth in the "magic" water and stretched out her tongue towards the spoon. The metal was red-hot and the wise man held it at arm's length, so that no deception was possible. Three times the girl licked the spoon and then the headmen gathered round to examine her tongue. There was only a very faint smear at the tip, which disappeared when she licked it.

"Clean," pronounced the fikki, and the woman turned towards the hillman she had saved. He was a fine figure in his indigo kilt and turban, with a sheepskin flung across his shoulder and his bare chest crossed with cartridge belts.

The woman looked up at him, smiling. There was a stir among the watchers, but the two who stood apart saw nothing but the expression in each other's eyes.

The Menace of a Crowd

TWELVE OR FIFTEEN miles after leaving Madai, we plunged into a region of sandhills covered with alga grass, and, while labouring up them, Ahmed entertained us with tales of brigands. Pointing to unpleasantly frequent cairns of stones, he assured us these were graves, but whether of the victims or the murderers it was difficult to discover, for it appeared that the Idrisi had waged such determined warfare on the marauders that there were hardly any of them left.

"In the Turkish times, the big sheikhs used to make much money stealing children and selling them in the towns," remarked Jusuf; "but now there is law and order everywhere." Perhaps it was only my fancy that he sighed.

East of us lay a wide expanse of desert, rising into low waves, where a few trees were visible, but never sufficiently uneven to hide the double line of hill and mountain farther inland. We were making for Midi, the second largest town, with a population of some 10,000.

It was very hot and we looked helplessly for shade in a waste of sand. There was not a tree or dune in sight, only two little mounds of stone. Beside one these we huddled to eat tepid water-melon and native bread. I was almost sick with the heat. Trying to burrow down among the stones for a few inches shade, I disarranged the cairn. There was something inside—rags of red stuff and a white fragment that, for a second, gleamed like flesh. My heart, or whatever it is we have inside us, somersaulted into my solar plexus. "What is it?" I asked with a gulp of nausea.

"You know our law?" returned the fat Jusuf, the Emir's wakil, who chaperoned me. "When a woman is unfaithful, she and her lover are taken into the desert, buried in the sand up to their armpits and stoned to death. Then more rocks are heaped above them and they are left as a warning to the foolish." His voice was quite unmoved. He knew exactly what lay under the battered stones. I could only imagine it.

Haradh, where some beautifully carved stone dogs were discovered in a recent washout, was left behind, and, as we travelled towards the coast, we saw great blocks of stone towering out of grass, grey and sun-dried. "Graves," said Ahmed. "Perhaps of the Time of Ignorance!"

I insisted on a closer examination. Many of the big coral slabs had fallen, but, of the hundred or so which stood upright, the largest were from eight to twelve feet high and three feet across, with a breadth of a foot.

"They are very old; no one knows how old," remarked one of our attendants. "Perhaps they belong to the Hillaliyeh; who knows but Abu Zeyd[1] may be buried here?"

The graves, which were intact, were edged with thick slabs of the same rock, and were about eight feet long, and the whole cemetery covered several acres, but there were no inscriptions.

Later, I invited some learned sheikhs to explain this interesting mystery. Sherif Hamud suggested that perhaps the stones dated

---

1 A legendary medieval Arab hero.

from the time of the Persian occupation, AD 600, but Ahmed Taher, whose father was known as "The Sheikh of Sheikhs," began to talk about ghouls. I listened, amazed, while a wild argument raged as to whether Ibrahim, the son of Mohammed, had really seen these unpleasant creatures when his straying camels led him near the forest of stones.

"The Hillaliyeh were Moslems," almost shouted the sherif, "and the Faithful are with Allah after death. How, then, could the man have seen ghouls?"

But Ahmed Taher inclined to the idea that Ibrahim's testimony of eye and ear must be accepted, and that this proved beyond all doubt that the graves were pre-Islam, belonging to those pagan times when certainly spirits walked abroad.

Midi is an imposing town when viewed from the east, for then it appears as if the whole central portion consists of large, solidly-built, stone houses, faced with ornate plaster work; but to the north it is fringed with Bedouin encampments, which give it a ragged and unkempt appearance. We arrived unexpectedly one exceedingly hot afternoon—the temperature varied between 80° and 86° Fahr. during late November, December, and January, but there was always a damp south wind, which made the climate very trying. The sheikh was out, but we were ushered into his reception room, which was exceedingly dirty and full of flies. "Bring the furniture," screamed a score of voices; and boys ran in laden with carpets and cushions, with which they proceeded to cover some of the dirt, though the flies still reigned supreme.

The room was typical of an old-fashioned Asir house, for it was about 40 feet long and 18 feet wide, and so high that it had rather the appearance of an aisle, with its ceiling supported on large beams, and painted in all manner of irregular designs. The arches that served as windows were protected by finely-carved shutters, above which ran a plaster dado of texts from the Koran, and between them the whole wall-space was covered with painted Indian plates. Further adornment was given by rows of mirrors hung so high that they only reflected the ceiling and numbers of pictures of legendary Arab heroes. A high and very narrow divan ran all round this remarkable room, with the exception of a space devoted to beautifully-carved travelling chests, inlaid with brass, and fitted with innumerable little drawers and trays. These are made locally.

Eight lean cats watched us with hungry eyes, so I went out into the sunshine, and, guided by the flutter of a woman's dress, I found an angle of house and outer wall devoted to a coffee hearth on a large scale. Here crouched several of the sheikh's harem, Abyssinian, Sudanese, Turkish, and Arabic, varying in rank from the wives and daughters of my host to black slaves captured as children "in the mountains across the sea," and sold in the markets of Yemen and Hedjaz.

"Don't you pull out your eyebrows in Egypt?" asked the mother of the sheikh, who had only one tooth, which hung out of her mouth like a tube. "I thought you were very civilized."

I looked at the black bar painted across her brow in lieu of hair, and the orange-pink powder falling from her embroidered head-dress, but, before I had time to answer, somebody else remarked in a tone of horror: "I have heard it said—Allah forbid!—that there are Christians in Egypt."

Hastily I protested complete ignorance of so dangerous a subject, but Fatma persisted. "If a Christian came to this country," she said, and spat vindictively at the name, "the people would 'eat' him!" and she made an unpleasant gesture of tearing something to bits with strong, claw-like fingers.

I tried to turn the conversation, but the crone's curiosity was aroused. "Had I thy grey eyes," she said, "I should not travel far in this country," and she recited with relish the tale of a Turkish doctor who had visited an inland village during an epidemic. "He had grey eyes like yours, and they were not sure if he were an infidel, but they dug out his middle to see!"

By this time, of course, my face must have been as anaemic as a suet pudding and the collar of my scarlet and gold dress seemed to be getting tighter every moment.

I was thankful when the old woman offered me a bath, and I hurried away, hoping that the apartment might be mercifully secluded, for I was beginning to imagine myself with luminous, sea-green orbs of incredible candle-power.

The bathroom, an empty, roughly-plastered cube with a hole in one corner of the floor to allow the water to run away, was in an outer court, and thither, a dozen women accompanied me with rose-water and various herbal pastes. It was only when the door was shut upon us and Haseena, an Abyssinian with gums so black and teeth so white that her smile was a curiosity, was ladling out water from the huge jar, that I remembered my beautiful olive-dye only reached as far as chest and elbow—and here were expectant slaves waiting to wash me!

The remarks about Christians hammered in my head as I fumbled with the choking folds of my habbara.

Then inspiration came. My fingers had closed round something soft and sticky in my pocket. It was a piece of soap and, without a moment's hesitation, I put it in my mouth. A little vigorous sucking and it was hardly necessary to simulate sickness, but I contrived some very realistic foam, and fear lent artistry to what threatened to become a most effective fit. The slave-girls were horrified. They knew all about jinns, and it was quite obvious that one or more of these evil spirits had taken possession of their guest. After my first gulps and splutters, they hardly looked at me, but, with amulets pressed to their eyes, and shrieking a medley of prayers, they stumbled blindly out of the door.

Fortunately Kamel Fahmi was attracted by the noise of the stampede and when I ran, choking, into the sunshine, I saw his face, which by this time had acquired a permanently anxious expression, peering round a forbidden doorway. Without asking any questions he hurried me to the distant rooms prepared for us and bolted the door, which looked as if only Aladdin could open it. The rest of that day was peace.

On the flat roof we breakfasted next morning—a curious meal consisting of figs, tarib (a junket made of sour goat's milk), marag (a sort of oily soup mixed with bits of fat), reddish-black doura bread, squashed dates which had come from Basrah by sea, very thick honey, with loucoums,[2] and water strongly flavoured with scent, for all the wells along the coast are brackish and unpleasant to taste, though apparently they have no bad effects on the system, except at the capital, Sabya, where the inhabitants suffer from swollen paunches.

While we were still eating, the murmur of voices gathered sufficient volume to attract my attention, and a cautious glance over the parapet revealed a group of horses and donkeys, with a large guard of soldiers, in the midst of a crowd which was momentarily swelling. The chief element consisted of pale, anaemic-looking men in futahs, striped purple and white, with little straw caps on their heads, which were shaven as clean as their faces, but there was a fair percentage of tribesmen of Beni Zeid, Beni Abs, the Ja'dah, and Beni Marwan, who had brought their flocks to market, and a picturesque contingent of hillmen of the famous Hashid tribe. These stalwart mountaineers, with sheepskin coats gaping over chests bare but for their broad cartridge belts, were clear-skinned and bearded, with black, well-oiled hair under indigo turbans. They had come down from their hills—which are so steep that

---

2 Turkish delight.

animals bought in the plains have to be carried up, as calves or lambs, and can never return—with Sheikh Ali Darhan, an ally of the Idrisi, whom I afterwards met in the house of Yehya Basahi, minister and rogue.

We descended to the street, where, to begin with, the crowd was quite good-humoured; but strangers were rare, and a habbara unknown, so they surged with undisguised amazement round the half-broken stallions provided for us to ride. The horses, maddened by the noise, bolted as soon as their heads were released, and the soldiers began beating back the people, who would have followed, with the butts of their rifles, thus turning good-natured chaff into angry abuse. Fortunately the crowd was so thick that the mass of humanity stopped the horses and, in a solid wedge, we swayed through the suqs amidst a riot of noise, smell and dust. The score of soldiers were unable to struggle with the throng, and, as more and more excited townsfolk swelled the mob and the ominous rumour drifted after us, "Are they Moslems?" changing to "By Allah, they are not of Islam," they got frightened and began hitting out wildly. Somebody was hurt, and the murmur of the crowd swelled to a roar. I never saw the soldiers again. They were submerged in a struggling mass, while Jusuf on his little white donkey was swept away by an eddy, impotent to resist, but shouting to me to follow.

The wide market square opened out ahead, with great stacks of dom leaves to be sold for thatch and a dozen camels moving the clumsy pestles of the sem-sem mills. I could not turn, but, with the clamour of abuse behind me and the sound of shots beginning to be audible above the tumult, I was impelled still farther away from my vanished guard. No one with any authority was with us, for the sheikhs were particularly bigoted and had refused to ride with a woman. I could hardly retain my seat, balancing sideways on a pillow and vainly attempting to keep my face hidden, and, at the same time, protect my head from the sunstroke which seemed imminent, for, through a single piece of silk, the Arabian sun has the force of a blow.

In this fashion I was swept along till, just outside the market, my horse stumbled and I slipped off among the half-naked throng. The soldiers, I was told afterwards, had formed up in a line and, kneeling, were attempting to stem the onslaught by hurling sand and stones, but my horse was sucked away in the human maelstrom, and, stumbling over unaccustomed draperies, blinded by my thick veil, I found myself powerless to resist the pressure. There were some unpleasant moments when all my Arabic left me, except a phrase which I kept repeating, and which I hoped meant, "There are many thousands like me in Egypt," and, after that, I have very little idea of what happened. There came a burst of firing, presumably into the air, and I found myself, breathless, crushed, exhausted, near an open door, which a stranger was doing his best to close as quickly as possible. The heavy wood stuck, and, with a supreme effort, I disengaged myself and almost fell across the threshold. Someone caught my arm and dragged me in, while an older man, grasping the situation with a promptitude unusual in the East, called to his slaves to put up the great emergency bars.

"Shut the door!" shouted everyone at once; but there was a moment of chaos while my rescuers fought the people on the threshold, dealing stout blows right and left. I was pushed up some stairs, while ominous crashes sounded below, amidst shouts and cries which in any other country would certainly have denoted a battle. Whispering women met me in the dimness and drew me on, up and up, till I found myself in the harem of Salim Ba Hassan, the Hadramauti, whose son was being married that day. Consequently, the crowd which surrounded me in the large upper room was wonderfully adorned.

There were a score of women and girls, ranging from three or four years old to sixty, but pre-eminent among them were Zahara and Ayesha, daughters of the house, and another Ayesha, sister of the merchant, for they were laden with gold jewellery in the shape of huge crescents, set with rubies, pearls, and sapphires, and their hair, rolled over great bundles of sweet-smelling herbs (chiefly berga-ush) was dyed a bright orange-pink, not red, with paste made of henna and marigolds. Leading me to the best divan, in a corner from where I could see the still-crowded square, a solid mass of faces all looking up at the house where I had taken refuge, they brought me most unpleasant syrups, diluted with rose-water, and sticky Turkish cakes, with which at the moment I was unable to cope. For the first time in a harem I saw the type which must have been the origin of the old Arab pictures—pale, oval face, heavy and smooth-skinned, slightly hanging full-lipped mouth, fine eyes, long and swollen lidded, but devoid of any expression except a certain vacant sensuality. Here, too, was the glossy black hair, high bosom, and the hips, "so heavy that they incommoded her walk," beloved of ancient poets. While waiting for the faithful Jusuf to come to my rescue, I talked about Egypt and the feminist movement among her women.

"I was born in this room," said Zahara, reprovingly, "and I have never left it! Women should be taken care of and given all that they can desire, but of what use is freedom?"

1924

Morocco: The Sultan of the Mountains

From Chapters I-III of
The Sultan of the Mountains:
The Life Story of Raisuli (1924)

Into the Days of
Haroun Er Rashid

66 You go to see my cousin el Raisuli—to write about
him," said Mulai Sadiq at Tetuan. "For what reason? Between Africa and Europe there is a barrier
higher than these mountains. You cannot cross it."

I had gone to see the old Sherif with regard to my journey to
Tazrut, for he acted as agent in Tetuan for his famous relative.
His house was most attractive with its little court lined with
mosaic and surrounded by white Moorish arches, from behind
which peeped his slave-women, their brilliant crimson dresses
showing through long coats of white muslin to match their turbans, corded with many-coloured silks. Mulai Sadiq is thin and
wiry, aged about sixty, bald, with a grey beard. He has an ill-kept
appearance, for he is an "alim" who considers that learning is very
much preferable to cleanliness. He was willing to talk for hours
of the adventures of "*the* Sherif,"[1] of whom he is the antithesis,
since his face is intelligent and sympathetic and his hands talk

---

1 Raisuli is generally called by his people "The Sherif."

even more expressively than his lips. When he got excited he took off his turban and thumped his fists on the ground, or flung them open above his head. I found him sitting on the floor, surrounded by immense tomes, with many others piled up behind him. He had to move a number before there was room for me to sit down, and then, with his spectacles pushed forward on his long nose, he began to talk about my journey.

"The Sherif will welcome you with great honour," he said, "but it is a long way and it is my duty to come with you, that you may travel in all respect." Thus it was arranged, and he went off to telephone to the secretary of el Raisuli in primitive Tazrut!

The great Hispano-Suisa car flung itself on to the road as if it would devour the strip of dusty white which fled before it. The old walls of Tetuan disappeared. Away on the hillside a splash of green marked Samsa, where legend tells of a Portuguese Queen imprisoned in a subterranean maze. The dew was still on the sugar-cane, mist on the river. Peasants were driving their flocks to market; the men rode on donkeys, idle hands crossed on the pommel, the women, their haiks[2] bundled above their knees to show stout leather leggings, their hats, the size of umbrellas, hiding their faces, trudged behind their lords, bearing huge bundles of firewood or sacks of grain. A figure swathed in a burnous, rifle slung across his back, appeared on the skyline, and there was the watchword of Morocco—a veiled country, alert and suspicious.

Up and up soared the road, an incredible feat of engineering, and never for an instant did the driver slacken his pace. By precipices where the wheels spun on the edge of eternity, by nightmare twists and spirals where the path slipped eel-like from beneath us, the Spanish car took us into the land for which Spain and Raisuli

---

2 A piece of woolen or cotton cloth worn by Arabs as an outer garment.

had fought their amazing battle. Right and left rose the mountains, their first slopes thick with scrub and grass, their summits barren. Here and there a police post guarded the road, two or three men, shirts open to the sun, with their horses, and a tent as brown as the rocks. Where the river Hayera trickled through a wadi,[3] wild olives grew in profusion. Cactus lifted its spikes above thickets of pink oleanders, the flower which the Arabs say brings death to any who sleep in its perfume. A Moorish village, the mud houses smothered under their weight of thatch, appeared among the boulders which strewed the landscape. On the hillside the Qubba of a saint drew white-robed figures to worship. A Sherif rode by on a mule with scarlet trappings, and a servant running in front, crying, "Make way for the guest of God, the blessed one."

The sun of Africa mellowed the scene, but, when a cloud crept over us, it showed a sinister land where the villages hid among rocks of their own colour and shape, so that one looked across a deserted prospect to the hills that tore the sky. A watchful land where a dozen of Raisuli's snipers could hold up a Spanish column. Ben Karrish appeared as a serrated white wall. Here, the Spanish post is built round an old house of Raisuli's to which the Sherif fled after the taking of Ain el Fondak. A few yards away is the mosque where he prayed for the miraculous intervention which his followers believe was afforded by the disaster of Melilla. A boy offered me flowers, a compressed bundle of morning-glory and yellow lilies. "There are but two good things in the world, flowers and women," he said.

"Won't you put the women first?"

"Ullah, they are the same thing! My master, the Sherif, has never refused the petition of a woman, but, Ullah, flowers are less trouble!"

---

3 A valley, a river; a ravine through which a stream flows.

Further on the road narrowed between wild vines and thickets of fig and dardara. "Raisuli's tribesmen used to hide there and pick off our men like rabbits," said the Spaniard who travelled with me. "Their chief is a strategist—we made war against shadows, and lost thirty men to their one."

Across the hills in front toiled a line of great, grey beetles which resolved themselves into lorries, packed with troops. The driver's eye brightened. "It is possible that we may see some little thing, after all," he vouchsafed, and spun past the nearest camion with two wheels down the bank. For an hour we overtook the various units of two columns *en route* for Dar Yacoba and the trouble that was reported vaguely "somewhere in the mountains to the East."

A cloud of dust which looked like a battle surrounded a mountain battery and a long line of mules laden with Maxim-guns. Far up among the purple crags smoke appeared. "Is there really something doing?" murmured my companions, but I was unresponsive. It seemed to me very much too hot for any comfortable warfare.

One by one we left the marching columns and came into the purple wilderness of Jebel Maja, whose height so impresses the Moors that they say the daughter of Noah is buried on its topmost crag, the only one that showed above the Flood. Far up on every hilltop appeared a fort, its isolation emphasizing the inviolability of the land it watched. Goats strayed across the road, but the herdsmen were invisible. Then came the stir of guarded bridgeheads, and again the name of Raisuli—"Here a man was killed on either side of him, when he stopped at the height of the battle, a mark for the whole countryside, while his horse drank." Rows of tents on the edge of a cliff, rows of mules tethered where those obstinate animals could have no desire to slip over it, showed us Dar Yacoba.

Then came the last steep kilometres to Xauen, the one-time city of mystery, of which men spoke in whispers, for it belongs

Photo Album

Rosita Forbes, author's portrait.
From *Unconducted Wanderers*, 1919.

A gate of Angkor-Thom, Cambodia. From *Unconducted Wanderers*, 1919.

Our houseboat near Ping-Shek, China.
From *Unconducted Wanderers*, 1919.

Rosita Forbes, author's portrait.
From *Kufara: Secret of the Sahara*, 1921.

Rosita Forbes as "Khadija."
From *Kufara: Secret of the Sahara*, 1921.

Rosita Forbes on her four-month
journey through the Libyan desert.
From *Kufara, Secret of the Sahara*, 1921.

Ahmed Bey Hassanein,
Forbes's co-explorer.
From *Kufara, Secret of
the Sahara*, 1921.

Our caravan approaching Aujela.
From *Kufara: Secret of the Sahara*, 1921.

Rosita Forbes, explorer, leaving Buckingham Palace
after an audience with the king and queen, 1921.

to the Ahmas tribe, cruelest and most savage of mountain folk. Twenty years ago they burned Christians in the market-place, and a certain street is still called the "Way of the burned." The men of Xauen had a secret language, and, if a stranger could not give the password at their gate, the most mercy he could expect was that his pickled head should adorn it, suspended by the ears. Xauen understands neither clocks nor calendars, and, when the Spanish troops entered in October, 1920, it was to find they had stepped back into the sixteenth century, from which the Jews, barefoot and bareheaded, hailed them with "Viva, viva, Elizabeth the Second!"[4]

Xauen's claim to mystery lies in the fact that it is so deeply embedded in a cleft of the mountains as to be invisible till one is fifty yards from the walls. "We have arrived," said the driver, and I looked blankly at the rocks and the deserted slopes. In another moment there was a town before us. By magic, white houses climbed one above another, madnas, tiled with the old faded green, soared from hedges of prickly-pear, and, below this huddled mass of roof and court, slipping like a cascade from the mountainside, lay the great Berber castle, time-mellowed, sun-bleached, relic of an Empire whose very history is lost. We left the twentieth century outside the gate with the car, which could take us no further, and, preceded by a black slave carrying my luggage, passed into the days of Haroun er Rashid and the Thousand and One Nights. Veiled women stole into doors that looked as if it was the first time they had been opened since the beginning of time. Each arch, each window, was carved exquisitely and differently. A muezzin[5] cried the noon prayer from a mosque which overlooked the Qubba of a Rashid from Baghdad. The dim musk-perfumed shops framed

---

4 A Spanish queen who died 200 years ago.
5 Muezzin—a Mohammedan crier of the hour of prayer.

the grey beards of Xauen's "ulema," a rosary between their fingers, their drapery flowing over the street.

One of these was a cousin of Raisuli's, a man prematurely bent and worn. "He has been called upon to defend the Sherif at moments when he would rather have been listening to his singing birds," murmured a Kaid. A tiny scarlet door, with a lantern that once must have belonged to Aladdin, led us into the Qadi's house. Slender Moorish arches surrounded a fountain, babbling to the swallows which perched in serried ranks upon the balconies.

Our host received us in a room whose ornamentation was particularly garish and crowded after the courts below. He had but two teeth, which hung from his mouth like tusks, but his manners were beautiful and unhurried. "The blessing of Allah, for you go to see the Sherif. He is a great man and the last of them."

Seated on cushions and leaning against a wall lined with strips of satin, yellow, blue and red, we conversed gravely and with long silences, as befitted a first visit. "With el Raisuli will pass much of Morocco," said our host. "You will not understand his ways—perhaps he will not speak at all—but, Ullah, his mind works all the time while he watches you. Nobody knows what he thinks, but he reads the minds of all men. That is his power."

"It is true," said the Spaniard. "He is an astute psychologist."

The complicated apparatus necessary for a tea of ceremony was brought in by slaves, whose waistcoats paled the heaped-up colour in the room. Our host beckoned to another greybeard and slowly, meticulously, the tea was brewed with mint and spice and ambergris. "The Sherif likes mint—it is his only pleasure. There must always be fresh stores in his house. Otherwise he cares about nothing. He has no eye for beauty. He has never known love for anyone or anything." Someone interrupted, "His son, Sidi Mohamed el Khalid. El Raisuli offered his whole fortune to anyone who would save his life when he was ill of fever." The

Qadi made a movement of protest. "It is his race which lives in his son—the Sherifs of Jebel Alan. Besides, there is the curse. . . ." "What curse?" But somehow the question was not answered. Sweet cakes and biscuits were pressed upon us. Long-stemmed bottles of scent were offered that we might sprinkle our clothes, but the name of Raisuli was no more mentioned.

In the coolness after the early sunset, while the mountain walls turned slowly indigo, I explored the town. Its narrow streets ran downwards, steeply cobbled, by way of the Mosque and the Square where the Jews might not pass for fear of defiling its holiness. The suq, so narrow that two could hardly walk abreast, was roofed with mats, till it twisted abruptly to the cistern of ice-cold water that the Arabs believe will cure most ills. A leper bent over it, his face distorted to the semblance of a beast, and the Sheikh who was with me blessed him as we passed. "In the great war," he said, "a German came here by night in disguise. He was the only European to see our town. Perhaps he came on business for the Sherif." The German, of course, was Mannismann, the evil genius of North Africa.

The Wild Land of Raisuli

LWAYS THERE WAS the echo of the personality which had so impressed itself on Morocco that the soil of the mountains and the texture of men's minds were equally impregnated with its forces. Here Raisuli saw a drunken Sherif, and, turning to the scornful onlookers, said, "The man is blessed of Allah. Your eyes see wrongly. He is in the throes of prophecy. Bring him to my camp." The Sherif was never seen again, and legend says he was corporeally translated to Paradise!

Here Raisuli took shelter from the advancing Spaniards and, from the walls of Berber Castle, made the prophecy that is repeated from one end of the country to the other: "This is my country and you are my people. Nothing will be taken from *me*, but after my death it will all go."

From Xauen it is possible to ride across the steep ridges of Jebel Hashim direct to Tazrut, but, because I wanted to see more of the country in which Raisuli had fought, we retraced our steps. Picking up the old Sherif, Mulai Sadiq, we continued by way of Wadi Ras and the Fondak of Ain Yerida, which was the Sherif's headquarters for many months of war, to Azib el Abbas. There we left the main road and swung down through a desolate region, grey with boulders, to Beni Mesauer, the constant refuge of el Raisuli when hard-pressed. The house of el Ayashi Zellal, his sworn ally and father-in-law, is hidden somewhere among the crags, but we left the highlands for Wadi Harisha, where the olive trees are like round tents by a stream lost in vegetation, and whole flocks shelter under their branches. For the first time I saw barley amidst the great stretches of millet. "These are the lands of the Sherif," said the Mulai Sadiq, who had pulled forward the hood of his jellaba[1] till only a long nose and a pair of immense orange glasses were visible.

"Everything that you can see from now on belongs to him," explained Mr. Cerdeira, the official interpreter between the Spanish Government and el Raisuli, who most kindly accompanied me to Tazrut, which he was the first European to visit, I believe. He added that, when Spain temporarily confiscated the properties of the Sherif during the recent war, they were valued at six million pesetas. Certainly these rolling downs, where villages were frequent, appeared to be excellent land for cultivation, though there are as many acres of great, heavy-headed thistles as of grain. The post of Suq el Talata appeared on a hill-top in a haze of heat, and, after that, we clung panting to the sides of the car while we negotiated a track that, as the Sherif expressed it, after he had hit the hood several times, "jolted our backbones through our heads." Sidi el Haddi, a valley where the stream made great pools between trees gnarled with lichen and thickets of the ubiquitous oleanders, gave us a little rest, and then up again by Sidi Buqir, a little white Morabit, where is buried one of the seven holy men of Beni Aros.

At last, when our throats were parched and our lips cracked, we had our first good view of Jebel Alan, on whose great peak was buried Sidi Abd es Salaam, the most famous of el Raisuli's ancestors,

---

1 A cloak with a hood worn by natives of Morocco.

and its twin mountain Jebel Hashim, the guardian of Tazrut. Below them, and most blessedly near, appeared the last big Spanish post, Suq el Khemis, and the little police camp of Sidi Ali. With a series of mighty jerks the car leaped up and over the intervening track and deposited us, much exhausted, in the centre of a crowd which represented both the old Morocco and the new. On one side were the officers of the police post, cheerily apologetic because of a combination of pyjama jackets and puttees, speaking Arabic like natives, and saying that it was so long (two years) since they had seen a woman that they had forgotten what one looked like! On the other were the envoys of el Raisuli, with a guard of his mountaineers. Prominent among them, because of his bulk, appeared Sherif Badr Din el Bakali, and behind him, his jellaba turned back over a purple waistcoat and girt with a huge silver belt, the Kaid el Meshwar ed Menebbhe. These brought me greetings from the Sherif and expressed many ceremonious regrets that his eldest son, Mohamed el Khalid, had not been able to accompany them. I learned afterwards that the said youth, aged eighteen, having consistently neglected his studies during the festivities consequent upon his father's recent wedding, had been put in irons by the Sherif, so that he might not be able to escape from his books!

It was then 108° Fahr. in the shade, and, personally, even in Arabia I have never felt anything hotter than the dry, burning wind, which appeared to issue from an oven among the hills. It was decided that while the Moslems prayed at the tomb of Sidi Mared, another of the sainted seven, fortunately conveniently near, the Christians should eat. We lunched with the hospitable officers, whose names I never knew, and a wonderful meal it was, not only on account of the inventive genius of the cook, but because no two people spoke the same language. Between us we mustered several different forms of Arabic and various European tongues, but the Tower of Babel would have been shaken by the efforts of the guests to communicate with their hosts! We gave it up in the end and sat outside, in the largest patch of shade, looking over the plain where the great weekly market is held.

Hearing that strangers were in the camp, some gipsies came and stared at us over the edge of the sand-bags. One man held a snake in his hand to which he was crooning gently. Without much encouragement they began their unpleasant performance. A wild-looking youth with hair standing on end seized a glass and began crunching it up in his teeth. The man with the snake held it at arm's-length and adjured it in the names of dead saints. Then, opening his mouth, from which foam dripped at the corners, he put out his tongue and let the reptile fix its fangs in it. Blood stained the foam and, with veins congested and eyes turned inwards, the gipsy began eating the living snake, first swallowing the head affixed to his tongue, and then chewing the body, which writhed up and struck him on the cheeks. All the time, the others kept up a curiously hypnotic chant which appeared to stimulate the hysteria or fervour of the performers, for, with a sudden shout, the eater of glass seized an iron mace which one of his companions was carrying. With this he struck his head so forcibly that the blood ran down under his matted hair. It was a disgusting spectacle, but evidently it delighted the remaining gipsies, who uttered bestial howls and flung themselves into a dance in which the maximum of contortion was achieved.

It was with great relief that I saw the approach of el Raisuli's dignified envoys. "If we would arrive tonight, we must start," said the Kaid, and, in another moment, there was the bustle of loading mules and mounting horses. The Kaid, evidently impressed by my boots, offered me his mount, a wild, grey stallion. "He is an Afrit,[2] so treat him with respect." I did not need the warning.

---

2 A devil.

The look in the Afrit's eye was quite enough, but, fortunately, it is almost impossible to fall off an Arab saddle. Immensely wide and padded, with a high pommel back and front, it is girthed over half-a-dozen different-coloured saddle-cloths and has silver stirrups rather like coal-shovels.

The procession that moved away from Sidi Ali was imposing, for half-a-dozen officers, on their way to an outpost at Bugelia, rode with us, accompanied by their troopers; but, after we had clambered up and down a series of precipitous ridges, they left us, and we were in the hands of Raisuli.

The country became even wilder, the wadis a tangle of vine and blackberry, with high-growing shrubs nameless to me as to the Arabs, who called them "firewood." First went the soldiers of the Sherif, stalwart mountaineers in short brown jellaba, with the rifles across their backs. They were followed by a couple of baggage-mules, behind whom rode a servant of the Kaid, a sporting Martini-Henry rifle ready for partridge or hare. His master was mounted on a gaily-caparisoned mule whose trappings went well with the gay colours of his turban and waistcoat. The Afrit and I danced uncomfortably behind him, generally sideways or in a series of bounds. Then came old Mulai Sadiq astride the plumpest of saddle-mules, his spectacles still balanced on the tip of his nose and a white umbrella over his head. Sidi Badr ed Din, his beard dyed with henna glittering in the sunshine, his horse almost hidden by his ample proportions, brought up the rear with the interpreter and some servants, who took off their outer garments one by one, to pile them on their heads against the fierceness of the sun.

For a couple of hours we rode across the mountains of Beni Aros, passing mud-built villages huddled under the shade of a cliff, their thatched roofs covered with wild vine, and wadis where the trees met above our heads, and grey foxes slipped away into the bushes. After this there was only a goat track, which ran on the edge of a gully thick with blackberries, or across open pastures where the shepherds went armed, beside their flocks. The sun slipped low behind us as we clambered up the last rocks, blackened by recent fires, to the Qubba of Sidi Musa. There, at a well under wide-spreading trees, we stopped to rest. The Arabs said their afternoon prayers, bowing themselves till the earth grimed their foreheads, but I noticed that they drank out of the same cup as their Christian guest, without washing it. If the fanatics of Libya or Asir did such a thing by mistake, they would consider themselves defiled.

In the sunset we approached Tazrut, a cluster of white houses and green roofs, with the tower of the Mosque rising beside a thicket of oak. Seen across a stretch of scrub and rock, it looked an ideal hermitage for a saint and an admirable post of vantage for a warrior.

Tazrut is the strategical centre of Raisuli's country. It lies midway between all his great positions and is within a day's journey of most of them, yet it is in the heart of the mountains, commanding a wide expanse of country in front, where the hills of Beni Aros are piled, fold upon fold. Behind is the great barrier range, to whose summits the Spaniards are pushing their advance posts, but which a few years ago was only inhabited by wild pigs and monkeys. We pushed our tired horses across the last mullah[3] and found ourselves suddenly among ruins. On all sides were traces of the Spanish aeroplanes, which had bombed Tazrut for two days in 1922. Here were rough pits under the rocks, where the inhabitants had taken shelter, and great holes torn by bombs and shells. Not a house was undamaged. Roofless, with gaping walls and doors made of new sheets of galvanised iron or the wood of packing-cases, they stood among cactus and thorn and curiously

---

3 Ravine, gulley.

shaped boulders. I looked again, for there was something very odd about these rocks, and then I saw that, on the top of each, crouched an immobile figure in an earth-brown jellaba, with a rifle in his hands.

We passed various camps where mountain-men sat at the doors of their tents, profiting by the coolness, and then, among piled stones and broken walls, where the earth was gashed open below a mass of plaster, there appeared a splash of colour. "It is the sons of the Sherifs," murmured someone, and I saw two vivid petunia jellabas, from the depth of whose hoods peered elfin faces with wild, tousled hair. In another moment we came to the paved road that runs between the mosque, miraculously untouched by war, the one complete building left in desolate Tazrut, and the dwelling of Raisuli. Slaves ran to hold out stirrups before the great arch which still kept some traces of its ancient carving. To the left was the domed tomb of Sidi Mohamed Ben Ali, a seventeenth-century ancestor of the Sherif; in front of us the passage leading into a space, half-yard, half-court. The compound was perhaps two hundred yards in length and, within its high walls, were various buildings. At one end was the Zawia, wherein were the rooms of el Raisuli, communicating with the old house which contained the family tomb and the women's apartments. This was sacred ground, and no Christian might enter, but, during the Spanish occupation, photographs were taken of the interior court, one of which is reproduced in this book. Opposite was a large structure, temporarily roofed with corrugated iron. This contained, on the ground-floor, a series of storerooms and, above, a couple of reception chambers, where the Sherif ate with his friends and followers. At the other end of the yard was an old thatched building, once a residence of the Sherif, now his son's school, with rooms for visitors above. Near this was pitched a great black-and-white tent, with a fig-tree shading its porch, and various smaller tents behind.

"This is your home," said Sherif Badr ed Din, beckoning me to enter, "and we are your servants." The pavilion was lined with gay damask and carpeted with rugs piled one upon another. It was about twenty feet in diameter and round the walls were mattresses covered with white linen, and rows of very hard cushions. There was also a table with two huge brass candlesticks and several long-stemmed silver flasks containing orange-water and homemade scent of roses, but presumably this was an ornament, for we always had our meals on the floor. As a peculiar honour, the Sherif had lent the chair made specially in Spain to suit his colossal proportions, and, sitting in one corner of its great expanse, I drank my first cup of green tea at Tazrut.

The moon had risen and, outside the tent door, the breeze stole whispering across beds of mint and poppies. The figures of Mulai Sadiq and Badr ed Din looked like ghostly monks, sunk under the hoods of their voluminous drapery. From far away came the sound of chanting. "It is in the mosque," said the Kaid. "Sidi Mohamed Ben Ali is buried there. It was he who won the battle of Jebel Alan (in 1542), where three kings were killed. The power of the Shorfa Raisuli began after that day, for Sidi Mohamed arrived with the tribes of the Jebala, when the Moslems were hard-pressed. 'Have courage in the name of Allah,' he cried, 'for I tell you a Christian head will not be worth more than fifteen uqueia today.'" The three kings referred to by el Menebbhe were Don Sebastian of Portugal, the Sultan of Morocco, and the Moorish Pretender.

After the prayers in the mosque were over, Sidi Mohamed el Khalid, released from his irons in order that he might perform his religious duties, came to see us. Fair-skinned as a girl, with an indefinite nose and hair clipped two inches back from his forehead and then dyed with henna and allowed to grow long, the boy greeted us shyly. His manners were clumsy for an Arab of great race, and he whispered instead of speaking out loud. When the Sherif Badr ed Din rebuked him, he said, "All we Moslems are savages, and I am the worst of them. My father wants to make me into an alim,[4] for the ulema[5] of Beni Aros are famous throughout Islam, but I do not like books." "What do you like?" "Only one thing, war. It is a pity that we have finished fighting!" "What do you do to amuse yourself now?" "I shoot. Will you come into the mountains and hunt monkeys? It is great fun! We go at night, when there is a moon, but it is very rough country; so we must leave our horses and walk. The monkeys come out one after another, screaming, and we shoot them." "I have no rifle with me." "That does not matter. You can have a choice of all kinds here, German, Spanish, French, or revolvers, if you like; but hunting is not so exciting as war."

After this there was silence, and Mulai Sadiq left us, to pray in the Zawia. Soon his voice was heard leading the aysha prayers. In spite of his age, his words rang across the compound, and it seemed to me that I was listening to the voice of old Morocco protesting against the Christians who trod her borders and penetrated even to the threshold of her sanctuaries.

---

4 A Moslem learned in religion and law.

5 A college composed of the hierarchy, the imam, mufti and caid.

Raisuli Himself

IT IS A long way from London to Tazrut and, during the whole journey, thoughts of el Raisuli had filled my mind. His name met me on the coast of Morocco and, wherever I went afterwards, I heard legends which magnified or distorted his personality. Small wonder that, sitting in his chair, a guest of his house, the moonlight sending fantastic shadows across the rough garden, my excitement to see this strange man grew until I forgot my hunger, forgot the tedium of the long ride. I only remembered that in a few moments I should see el Raisuli.

It was very still, except for the crickets. Even the breeze had stopped. The chanting in the mosque died suddenly, and Sidi Badr ed Din rose. "The Sherif comes," he said. With racing pulses, I turned to meet a presence which blocked the way beneath the bushes. An enormous man stood before me. At first glimpse he seemed almost as broad as he was tall, but it was the breadth of solid flesh muscle, not of fat. His round, massive face was surrounded by a thicket of beard, dyed red, and a lock of terra-cotta hair escaped from under his turban. The quantity of woollen garments he wore, one over another, added to his bulk, and when, seating himself in a chair which seemed incapable of supporting his weight, he rolled up his sleeves, baring arms of incredible girth, I found myself looking at them fascinated and repelled, while he gave me the usual courteous greetings. "All the mountain is yours. You are free to go where you will. My people are your servants, and they have nothing to do but to please you. I am honoured because of your visit, for I have great friendship with your country." His voice was guttural and rich, but it appeared to roll over his thick lips from a distance which made it husky. His manners were gracious and his dignity worthy of his ancient race. After a few minutes' talk I had forgotten the unwieldy strength of his body and was watching his eyes, the only expressive feature in Raisuli's face. They were watchful eyes, dominant and fierce, in the midst of flesh, which it seemed to me they used as a veil. Sometimes, when he spoke of small things, they softened till they were almost wistful, but generally they watched and judged and revealed nothing.

I presented the gold-sheathed sword I had brought, with the Arab saying, "There is but one gift for the brave—a weapon." The Sherif smiled. "You ought to have been a man," he said, "for you have speech as well as courage." Then I offered him some rolls of vivid-coloured brocades, purple, orange, rose-red and emerald-green, with heavy patterns in gold and silver.

"I heard, even in England, that you had been recently married, and I hoped, perhaps, that you would give these to the Sherifa with my greetings."

Raisuli accepted the gifts with the simplicity of every Arab who considers that generosity is as common as sight or hearing, and it is rather the donor than the recipient who is blessed. Then a row of slaves appeared, with brass trays on which was every form of meat, with chickens, eggs, watermelons and grapes. These were placed on a leather mat on the floor of my tent, and the Sherif, with a soft "Bismillah," bade me enter. "Tomorrow I will eat with you, but today I fasted all the day; so I ate an hour ago, after the aysha prayers," he said, and sat down on the thickest mattress, to make conversation while we fed. Occasionally he picked up a quart-jug of water and drank it in two or three draughts. Mulai Sadiq crouched beside him, looking like an old hawk, as he peered at one dish after another, picking out the tenderest portions with bony, but unerring, fingers.

It was hot inside the tent, and the Sherif moved restlessly in the middle of a discourse which revealed an intimate knowledge of European politics. I offered him one of those little mechanical fans which are worked by pressing a button, and I think he preferred it to any of my expensive gifts. "Allah, it is good! In this way one has the wind always with one." But his thumb was so thick that it was very difficult for him to hold and work the slight machine.

We talked far into the night, till my head was whirling and my eyelids fell with automatic regularity. For us the day had begun before the dawn, and there came a moment when, my answers having become so vague as to be incomprehensible, the Sherif noticed my exhaustion. "In the pleasure of your conversation, I forgot that, after all, you are a woman," he said. "Sleep with peace." Without any loss of dignity, he heaved himself up, and his face was unexpectedly kind as he made his formal farewell. "Tomorrow we will talk of many things," he promised, "and you shall begin your work, but Mulai Sadiq is my biographer. He knows my life better than I do, and as for these two men," (he indicated Badr ed Din and the Kaid) "one has been my political adviser for fifteen years, and I have been in no battle without the other for twenty-five."

During the time that I stayed with el Raisuli, I was hardly ever alone, and counted myself lucky if I had four hours uninterrupted sleep at night. By 6 AM the place was astir, and I used to hear the Haj Embarik, a man from Marrakesh, who had travelled a good deal and understood my Eastern Arabic, murmuring outside the tent. I knew that he was wandering about with a ewer of hot water, kicking the tent-ropes to attract my attention; so I had to throw off my tasselled blankets of red and white camel's hair and prepare for a strenuous day.

Breakfast consisted of a bowl of thick vegetable soup with bits of fat floating in it—the "harira" that is given to children during the great fast of Ramadan. After that there was a painful gap so far as food was concerned till 3 or 4 PM, when an immense meal of many meat courses made its appearance, borne shoulder-high by a line of slaves. Sometimes, when Mulai Sadiq announced that he was tired, we were provided at odd hours with green tea and very sticky pastry, sweet and heavy.

El Raisuli is always out by 6 AM, and any one of his friends or his household may approach him in the garden, where he holds an informal council, seated on a broken wall or the steps inside one of the doors. Before noon he retires into the Zawia, where none may go to him unless he specially sends for them, except his eldest son and the ten little slaves, all under twelve years old, who attend on the harem. These small boys are rather like monkeys, but sometimes, when they are feeling important, they wear huge cartridge-belts over their inadequate shirts, and oil their top-knots till they look like coils of silk. Besides these minute servitors, there are fifteen slaves, coal-black men from the Sudan and Somaliland, under the orders of old Ba Salim. They are not allowed into the house, but two of them, Mabarak and Ghabah, are the personal attendants of the Sherif. When he rides on his roan stallion, they walk one at each stirrup. In battle they range their horses on either side of him and each carries a spare rifle, for el Raisuli never fights with less than three. During my stay at Tazrut, they were assigned to my service, which was one of the highest honours the Sherif could pay to a guest.

About 4 or 5 in the afternoon, el Raisuli makes a second appearance, and, from then till midnight, or a much later hour, he transacts work and receives messengers, with the numerous reports and petitions that come to him from all over the country. The interviews I had with him were nearly always in my tent, or in the garden, or in one of the guest-rooms where a slave would hurriedly spread mattresses and rugs. The Sherif is a facile raconteur, and his memory is astounding. He never hesitates for a date or a name, but his eloquence consists more in the wealth of his similes than the richness of his language. His vocabulary is small, and he uses the same words continually. He recounts conversations word by word, with an annoying repetition of "qultu" (I said to him) and "qali" (he said to me). Obviously he is used to telling the story of his life, but this is natural, for very little Arab biography is written, in any case, till long after the death of the subject. Facts and anecdotes are handed down verbally, and it is part of the work of disciples to know by heart the life of their master, of schoolboys to learn the history of their ancestors.

The Sherif did not tell me a consecutive story, for often he would think of incidents that he had omitted, and indulge in much repetition in order to bring in a certain anecdote, but at different times he reviewed most of his life with a wealth of detail. Of course the episodes that most interested him and upon which he dwelt at length were often not those which would appeal to a European biographer. On the contrary, he showed no interest in events which to me were of historical value, and it needed a great deal of tact and patience to induce him to talk of them at all. At times his point of view was so biassed that it was palpably incorrect, but his story, even though it often either exaggerates or lacks detail, is a record of an amazing life—a web of philosophy and atrocities, of war and psychology, of politics, ambition, and Pan-Islamism.

When he became interested in his narrative, the Sherif lost all sense of time. Once he talked from about 7 in the morning till nearly 3 PM and often he would arrive before dinner and, hardly troubling to eat, talk without a pause till 2 or 3 AM. Mulai Sadiq and Sidi Badr ed Din acted as a sort of Greek chorus, reinforced on certain occasions by the two favourite slaves, who emphasised the story with murmured confirmation. When the Sherif was in the Zawia, his cousin permanently kept us company, while others dropped in for an hour or two's "short talk." My notes were always scribbled in the wildest confusion as I grasped the meaning of the Moorish dialect, or as the interpreter rendered it in French, but I got quite used to writing them up while a violent argument was going on between the Spaniard and three or four Arabs as to whether a soldier found wounded in the mountains had been fired upon by a tribesman, or had accidentally shot himself. The Moorish voices rose to a pitch that would indicate incipient murder in any other country, as they revelled in the game at which they excelled—prevarication!—and I admired the persistence of the interpreter in outscreaming them. The fate of that soldier haunted my stay at Tazrut, and it was with the greatest difficulty that I managed to exclude him from my book!

1925

A Thousand Miles
of Abyssinia

From Chapters I, II, V, and XVII of
Red Sea to Blue Nile: Abyssinian Adventure (1925)

Anticipation

66"IT IS A very good boat," said the Parsee doubtfully, "but it is not for passengers." His gaze wandered past me out of the window, to where a tramp of perhaps 130 tons with an incredible list to port was anchored in the harbor. "There is one cabin, certainly," he continued, and pushed back his sweat-stained fez to scratch his head with a toothpick.

"We cannot both sleep in that," I protested, thinking of Jones, my cinematographer, and the enormous tins of films from which he refused to be parted.

"Sleep in it!" echoed the Parsee with horror, "but nobody can sleep there!"

Somewhat bewildered, I left the office with a dirty slip of paper which entitled me to the hospitality of a Persian cargo boat between Aden and Djibouti, but a few hours later the mystery was solved. The "cabin" was a hole, apparently in the bowels, and water swirled gently back and forth across the floor. The blankets on the shelf which served as a bunk were bright pink and the cockroaches it seemed found them comfortable, for they lay there in heaps, waving their whiskers with that horrid watchfulness that makes cockroaches so unpleasant. After one glance

Jones and I mutually offered each other the sole use of the cabin, and clambered up on deck. The moon was a magic lantern projecting the rocks of Aden flat and black against a sheet of silver. The sky was a net so heavily weighted with stars that it drooped above us. By standing on tiptoe it seemed as if one could steal one of the lights of the Milky Way and set it, twinkling, on the table. By the radiance of these myriad sky candles, and rolled in blankets as the breeze freshened, we ate gray matter, pounded into unnatural shapes, which an Arab assured us was fish. I had a bag of dates which I shared with a Levantine and a portly Sayed[1] from Hadhramaut, who was going to Addis Ababa to visit a cousin. He was very distressed because he was unable to discover from a little wizened man who spoke the language of Damascus, whether the Abyssinians were civilized enough to understand the making of a certain floury paste flavored with oil, pepper, and nuts, which he considered essential to his sustenance. I fell asleep in the middle of the discussion, and woke to find the Levantine politely fanning the flies off me. Somaliland was a bed of violets on the horizon and the Sayed was talking of dogs. "The Saluki should have feet fringed like the eyes of a woman," I heard him say as I went in search of breakfast.

While the tramp ploughed her way, with much grunting and rolling, over a sea of glass, the wizened one produced a bundle of quilts and, from inside it, a terrier puppy. A couple of natives drew nearer, their mouths open, obviously hoping that this was a new form of conjurer! "See now, here is a real dog," said the Syrian, but the Sayed only snorted. For him the greyhound was the only animal worthy of such a name.

"It isn't a dog at all," he announced, "it's a—it's a boojie!" The insult was so great that conversation languished till the rattle of

---

1 A Moslem holy man.

the anchor-chain announced our arrival at Djibouti. "Allah be praised," said the Sayed, clearing his throat with the noise of an exhaust. I ventured to agree with him and was promptly submitted to an inquisition as to how and why I had come to this "land of strangers." When I confessed to a roundabout approach by way of Palestine and Syria, Iraq, and Persia, the old man gazed at me with dismay. "Allah pity you," he exclaimed, "traveling is not fit pursuit for women."

The Arab doctor took us ashore in his launch and a veritable "open sesame" of a document presented me by French officialdom prevented inquisitive douaniers sticking their fingers into raw film on the theory that it might be tobacco or opium. We walked to the hotel through valleys of pink hibiscus and I decided that Djibouti, white and neat and empty, looked as if it had just been washed and dumped out in the sun to dry. The check tablecloths and the crisp yard-long breads, with the flasks of red and white wine reminded me of Southern France, and the patronne, who insisted that Jones must sleep in the "lingerie" since the hotel was full and it would be a crime to send him to the desolation of the rival inn, had the accent of the Midi. Djibouti was busy exporting hides and coffee and importing Maria Theresa dollars and she did her business in a soufflé of different languages, which made her seem very cosmopolitan. Even the Somalis wore their white tobh[2] draped round their waist and flung over the shoulders—cape and kilt in one—with an air of sophistication, from which I am not certain whether the addition of a felt hat detracted or not. Consequently I understood the horror of the British Consul, when a fair young thing recently passing through as a "Complete Sportswoman," asked him if she could wear shorts in the train to Addis Ababa!

---

2 Arab word for dress, shirt, or cloth.

That train, alas, departs at dawn, so in darkness we sampled Madame's exquisite coffee, paid the very last extra that her thrifty ingenuity could conceive and went out to find a gharry. "Better take one each," said the Somali porter, looking at us as if he thought our combined fifteen stone were more than any one animal could be expected to pull. In silence I looked at a broken horse tied together with harness made of rope. Equally silently Jones prodded the ghost of what might once have been a packing-case or a cubist toy.

"Yes, we will go singly," I said. "Better sit well in the middle." My warning was justified, for a wheel came off after 200 yards and the journey was finished on foot.

There was nothing ghostly about the station except the half light which turned the yelling mob of porters into a white wave of humanity that threatened to engulf us as it had already done our baggage. The Somali idea seemed to be to weigh every item as many times as possible and hurl it with vociferous violence on to a pyramid of crates in the van.

"My camera!" moaned Jones as a score of hands swept it from him. The tripod was thrown on the head of a merchant in a gold turban who, naturally objecting, dashed it to the ground. The uproar must have gone to my head, for I found myself leaping the counter and wresting our more breakable possessions by main force from the crowd which, under excuse of weighing, seemed to be determined to stamp and tear them to bits. Finally, by a combined rush, we bore the cameras through the gate and, piling them on the platform, breathless, heated, bruised, sat on them until the stationmaster came to the rescue!

After this our leisurely progress across Somaliland was peaceful. The train rested before most hills or after any very violent corner. It stopped when the driver wanted a drink, or the mechanician tested the wheels with a spanner nearly as large as himself. Most obligingly it pulled up at mid-day in the shade of mimosa trees before a little estaminet where we ate macaroni and goat's meat with appetite. The Sayed greeted me warmly from a bench where he discussed women with an acquaintance in a magenta turban and a blue frock. Divorce is much practiced in Southern Arabia, so I was not as surprised as his companion when he announced that he had already had over eighty wives.

"Inshallah, you will live to make up the one hundred," gasped the turbaned one, but the Sayed was indignant.

"My gray beard is the result of wisdom, not of years," he retorted with a scowl. "I hope, indeed, that the number will be two hundred."

I choked over my coffee, for most intimate details followed. . . .

All afternoon the train dawdled through sand and rock. "Dust devils" whirled up like great columns of smoke, and occasionally one broke over the train, smothering us in grit. After leaving the border hills, it was a monotonous country of black stones and red earth, but gazelles ventured within tantalizing range and a hawk or two hovered over some invisible prey. Towards sunset the advance guard of the Abyssinian mountains broke the line of plain. Between the foothills rolling upwards, amber and rugged, there was a forest of scrub. Thick green bushes with juicy leaves, a mist of gray acacias and skeleton thorns, with hundreds of hanging bird's-nests, gave promise of the changing country which lay beyond Dire Dawa and the gates of Ethiopia.

"Attractive land to camp in and plenty of shade," I suggested, but Jones spoke learnedly of visibility and light values, so I retaliated by spreading out the largest map and planning optimistic routes. That is the charm of a map. It represents the other side of the horizon where everything is possible. It has the magic of anticipation without the toil and sweat of realization. The greatest romance ever written pales before the possibilities of adventure that lie in the faint blue trails from sea to sea. The perfect journey is never finished, the goal is always just across the next river, round the shoulder of the next mountain. There is always one more track to follow, one more mirage to explore. Achievement is the price which the wanderer pays for the right to venture.

So the routes I planned to Lalibela grew more and more complicated. Abyssinia can offer every contrast of mountain and valley, desert, river and forest, of walled medieval town and thatched mushroom village, of troglodyte and hillmen, priests, courtesans and savages, of courteous simple hospitality and the glamour of ancient violences, but Lalibela is her jewel, secret and unique. The dozen legendary churches like Petra "rose red and half as old as time," are hidden among the rocks and thorns of Lasta. Built by slaves or angels, by Egyptians, Phoenicians, or Arabs, the glamour of these subterranean marvels was as strong for us as for the 500-year-dead priest, the Portuguese Alvarez, who first described them. Since then, the red mountains have revealed their secret to scarcely half a dozen Europeans. The monks who guard the monoliths babble of their miraculous construction and add to its mystery by showing records so old that a breath might destroy them, with paragraphs in Arabic interspersed between the Geze.[3] Lalibela then was our goal, and it lies in the heart of Abyssinia with innumerable ranges as its walls, rivers as its moats. . . . I returned to the friendliness of my map and planned a route, whose charm was the extent of ground it covered, most of it perpendicular!

We arrived at Dire Dawa while I was hesitating between Massawa on the Red Sea, or Wad Medeni on the Nile, as the pleasantly far-away end of a journey so tortuous that I had given up trying to excuse it.

---

3 The ancient tongue of Ethiopia.

There was another battle over our luggage, during which various articles dripped out of my flea-bag which had burst a strap, and then we were escorted to the hotel by a kindly Armenian merchant who adopted us at sight. My bedroom opened on to a thicket of bougainvillea pierced with scarlet poinsettias, and a heavy-scented creeper hung like a curtain round my door.

"From the moment you enter Abyssinia till the moment you leave it," warned our new friend, "you will never meet an honest man."

Later I decided that many Abyssinians are honest with money, none with their thoughts, but, for the moment, I accepted the verdict literally and a stolid Ethiopian called Esheti as bodyguard.

Next morning we two went to the market with a bagful of the smallest coins I could procure—they were piastres and worth about 3d. each, but they had remarkable buying powers. We purchased grain, coffee and sugar for the caravan, and huge sacks of salt to barter for eggs and milk in the interior. Then we strolled round the square crowded with the usual half-civilized, half-commercialized medley of races that haunt railway outposts in Africa. Somali women crouched under straw shelters, their hats rolled in nets, their throats laden with beads—yellow seemed to be the fashionable color—and a strip of red cotton wound gracefully over one shoulder. They sold goat's butter in woven bowls, milk smelling of the smoke with which the calabashes[4] were dried, and thick lumps of tobacco set out on leaves. White-robed tribesmen passed hand in hand, with yellow clay on their heads, spears across their shoulders, sometimes swinging a pole at each end of which was a bundle of living birds. Townsmen and townswomen were almost indistinguishable with their white muffled *chammas*[5] and close-cropped curly hair. Two or three widows with shaven

---

4 Gourds made from dried pumpkins.
5 The white, sheetlike wraps worn by Abyssinians.

crowns sheltered by the most curious little pagoda-like umbrellas of straw, dragged their saffron robes through the sand. A madman wound up in rope till he looked like a black parcel bursting from its wrappings, cried out for alms. A musician with a scarlet turban sat under a mimosa tree playing on a stringed gourd, and, near him, a dog gnawed at a bullock's head thrown in the dust. It was the gate of Africa with her glare and heat and smell, and when marriage music burst suddenly from a fenced compound, there was a hint of the spell which underlies such things.

"It is a friend of mine who marries his daughter—she is fifteen and the bridegroom is twenty-two," said Esheti, as the beat of drums swelled into a rhythmic clamor. "Come and see—there will be much dancing and noise."

He led the way, smiling, into a court full of servant girls and slaves, beggars, lute players and small boys who made the most frightful gurglings with fingers stuck down their throats. Half the yard had been converted into a great tent, and, when a charming host in spotless white garments bordered with green had begged us to enter, we found several hundred people, men and women, seated on the floor round an open space. There was an inner circle of men with rifles and among these danced ebony figures, white turbaned, white swathed, with long-stemmed flasks of oil, with which they sprinkled the multitude, who kept up a sonorous clapping of hands. The very black faces and very white garments made a curious contrast and, in the dim light, it was almost as if patches of shadow drifted up and down on a frozen sea.

In one corner some women held up a square of white muslin within which Esheti informed us was the bride. "The men jumping there are relations," he said, "they dance and shout to keep away evil spirits, but presently they will all drink *tedj*[6] till they forget!"

---

6 Mead.

Before I could ask for further explanation, the multitude began to surge out into the yard where there was a group of gaily-caparisoned mules. The bridegroom, wearing a blue and white veil and a dark cloak, was assisted to mount by three friends, who apparently acted as groomsmen. The bride followed. Lengths of gauze were held over her like a tent, but the instant she was in the saddle it was all swathed round her and surmounted by a Stetson hat! Not to be outdone, the bridegroom and his attendants assumed the same headgear on top of their veils, and the procession crowded down the narrow path, a mass of wild, leaping figures, preceded by musicians playing on oddly shaped stringed instruments, the bearers of the sacred oil, and ragged figures carrying platters of food draped with scarlet cloths. I wanted to follow them to the feast, but Esheti was stern. "The morning is gone," he reproached, "and there is much to do about the caravan." Apparently he felt a friendly or possibly a financial interest in us, for he announced that he would find us servants and muleteers, as well as baggage beasts and "strong fat animals fit for your superiority to ride."

Thereafter I interviewed guides who would not go as far as I wanted, and others, more crafty, who promised everything with a volubility that did not compensate for their sly glances. I communed with cooks, who seemed not to know the difference between a chicken and an egg, and culinary experts who wanted to take a grocery store with them. Mules by the dozen crowded the streets outside, but they were all lame or had sore backs. An escort of soldiers was necessary, but when what looked like a battalion paraded for inspection, most of them seemed uncertain as to the reliability of their rifles. There were no English saddles to be had, and the Abyssinian ones were not only seats of torture, but had small stirrups supposed to be held between the toes. The caravan leader—known as the *khabral*—who had been recommended to me, had vanished into the mountains, and all that was known of him was that he would certainly return to-morrow, or after to-morrow, or sometime. In fact, as usual in organizing an African caravan, there came a moment when, having investigated all forms of transport from camels to little gray donkeys with black stripes on their shoulders, and seen the last of the guides who knew all the country except where we wanted to go, it seemed as if we should never get started at all.

Then, one morning Esheti appeared with a thinner and blacker edition of himself. "This is Gabra Gorgis—he will be your cook," he announced, and from that moment things began to go better. Gabra Gorgis looked at my stores with pity. "We will now go to the market and buy what is really useful," he said, and I spent an instructive morning bargaining for oils and spices, small bundles of leaves for flavoring, curious pots and pans which Gabra Gorgis insisted were more suited to wood fires than our enamel ware. We also laid in a store of highly ornamental cups lest "the great should come to visit our camp," and some padlocked cases to prevent the soldiers or muleteers taking too much interest in our food. The next day everything happened at once. Six soldiers were produced by the Armenian merchant, and another half dozen to act as guarantors during their absence. This system undoubtedly facilitates trekking with an unknown escort, for each servant, soldier or guide must leave at the starting-point some reliable guarantor, a *dalmin*—literally one who will be faithful for him—who is responsible to the local authority for the behavior of his friend.

The warriors had scarcely departed to buy sandals and blankets, which are a part of their wages, though I believe they generally sell before starting, when a "boy" with a wistful expression was dragged into my presence. Gabra Gorgis insisted that he was a pearl of servants, and in answer to every question, the youth said, "I can wash clothes beautifully!" On the strength of this, and his expression, I engaged him, in spite of a name which began with Gabra Miquael Gallav—the end I never could pronounce.

There was a rumor that a troop of fine mules had arrived from Harrar, and we rushed down to the grain market to engage them as soon as they had unloaded. On the way a tall man saluted my companion, and Gabra Gorgis literally threw himself upon him, clutching him by the shoulder as if afraid he might take flight, and shaking him to be quite certain he was real. "There are three men looking for thee in the mountains, thou fox!" he exclaimed by way of explanation, "come now with us and choose the mules." In this way Omar the *khabral* was added to our party. He was still protesting when we reached the group of acacias under which the mules were rolling free of their sacks. "Do not look too closely, lady, I beg of you," murmured Gabra Gorgis, but miraculously we were able to pick out a dozen sound beasts and when on our return we found a mournful Indian tailor had brought our mosquito nets, and a tinker had unearthed some rusty English stirrups, our spirits rose in anticipation of speedy departure.

Of course there were further delays. The coinage of Abyssina consists of Maria Theresa dollars, 80 per cent silver, worth approximately three shillings (about seventy-four cents) each, and of an incredible size and weight. A sack containing £50 worth of these was as much as I could lift, and four such bags form a mule load, but, as there is no change in the interior, dollars are of very little use except for a Croesus. You can buy twenty eggs or two chickens for a piastre, and a sheep for three quarter-dollars, but unfortunately all these coins are more or less mythical, and you have to go out into the market with your beautiful shining white dollars, and haggle for piastres and quarters at an inflated value. There is another snare for the unwary. The quarterthaler is stamped with a crowded lion, but if the beast has his mouth open and a particularly flamboyant twist to his tail, the tribesman will not accept him, so Jones and I spent weary hours bargaining for neat quiet lions, with shut mouths and slinky tails. At last we came back, burdened with small sacks, dumped them into a suit-case with a sigh of relief and attempted to lift it into a corner. Both handles broke at once. We sat down on the floor and looked at each other mutely. . . .

There came a voice from outside—"Lady, the soldiers say it will be wet on the mountains and they cannot buy any stuff here to make a tent, and the poles you ordered in the suq are too long for the mosquito nets, and Gallan has fever, so that his insides shakes." Another voice broke in—"It is not fever that he has—the bad one has been eating *kat*! Lady, shall I tie the stirrups on with string, for your legs are too long for this saddle." We were no longer mute!

That afternoon every member of the caravan asked for advance pay, on the ground that he had a sick wife or a child whose small-ness was measured by an appealing hand a few inches from the ground. As every man appeared later with a bundle of fresh green leaves in his belt, I imagine that most of the money was spent on *kat*, a drug which alternately stimulates and depresses, and which is supposed only to be eaten by Moslems.

The Arks at Harrar

IT HAD BEEN arranged that we should start at six, so at five AM, in complete darkness, before the cocks had begun their crowing match, we were dressed and looking out for the arrival of our mules. Gabra Gorgis and Gallan carried out the baggage, muttering their discontent. "Everything's always an hour or two late in this country," I assured Jones, when a gray light crept across the verandah and there was no sign of a beast.

"I do not believe the mules are in town yet," announced Omar, returning from his fifth survey of the street. He explained that, to avoid expense, the *nagadis*[1] always send their animals to feed in the hills and brought them in just before they were wanted.

When the sun rose we were all sitting on piles of luggage at the edge of the street, looking almost as foolish as we felt.

"What about another breakfast?" I suggested, remembering the excellence of the hotel coffee. It so far cheered us that we discussed the Arab saying, "There are three starts and then there is a real one."

"I dare say we'll be off by noon," remarked Jones.

---

1 Head muleteer.

At nine came a rumor that the last that had been seen of our mules was a disorderly mob galloping away into the mountains. About mid-day the messenger we had sent to inquire into this story returned, trying to look depressed, but really delighted with the unexpectedness of their information. The mules, they said, had been attacked in the night by hyenas, one had had its leg eaten off, and the others had stampeded. Their owners were still chasing them. The story grew rapidly, and the last I heard of it was that a lion had eaten the *nagadi*!

As unobtrusively as possible, we returned our baggage to our rooms, changed into civilized garments and went out to watch the arrival of Dejezmatch[2] Imaru, the Acting Governor of Harrar, who had been attending the wedding of Ras Tafari's daughter in Addis Ababa.

The procession was attractive. First came soldiers of all sizes and shapes, "simply swathed in cartridges," as Jones expressed it in the intervals of working the cinema. These were the personal body-guard of Ras Tafari, trained by former non-commissioned officers of the King's African Rifles, uniformed in European khaki. The Dejezmatch followed on foot, a slight man with a distinguished carriage, which his wide black cape and rodeo hat did much to hide. Behind him came his officials, a mass of very white draper-ies, with here and there a splash of scarlet bordering a cloak. There were women holding absurd little pagoda parasols over an infin-ity of plaits so finely braided that they looked like a net. Porters staggered under loads of steel dishes, or perhaps they were shields. Horses, with tassels swinging from their lion-embroidered sad-dle-cloths, were led by retainers armed with rifle and spear, and the rear was brought up by fuzzy-headed mountaineers, lepers, beggars, a few dozen dogs and a stray goat.

---

2 General.

We had only just packed away the camera when a message came that His Excellency would like to see us, so Jones and I went up to the little Government House, built on a hillock in the middle of Dire Dawa, and surrounded with verandahs from which there is a glorious view of hill and valley. It is approached by a mass of steps, which soar up almost perpendicularly between very drugged looking lions. "There's something missing in those animals, but I can't think what it is," murmured Jones, as we plodded up flight after flight between the disappointed thousands who sought audience of the great man.

Dejezmatch Imaru received us in a big, almost empty room, hung with red, the lion predominating in the canopy and decoration of a chair of state. He spoke a little French, and the mystery of our summons was soon explained.

"In the *Illustration* last year," he said, "I saw your picture with an Arab Chief! I remember it because he was the largest man I had ever seen. I did not know anyone could be so monstrous." I laughed and told him about the Moroccan Sherif Raisuli, whose girth was so vast that he had to have a special door and a special chair made for him. Imaru has a thin, intelligent face, and his smile comes just often enough for one to appreciate its attraction. After he had volunteered to send a wire to Ras Tafari asking for a special firman to facilitate our journey through the mountains, he invited me to come and see his wife.

In a room furnished with gilt French chairs and tables, a woman was sunk in an armchair, inert amidst her wrappings, which lapped up to her lips white fold on fold. Her fine black eyes were lashed as thickly as a deer's, her hair meshed so intricately as to suggest embroidery, but she was tired after a long journey, or too shy, perhaps, to speak more than a few formal words of greeting. Servants brought glasses of golden *tedj*, the drink made with honey and bitter herbs, of which Baudelaire wrote—"*Le plus grand délice, c'est de boire l'hydromel dans le crâne d'un enfant.*"

We discussed travelling, and the Ras was of the opinion that a mule caravan was infinitely preferable to a train. "From the railway," he said, "one sees nothing of the country but its dirt, and one eats and breathes that as well. You are wise to ride; you will gain everything but time." He smiled, adding: "Shall we ever consider that quite as precious as you do, I wonder?"

When we returned to the hotel we found a depressed group of animals clustered round the steps in charge of a *nagadi* who surely was Ham the son of Noah. His face, in its thicket of white hair, was noble and square and lined in broad valleys, between which showed the moulding of the bones. His eyes were deep set and candid, with the look that is neither old nor young, but very wise. Unfortunately, his dialect was incomprehensible to everyone in the caravan except his muleteers who, for our benefit, translated and elaborated his few words—I don't think he ever used more than half a dozen consecutively.

It was difficult to reproach such an individual for anything so incomprehensible to him as a day's delay, and it was awkward to have to point out that, whereas I had certainly chosen sound mules, most of those he had brought had backs as raw as meat in a butcher's shop.

"He says it does not matter," announced a curly-headed black Pan who should have had a pipe in his belt. In despair we saw the mules driven into a yard, saw the door locked, and announced once again that we should start at six.

At three-thirty there was a thunderous knock on my door, which must have awakened everyone in the street.

"Is it time yet, lady?" asked Gabra Gorgis.

"It is not," I retorted, wishing I could remember a really satisfactory Arabic curse. The next hour was enlivened by songs from the escort, waiting in the street, and after that we gave in.

Most of Dire Dawa turned out to see us start, and I felt the way we meandered up the dry river bed outside the town was hardly worthy of the interest we excited. A couple of soldiers went first, their rifles in their hands, immense curved swords sticking out behind them like tails. Laden with every form of box, bundle and sack, the mules drifted purposeless after them. Jones and I vainly tried to keep our mounts straight, but, after the first exhausting mile or two, we realized that you don't ride mules unless you're born and bred to them—you merely sit on them and try to avoid the heels of their neighbors. During our progress through the sands of the Harri valley I thought longingly of camel caravans, for a camel can only kick one way, whereas a mule has something magic about his joints and can kick equally effectively in all directions and with all feet. Jones just missed a blow on the shoulder from a white beast with a torn ear, and a hoof glanced off my wadded saddle-cloths before I learned discretion. It was very hot, and a slab of chocolate in my haversack melted and ran into my brush and comb before I noticed it dripping down my boot.

The dust was thick in the river bed, for it is the main road of the hill villagers coming to market their produce in the town. We met troops of donkeys laden with fodder, and camel strings tied head to tail, driven by half-naked blacks, the whole of their luggage, comb, toothpick, tobacco and ear scratcher, stuck in their flaring hair. The women were the heaviest laden of the beasts of burden. They passed us in scarlet-robed groups, bent double under stacks of firewood, with a baby or a bundle of chickens slung on their hips. Sometimes their hands were full of calabashes, a towering pumpkin was balanced on their heads and a goat wrapt in the sash round their waists. Herds of small humped cattle browsed under the sheltering fans of the mimosas and, as the scrub thickened at the foot of the hills, we came upon charcoal burners surrounded by blazing stumps and flocks of goats in charge of small naked imps.

The great thorns grew closer till they made above our heads a curtain splashed with the sudden scarlet of wings, or rent by the weight of creepers. Then we began to mount and the world spread out before us like a map. The track was narrow and scarred with boulders, in places almost perpendicular, and it twisted and doubled back on itself, till we saw the path we had traversed as a series of incredible spirals, dropping from rock to rock below. The mules slipped and staggered. Twice the ropes broke and loads crashed down between the stones, while the beasts lashed themselves free.

We made slow progress, for at every corner where the track hung on the edge of space, a crowd of little gray donkeys over-burdened with sacks of coffee, slithered helpless amongst us, adding to the confusion of our laboring beasts, and causing a storm of abuse from the drivers. When, for a change, the trail pitched downwards between torn-up roots and under hanging boulders, we walked, for it seemed that at any moment the saddles might slip over the mules' heads. Once, as Jones remounted, the girth broke, and he fell backwards on to his shoulder. The Abyssin-ian harness is as frail as it is clumsy, and every strap is knotted, mended and reinforced with string, except where its discrepan-cies can temporarily be forgotten under a saddle-cloth.

Suddenly we found ourselves on top of the last ridge, and with a glance backward at the blue of cupped valley and wooded moun-tain, sweeping down to the plain beyond Dire Dawa, we saw before us the plateau, a tame land of cultivation with the sheen of a lake between thatched mushroom huts. Flowering euphorbias and cactus bordered our way. Flocks and herds rested in the mid-day heat wherever stacked sugar-cane or durra offered them shade. Men and women were sleeping with cloths thrown over their heads and, one after another, our escort pointed out that the climb had been steep! The blackest soldier, a second Gabra Gorgis, who was an engaging ruffian with a scar from temple to chin, muttered something about fever. Another was more honest. "We are all tired," he laughed, "because yesterday we drank too much *tedj*. We sang all night and we're sad this morning."

Balla Lake drifted into a haze which shimmered over the scattered villages, fungus rings on the slopes, surrounded with hedges of euphorbias twenty feet high. After about seven hours' march, we arrived at another lake, Arameya, its waters ruffled by a sudden wind and laden with duck. There were red-eyed spoonbills, huge bald-headed coots, divers which seemed to have no heads at all, and quantities of waders, black and white birds, stepping daintily on spidery pink legs.

Enchanted by its pictorial possibilities, we camped on low ground near the water, surrounded by poplars which formed inadequate shelter against the wind. Gabra Gorgis had been buying food along the way, a gourdful of milk, a thin chicken. Now he collected a few stones and an armful of wood, and having piled everything round him in apparently inextricable confusion, in half an hour he produced a marvellous meal. After the third course, which, if it was the athletic fowl, was most intriguingly disguised, we ceased to feel hungry. Jones produced the inevitable pipe—he only took it out of his mouth to eat or when his face was glued to the back of a camera—and I one of my last treasured cigarettes. We talked of the wonderful pictures we were going to take till the sun went down and a gale threatened our tents.

The soldiers and muleteers had established themselves on the lee side, waiting for their feast of sheep. Whenever a caravan starts on a long journey, the escort claimed the sacrifice of a sheep to bring it luck. In Abyssinia it really is a sacrifice, for the animal is led into the middle of the circle, its throat is cut, and before the body has stopped quivering, half a dozen knives are slashing at flank and quarter. The raw warm flesh is disposed of in a few mouthfuls, and five minutes after the initial knife-stroke, there is nothing left but the bones and the blood smeared on cheeks and fingers. I saw Omar lead a sheep towards the group near my tent, and fled precipitately into the darkness!

It was a miserable night. As the escort were without shelter, we were obliged to share our blankets. By eleven it was bitterly cold, and the temperature dropped lower with every hour towards the dawn. We had not expected mosquitoes in such a wind, but we found the tents full of them—"As big as rats," said Gallan, upsetting himself into the net. I got up a dozen times to conduct a wholesale slaughter, and still more often to see if there was anything else I could put on. The soldiers coughed themselves hoarse on the other side of the canvas and, between spasms, intoned what I imagined were tragic dirges, but I could not understand their Amharic. We were all glad when the dawn came, though Jones and I, stamping round and round, muffled to the chin, while we ate stale bread and hardboiled eggs, tried to conceal our shivers, and ended by comparing bites!

In the shelter of a cactus hedge, squealing, kicking, the mules were loaded. We set off down the broad path between millet stalks and plough. We passed threshing-grounds where men beat the grain with flails and small walking haystacks that resolved themselves into overloaded donkeys. The road was full of traffic, chiefs on horseback surrounded by rifles, men on mules, men on foot, all hastening to meet Dejezmatch Imaru, or to watch him pass. A personage with a gold-bordered cloak passed on a white Arab pony. I turned to look at the spearmen who ran behind. "They're far more effective than guns—" I began, but the sentence was never finished, for my mount, objecting, plunged sideways, the girth broke, and in an avalanche of saddle, water-bottle and haversack, I pitched head first into a bush. A babel of voices followed me, a scurry of running feet, but it was the mule's heels which brought me out, unhurt, but a pincushion of thorns, which Gabra Gorgis extracted one by one, a new condolence with each.

The morning offered no further incident, and by noon we were camped amidst coffee plantations on a shelf of ground overlooking Harrar. Pepper trees provided shade for the tents. A path bordered with wild rose and lilac slipped steeply to the mass of old walls, golden brown and crumbling, that were built in the 15th century. Further away the white modern buildings lay in a splash of sunshine, their towers piercing the mountain mist.

Just outside our camping ground, divided from it by a bank of flowering creeper, a stream widened into a pool. Here most of the population seemed to be washing either their clothes or themselves. Ebony figures were silhouetted stark against the water. Hides, spread in convenient hollows, provided tubs full of lather, wherein women rinsed and pounded till the whole ground was covered with white heaps of linen. It was spread on the hedges, flung across branches, laid out on bank and furrow. Long strips were held down by urchins. Cloths dripped from every wall. As we went down to Harrar, each angle of the stream, each ditch held its quota of washing. Every human being was scrubbing some scrap of cloth. We demanded explanation as women hurried past us, dripping piles on their heads, smell of soap preceding them, and learned that it was the eve of Timkat, the great feast of Epiphany, when, from all the churches, the Arabs would go in procession to the pool for the yearly blessing of the water. Everyone must have a garment, "white without reproach," and everyone must struggle for a few drops of the holy water.

Ethiopia has been Christian for nearly 1,600 years, and as the Champion of the Faith during centuries of struggle with Islam, she claims not only an older but a purer conception of it. Legend has it that Makeda, Ruler of Axum, was the Queen of Sheba who visited Solomon 1,000 years before Christ. By him, she had a son, Menelik the first, the ancestor of the present reigning house, and the originator of Judaism in Ethiopia. He was educated at Jerusalem until he was eighteen, and the Abyssinians believe that, when he returned to Axum, this founder of a three thousand year old dynasty brought with him the Tablets of Moses, perhaps even the Ark of the Covenant in which they were kept. There is a story that the original tablets are preserved in the old capital, and another that the Ark is buried somewhere below its walls. In any case, every orthodox Abyssinian Church has a copy of the Tablets of the Law and at the feast of Epiphany, the arks that hold them are borne in procession through the town.

At sunset we stood on the hill above our camp and watched the crowds swell up towards the red-draped shelter prepared for the Tablets. From a distance it looked as if the sands had blossomed. The sound of drums, shrill pipe music and triumphal songs came up from the gardens where the bloom was like golden butterflies and Canna lilies stood guard against the bougainvillea. Slaves hurried by with the last bundle of rugs for the tents of the devout. Women followed, carrying baskets of bread, or calabashes on their heads The drums rolled nearer, and from every side came priests, monks and deacons, rosaries at their waists, the crutches on which they lean during the long church services carried by excited followers.

The mob seethed and eddied till it was like a sea in foam. Suddenly the songs merged into a cry of adoration. Every figure seemed to fold up, as, with heads bowed to their feet, they acknowledged the approach of the arks. Very slowly between the trees came the lute players and the monstrous barrel drums. Horns flashed up above the rifles of the escort, and amidst clamor of voice and music, eddy of gun and spear, there swayed, like poppies, the gorgeous velvet umbrellas gold embroidered, lilac and red and purple, under which walked the arch-priests. The sunset picked out the gold in each flaming vestment, blazed on the square carved crosses, lit every fringe and bauble. Against the mass of color in which silk and velvet and jewelled embroidery ran riot, the censers swung their trail of smoke, the mighty crosses swayed.

Between the poppy heads that were umbrellas, two figures, their humanity smothered in the stiffness and the richness of brocade, bore the Tablets on their heads, covered in exquisite stuffs so that nothing could be seen but their shape.

Unnoticed, the sun went down behind the hill, but in the hollow where the tents were pitched as close as mushrooms, the clamor swelled again. The arks of the Trinity and our Saviour passed down towards the pool and behind them walked the Governor Imaru with his chiefs and his soldiers. For a moment I thought the sunset was reflected on another wave of white which surged up from the town, but a thousand welcoming voices cried, "St. Michael!" The third ark passed on to join the glamour of gold and jewels beside the water.

As we walked slowly back through the coffee trees, we could see the last procession, Saint George's, winding down the mountain from the Church on its crest. To the age-old cry of women, that gurgling ululation that is the throb of Africa's rejoicing, it came, a Christian token against a setting of pagan violence. There was a fight now in the valley, but nobody knew why it began. A man staggered out with a bleeding head. A scrum of struggling figures swayed round the original combatants.

All night long the drums crashed from the hillside, while the priests kept vigil beside the arks, and the devout watched and prayed and ate thin sheets of Lenten bread, the great men in their tents, the soldiers beside their stacked arms, and the poor rolled in their newly-washed rags.

Chiefly Mules and Marriages

DEDER SEEMED TO me the first of our mountain camps, not because it was higher than any others—according to my aneroid, the altitudes on this trek varied between 6,000 and 8,000 feet—but because the tents were pitched on such a slope, that everything slid gently out of them. I went to sleep with my feet hanging over the edge of the stretcher, and woke with a bump to find that myself and the flea-bag had followed them.

By this time, reversing the usual proceeding, we used to dress at night to go to bed, and undress in the morning for the long hot ride. Consequently, muffled in jerseys, scarfs, a coat or two and a mule blanket, it was rather difficult to extract myself from the narrow canvas. I had just done so when there came a crescendo of grunting squeals, a stampede of hoofs, shouts, a shot, and more squeals. Seizing a revolver, I burst out of the tent to see a dark mass scudding into the night and a confusion of blanketed shapes.

Desta dashed past me with a rifle. "Hyenas!" he shouted, and the next moment something loped clumsily out of the shadow. I had a shot at it, but missed, and then every one seemed galvanized into sudden action.

"If you waste any more ammunition, the whole village will come to the rescue," I remonstrated with Gutta.

"Let them come and find our mules," he retorted.

We spent the rest of the night looking for the beasts, and started in the morning with two short. As we rode through an exquisite valley where the forest trees were burdened with clematis, orange honeysuckle and a flaming scarlet creeper, I preached on the subject of the old Arab saying, "put thy trust in God and a rope on the leg of thy camel," but learned that the mules had torn up pegs and broken heel ropes.

"Two things bewitch them," said the *nagadi*, "camels and hyenas." It was the longest speech I ever heard him make.

We had a good cinema "bag" that morning, for in one place we had to climb on hands and knees, while the mules sidled up sideways—I am sure they have crab blood in their veins. While Jones was turning the handle down below, some Gallas passed and, with hands clasping the most potent of their amulets, they bowed to the ground to propitiate the unknown power!

After this the track wound monotonously through the valley of Burka, beside whose stream we lunched. To reach the only shady tree we had to cross a deep ravine and Omar was so anxious to help us that he pulled at the wrong moment, precipitating Jones and himself into the water. The rest of our followers cast themselves, shrieking, to the rescue, and each seizing an end of their victims' clothes or one of their limbs, dragged and pushed with such lack of unanimity that Omar was nearly drowned and Jones reached the bank coated with mud. It fell off him in cakes as we left the valley in the afternoon blaze. Shortly afterwards one of our lost mules was recaptured and branded in front of us with an iron thrust into a charcoal-burner's fire. I had hardly got over this unexpected sight, when, clambering up between slippery boulders, which necessitated an infinity of heaves and twists, one of the baggage beasts fell, failed to rise under the weight of its pack, slipped horribly and broke its leg.

For a moment the babel was deafening, and then I realized that the muleteers were trying to beat the wretched animal to its feet. Seizing Demessi's rifle, I plunged down the rocks, prepared to shoot the beast myself, but the *nagadi* interposed with a knife. "Why waste good bullets?" he said. While I was still stuttering at him in the middle of an avalanche of cast loads and resentful hoofs, somebody came to the rescue with a couple of shots. The storm of protest and explanation spent itself in a perilous reloading.

It is curious that the Abyssinians have so little consideration for animals, for they are kindly in their dealings with their fellows, and, in the south, where they are used to contact with strangers, hospitable in their relations with them. Constantly small gifts of milk, durra, bread, or ale were offered us by passing villagers without any apparent expectation of reward. The muleteers used to pick sugarcane or millet as they passed and the owners, working, half naked, in their fields, laughed and wished them a good journey.

At certain stages, when the track was so steep that the loads had to be lightened, we were obliged to rely on local porters, and these were recruited in the most arbitrary way. The soldiers would see some men lounging in a village, go and pull them to their feet and, amidst cheerful protest, dump anything from a tent to a tin of paraffin which always leaked, on to their shoulders. With remarkable good humor, the hillmen carried such burdens to the end of their districts when a new set of porters were requisitioned. If we gave them the smallest coin, they thanked us profusely and kissed our feet. The Abyssinian manages to do this with a shy, swift dignity that is very attractive.

The *ballambarassi*[1] told me that in olden days any stranger might claim the right of transport through the village lands and that the custom still held good in the mountains, but I think much was due to the munificent orders of Ras Tafari, with whose firman we traveled.

The fourth night we spent at Tullu, a district of small hovels, wide spread over the slopes round a valley, where table-top mimosas sheltered our camp. The muleteers grumbled over the loss of the mule, insisting that we marched too far each day. Gabra Selessi, the kindest and most patient of companions, explained that the *nagadis* consider a five hours' march sufficient in mountain country, and they cut it short at midday, idling through the afternoon, eating their one solid meal at night, but he comforted me with the courteous assurance: "My only desire is to march as long as you like, to stop whenever you wish, and to make all things easy for you."

That night I made sure that the mules were safely tethered, doctored Gallan to the best of my ability for an ailment which gave him a temperature of 102, and which he thus described: "A mule stood on my foot and gave me a pain in my thigh, so now my head bursts," and, coming back to my tent in starlight, heard Omar's voice describing his vain search for food among the *tukels*.[2]

"They are not people in this district, but hyenas," he was saying. "The instant they saw our rifles, they ran away, shrieking. It was useless that we followed crying: 'Of your kindness sell us a few eggs. By your pleasure! Do us a favor. We shall be grateful, Allah bless you.' They did not wait to listen. The sight of us cleared the hill-side!"

I think the escort must have gone to bed hungry, for they were ready to start by seven next morning, an hour after I had shouted

---

1 Lieutenant.
2 Mud and thatched huts.

the usual reveille. The day's march consisted in climbing over two steep passes between which lay the valley of Hirna. The first was clothed in forest. We rode below curtains of strongly-scented purple creeper, with shiny green euphorbias lacing thickets of tall trees, their branches bearded with ferns and the froth of seeding clematis. Our pleasure was somewhat spoiled by the persistence with which one of the local porters waved in front of us a bunch of living fowls tied by their legs to a stick. At last I insisted they should be killed, and a fury of discussion raged. When, my vocal chords proving inadequate, I managed to inquire the reason by signs, I learned that all our porters were Gallas and either Moslems or pagans, and they would not carry anything killed by the Christian Abyssinians. "Well, let them kill the fowls themselves," I suggested, but Omar pointed out that our cook could not possibly handle any bird slain by an infidel's knife. The deadlock seemed absolute till it occurred to the soldiers that if they killed the birds and put them into a sack, the Gallas might be induced to carry it at the end of a pole!

We spent an hour photographing the harvesting of durra, a picturesque scene, where black giants, nude but for a loin cloth, wrestled with the fourteen-foot stalks, and girls, supple as a Grecian frieze, bore away the grain in baskets on their heads. An old man passed, bent under a mass of empty gourds. They looked like bloated balloons frozen to his shoulders. He glanced wistfully at my white mule. "A good beast," he said, "he runs like water, but my feet are stones under me." A piastre cheered him considerably and he clumped away singing.

At Hirna, a large village, the market of the neighborhood, with a few Greek or Armenian storekeepers, we received a shock. It was barely noon and we were walking briskly, a cold wind in our faces, when Omar pointed out a medley of baggage and unsaddled mules scattered over the green. Closer inspection proved that the *nagadi*, taking advantage of our absorption in photography, had calmly camped for the day. Doubtless he thought the pitching of his shelter and the uncording of all the luggage, while his beasts wandered down to the stream, would convince us that another start was hopeless. His expression was a blend of amazement and disgust when I hustled the soldiers after the mules, had them driven in at a trot and ordered an immediate reloading. It wasted half an hour, but it taught the *nagadi* a lesson and we proceeded up the next ridge in what Abyssinia would consider silence!

In spite of all these delays we reached Debasso and a hillside thick with dog-roses in time to see the sunset over Kunni, the mountain of forests. Round a blazing fire, our followers, each a little separate tent in his blanket, with only eyes and nose showing, roasted the durra they had stolen in the valley, and talked of their battles and, alas, their insides! At a cluster of huts near by, a wedding feast was in progress. The bridegroom was a Christian merchant from Hirna, so we were invited to drink *tedj* and eat *fet-fet*, little round pieces of meat steeped in the hottest of sauces. The guests, seated on the floor, with a spoon and a knife each, used sheets of the native bread (*anjera*) as table and napkin combined. The bridegroom, smelling strongly of scent and oil, was fed by the four groomsmen who sat one on each side of him, and they cut titbits of raw meat from the sheep hanging by its legs from a pole held by two slaves and pushed them into his mouth. Behind the shelter of a few yards of muslin, held up like a tent, some girls performed the same office for the bride. Once, when the bridegroom choked, two or three friends precipitated themselves to hide his face under their *chammas*. At intervals the women who feasted in an adjoining yard could be heard singing, and occasionally, without warning, some man leaped to his feet, emptied a cow horn at a draught, and holding it upside down, sprinkled the guests with the few remaining drops.

After a last *feu de joie* had wakened every dog in the neighborhood, the bride was led into the hut and seated on a couch while her father read a list of all her possessions beginning with two oxen and ending with a felt hat. Four times oil was sprinkled over her from a slender flagon; she sipped a horn of *tedj* from which every one else drank in turn. Then the muslin screen was folded round her while she embraced or talked to her mother.

The number four is considered not only lucky, but almost sacramental, as the Fetha Negast[3] states that there are four patriarchs, four gospels, four rivers in the terrestrial paradise, four winds, seasons and elements, and four quarters of the earth. Consequently the bride came out from her muslin screen with four branches of olive held over her and the same number of amulets hung round her neck. We wanted to wish her luck, but a fellow guest insisted that she must not speak to a stranger on her wedding-day, so we left her amidst the songs and the scented heat of her hut and went back to the camp fires. There were three of them and, in every one, bread was being baked in thin cakes spread on a stump and plentifully sprinkled with ash.

"To-morrow we shall be in Kunni," said Gutta, "and there will be whole trees to burn."

"Monkeys too," smiled Desta, "and I shall want to shoot them, but the lady will say they are beautiful and she loves them as a son, like the black and white ram at Deder, which she would not let me kill."

There was a general laugh at the memory of how I had crept out at night to release an engaging animal destined for a feast of raw meat. I went to sleep to the echo of native voices, for I think most of the country folk came in to sit by our monster fires and exchange fragments of dried meat, as stiff as hide, for the gossip of

---

3 Books of law—religious, civil, and traditional.

the road. I woke to the heaviest dew of the march. My boots were so stiff that it took me nearly ten minutes to stamp into them and my clothes were like a sponge. I heard Jones come out of his tent, and then, after a clatter of tins, his voice sounded cheerfully, "They're dry as a bone!"

"What do you mean? Have you been sleeping on your boots?" I retorted crossly, as the second strap broke.

"The films, of course," answered my single-minded companion, rubbing his hands which were numb, though raw in places from the extremes of sun and wind.

The only other trial of this mountain trek was the lack of water. If there are large springs, they are hidden beyond ken of the villagers who drink from the most appalling holes where cattle and goats wallow, or from slow-running streams putrescent with slime. Most of the huts are built at a considerable distance from water, and often we had to send our men some miles into the hills to bring back a supply for cooking and drinking. Washing was out of the question. Sometimes, for three or four pence we could buy a gourdful of water, muddy and unpleasant both to smell and taste, but, after the first few days, we ceased to argue about the doubtful contents of our bottles.

"Shut your eyes when you drink and trust to luck," suggested Jones.

Fortunately there was always some sort of muddy ditch or pool where the mules could be watered if, during the day's journey, we crossed no streams.

The sixth day brought us to Kunni, two mountain masses sheathed in forest. All the morning we watched clouds slip over the dark summits, and at midday we rested under some olives to enjoy the view. Sunlight and shadow flickered over twin valleys, the large new village of Sabatafero like a crop of mushrooms in the northern, a half dry lake gleaming in the southern. Reflectively peeling eggs, very, very hard-boiled, Jones and I congratulated ourselves on the beauty of Kunni and the morning's catch—some attractive scenes of Galla women pounding maize in huge earthen jars, half a dozen men flower-crowned, rethatching a *tukel*, and a crowd of oxen stamping the grain from straw. Omar interrupted us, "The *ballam-barassi* wants to know the hour—his watch is asleep." Startled, I must have pinched the egg I held, for it shattered my complacency by erupting over me in yellow slime.

"Misfortune," exclaimed Omar, "it would soon have been a chicken!"

Jones choked and crushed his handkerchief to his nose. It was the worst egg of a long native experience, and it ruined my long-suffering breeches!

We camped on the ridge between the great forest peaks, because the *ballambarassi* wanted to be near the remains of what had once been a large village graced by a residence of Ras Macon-nen, father of the present Regent. The majority of the people have now moved down to Sabatafero, wisely, I thought, after two tents had collapsed in the gale which blew over the pass. It was an unpleasant night spent chiefly in knocking in pegs and tightening ropes. In the end I gave up all hope of coping with the whirlpool of screaming canvas which strained the poles to breaking point. Miserably I dragged my flea bag into a sort of furrow below a bank, burrowed right down into its eight-foot length, stopped up the entrance with my pillow, and slept till a cow butted me gently to discover if I were edible.

There was a marvelous rose-pink light on the hills against which the trees were carved ebony, and a rime of frost on the grass. Jones and I took turns to nurse the coffee pot, the only warm thing in the universe. Generally we walked and rode through alternate hours, but that morning we tramped steadily till the sun melted the frost and the forest paths were jeweled, every creeper sparkling, the branches whispering beneath their weight of crystals. Down we went by crooked, stony paths, over tree trunks or under them. Occasionally a goreza, a large monkey, his black face surrounded by a white ruffle, slung himself whimpering over our heads, or a caravan of them, climbing heads to tails wheeled into the distance. Omar told us that the Gallas put down a pan of beer in some glade dear to the monkey heart, and when the inquisitive gorezas have sniffed and tasted sufficiently to make them drunk, they are easy prey for the watching spearmen.

After three hours' march we were passing the last trees, table-top mimosas with purple convolvulus clambering up them. Behind us the mountains in their close-fitting mantle of forest, looked like rough velvet. In front was a wide sweep of grass, alternate plain and hill, with crests a little sharper than the English downs. Fields made a patchwork of gold where men flailed the barley with long-handled swingles, or of emerald green where bananas and coffee grew near a stream. Dotted through the cultivation were watch-towers that looked like flat beehives set high on bundles of stakes, a precaution against the depredations of wild pig.

By noon we were riding through Boroma, where the grass grew saddle high and our caravan looked like field mice. Beyond the smooth, sun-kissed downland, the ridge of Lagardin loomed a misty blue that never came any nearer. We passed through Badessa, an ugly village of haystacks, windowless, but with low doors cut in the fourteen-inch thickness of the straw, where small boys play hockey with sticks of sugar-cane and the hard yellow fruit of amboy.

An hour later we realized that we had lost both luggage and mule-teers. A furious search along the route we had traversed revealed the mules idling placidly on Badessa green and the *nagadi* entrenched in one of the haystack houses. I cut short the screaming which followed by a revolver pressed into the back of the nearest muleteer.

Much surprised and a little amused, he trotted briskly round the recumbent beasts, adjured them to their feet, and we left the village—and the *nagadi*—in triumph, driving our caravan before us. All this of course had wasted much time and, as we were inexpert muleteers, we lost considerably more gathering stray beasts back to the fold whenever a patch of anything edible bordered the track.

At last Omar announced we had reached Habro, so where a clump of trees gave promise of water—a muddy black ditch that stank—we camped. It was pleasantly warm, but there was a fairly strong wind.

Jones and I, tired after our rodeo efforts with the mules, were drinking sour milk and coffee in his tent, when there was a shriek outside. It was feminine enough to be recognizable as the voice of Walata Sabat, the *ballambarassi*'s slave, and it was followed by a crackling roar which brought us out at once. Obviously the maiden had lit a fire on the edge of the long grass which stretched for miles across hill and valley. There was a pile of corn cobs at her feet and behind her a sheet of flame. For a moment we thought the tents were threatened and, together with every member of the caravan, rushed headlong to beat out the blaze. Jones seized somebody's blanket, I a saddle rug. The muleteers had produced some hides—relics I suppose of their raw meat feasts, and the soldiers tore up roots and green branches, but the fire licked up into the wind and, scrunching joyously, ate its way up on to the hill, regardless of our efforts.

"There is no fear for the camp," shouted Gabra Selessi's headman, as the red torrent charred a stretch behind us and flooded slope after slope. Jones's natural instinct re-asserted itself! In a few seconds he had his camera out and, whenever I looked back from directing the salvage operations—there were thatched huts on the other side of the hill—I saw an eager, sunburned face, hair on end, peering over a lens always at some new point of vantage, while on all sides of it crazy figures were belched out of the smoke clouds, silhouetted for a minute against the glare, and absorbed once more into the whirl of wind, flame and shoulder-high grass.

Eventually Gallas from the neighboring villages came at a run. Amidst a turmoil of shouting, they cleared a huge space before the fire and, from the edge of this barrier, beat it into impotence.

"I say, I am afraid I upset the coffee getting my camera," said Jones, rubbing his forehead into blacker smears, "but it would have been cold anyhow!"

A figure, crouched in the lee of the tents, was trying to blow a few sticks into flame. "There can be no fire in this wind," it muttered, and we realized that Gabra Gorgis's soul was entirely concerned with the tragedy of the wasted coffee!

We had passed two wedding processions that day which the cook had assured me was unlucky. He remembered his warning as, with charred hair and sweater, I went towards my tent.

"I told you that one thing may be good but the double of it is always bad!"

I laughed and dreamed of marriages and women.

The Palaces of Gondar

THERE WAS AN air of doubt around our departure next morning. The guide plunged left handed into a thicket which branded us afresh. A small boy rescued us and set us on what he assured us was the "head road" for Zos Gorgis. After a mile this trail lost itself in green bushes with most deceptive self-colored spikes. For some time we struggled through a maze of scrub, the guide smiling but entirely vague. Then Jones and I alternately discovered tracks which lost us a little more hopelessly. After two hours, three or four of us were climbing straight up the mountain side, dragging our mules after us. From the midst of the speared thicket below came a despairing chorus of whistling and shouting.

"The luggage is divided into three parties," translated Hassen. "Atto Belacho is lost with one. A mule is missing. The man who went to find it is also lost. They are all lost."

The chorus of plaints and appeals certainly came from half a dozen different places and some were very far away.

Jones and I looked at each other guiltily.

"They'll never get up here. It's downright impossible," said the hot and suddenly bearded youth in a torn and muddy leather coat, his puttees and skin equally frayed, his sun glasses cracked across, an angry mule suspended from one very sunburned arm.

"I don't care," I said recklessly. "I'm going to get to the top and see where we are."

Speechless, panting, slipping, we scrambled on till a final rock tipped us unexpectedly into a haystack perched on the edge of the cliff. A field stretched beyond, and, above it, the unnumbered hill that might be the last crest or merely one of an infinite series.

Fortunately for our tempers it was the last. It was crowned by a few hovels, where women danced and wailed the week-old loss of some relative, staring at us curiously while they beat their heads and wrung them as if after washing. When the groom spoke to them, they shrieked and ran away. Abashed, for he was a personable youth, he grinned at us.

"They are not used to strangers!"

We were immediately under the mighty crag of Zos and a splash of red on the ridge in front of us showed the carved rock façade of Gorgis, an underground church. Having dispatched Hassen to obtain some further specimens of guides, we returned to encourage the caravan. For an hour we waited at the top of the cliff, shouting directions and encouragement.

"I simply daren't go down," I said.

"I don't want to have to see them come up," retorted Jones.

When the last beast had, in some incredible fashion, caterpillared over the top, we selected the least dull-witted of Hassen's recruits, crossed the sugar-loaf range and slowly, very, very slowly, wound down through sand and rocks and multiple flat hillocks, each crowned with euphorbias and a village. Description of that day would surely be as wearisome as the unending hours of it.

At each village, perforce, we took a new guide, for the old one, having lost his head, or the track, or both, abruptly left us, generally waving his arms in two directions. Northwest—"there is Gondar," and southwest, "that is the road. Tamallas! It turns."

It turned and we turned! Once, in the early afternoon, we strayed into half a dozen villages, which, by adding a syllable to their generic names (Mederdinje instead of Mederje) we could fit into a place on the map. There we took three guides and a policeman and, for two of the noisiest hours of a journey distinguished by its lung power, we wandered round and round, chiefly with our backs or right shoulders turned to Gondar. Whenever I pointed out the right direction by compass, all the guides agreed, and, with forked canes waving in three different directions, they announced simultaneously, "That is the head road. Tamallas. Tamallas!"

We crossed another river and Woldo Sambat regained his interest in life.

"Truly I lost my head a little," he said. "There was so much talk, but now, with my eyes shut, I could not miss the road to Gondar."

He strode ahead and, while Jones and Gabra Gorgis searched among the stones for a pocket of clean water, I followed numbly. After three hundred yards the track disappeared into a stretch of cotton. Without interest or feeling, I sat doubled in the saddle, while the guide hesitated, saw two blacks approaching and demanded:

"Where is the road?"

"Eh?" grunted one.

"Au" (Yes), said the other.

Woldo Sambat repeated his question.

"Tamallas. It turns," said both slaves at once.

We camped in the cotton field and it rained.

Much later, when coffee and the prospect of an entirely new guide had cured our sense of humor—Jones had been making bitter remarks about my short cut to which I had responded in kind—there was a stir outside.

"One of the great has come to visit you," shrilled Gabra Gorgis and, unwashed, mud-stained and torn, we had to receive a personage, very black of cloak, very white of *chamma* and spotless trousers, the *Feterari* Tabaja, with twenty rifles around him and a smile as twinkling bright as their barrels. We exchanged our best and most complicated compliments for half an hour and then a note of reality crept into the conversation, for he offered us a guide!

"What sort?" asked Jones.

In the end the *Feterari*,[1] smoking a gold-tipped cigarette out of curiosity and by the wrong end, suggested that, as he was returning next day to his house on the Gondar "road" we should ride with him. Thankfully, I agreed and my visitor departed, after pressing upon me a bunch of fowls, in exchange for which he would only accept soap. "For," said he, "my servants say their clothes are so dirty they will be ashamed to walk in front of you, but must keep far off." The idea of playing hide and seek among the hills with a guide determined not to be seen was unattractive, so I doubled my subscription to cleanliness!

Our departure the following morning was most impressive and it was watched by all the villagers, who followed us for stages suited to their rank. First went the *Feterari* on a mule smothered in silver and scarlet, with a funny little page, possibly a Yemenese, smooth, olive-colored between the folds of a red and white turban and a striped cape. Behind him came two youths, one carrying Tabaja's topee,[2] generally on his own head, which disappeared completely inside it, the other a black woolen cape and a clothes brush. Sandals and rifle were borne by an older pair and the rear was brought up by an assortment of men-at-arms and servants with eight-foot canes.

---

1 Colonel.

2 A pith hat or helmet.

At the large village of Talla, we were assured that we were now on the main road, but, unfortunately people had been inconsiderate enough to plant cotton or grain across it, so we were never able to verify the statement! We passed lots of villages, all of whose names were unanimously produced for my information, but none of them appeared on the map, while no one from the *Feterari* to the oldest local inhabitant was able to recognize any of the places charted except Dabosje and Mariam Waha, both of which they said were far away, so we were still mystified as to where we were and when we should reach Gondar.

At one hut, a boy sold me a quart of milk for a pencil and, as he could neither read nor write, we wondered why he wanted it.

"He will take it to a wise man who will write him a charm to cure his belly," said Hassen.

"Wouldn't it be simpler if I gave him some medicine?"

"Better not," urged the interpreter. "These people are very ignorant." I remembered one of my earlier efforts to cure a boil with boracic ointment, when the patient had returned to say he did not like the taste, but had managed to eat the whole tube by mixing it with honey!

That day the land smiled at us with gold of barley and wild flowers and a twelve-foot bean, with pods like green balloons. When the hills, tinted like an American autumn with the vermilion-barked thorns, encroached on the farms, they were full of gazelle and guinea-fowl. One of the *Feterari's* soldiers tried a shot at a flock of the fat gray birds, while they stood watching him fifteen yards away. He missed, though he rested his rifle against a tree and, sitting down, aimed comfortably for several minutes.

"The Abyssinian can never hold his gun steady," said Hassen. "His hand always shake, because he eat lots of pepper and salt which make him thirsty and then he drink too much."

By mid-afternoon we reached Tabaja's property and, after vainly urging us to spend a night there, that he might provide us with all forms of food and fodder, he let the caravan proceed with a parting gift of ale, but insisted that we must visit his house. It was a huge round hut, with a corner partitioned off for a donkey, whose tail acted as a fly-whisk if one sat on that side of the wood fire. A third of the remaining space was taken up by a stack of raw cotton and by half a dozen great mud barrels full of the same product.

"I do nothing to my plants, just leave them alone and they bear three crops a year. Now the country is white with their bloom and I shall not even pick it. What can I do? My house is already full of it!"

"You could get a good price in Addis Ababa."

"That is far away," said Tabaja indifferently.

We sat on a log covered with several hides, till someone brought a chair made of a triangle of gnarled branches, the seat plaited from leathern thongs. In a corner a nut-brown woman with hair close-plaited, showing the greatest beauty of the Abyssinian, a well-formed head, was weaving a basket of many colored grasses. She took no notice of us except to hand a gourd to a slave with a gesture in our direction. The milk it contained was full of extraneous matter, but very refreshing. On the strength of it we marched till four, and camped in the bush close under the range of hills beyond which, we were assured, lay Gondar.

"A day's march," said the groom.

"We shall be there before noon," prophesied Hassen.

"You will not see it by night," muttered Atto Belacho, who had a cut foot.

That night the robbers made a more successful raid on our mules and succeeded in capturing the best of them, as they returned from watering. Atto Belacho, who would not spend a bullet or half a salt to feed his caravan, trusting to Providence or me to provide barley, took the loss with a smile and a shrug.

"It is luck," he said, and left me amazed at the mentality which will venture nothing for success, but accepts the worst failure with equanimity. An Abyssinian is a bad gambler but a good loser. We sent a messenger at once to the *Feterari*, asking help for the recovery of our mule, and his answer convinced us that the Ethiopian bears other people's losses even more placidly than his own.

"Anything lost in this district is never seen again. Robbers, villagers and headmen are in league and they all share the profits," replied the guardian of the law.

There was nothing left for us but to get as far away from such a province as possible, so we marched for ten and a half hours next day, passing Dankaz midway, but Gondar remained mysterious and aloof.

"How far is it?" we asked a peasant at midday.

"Two hours," he answered cheerfully, and looked round to add, "you won't get there to-night."

Much puzzled, we addressed the next passer-by.

"It will be an hour from where you put your tents to-night," he said.

"Where do you mean? Where do you suppose we shall put them?"

"How should I know—it depends on your walk," he answered.

All morning we climbed up to the narrow tableland on which wind-blown Dankaz perches. We saw Lake Tsana, a sheet of opal and turquoise in the distance, and all afternoon we labored down the rock shelves on the further side. Rain spat at us as we reached a valley and shepherded our caravan with revolvers ready across a river, which wound back and forth across the track in a persistent way that suggested collusion with the robbers.

We camped just as the clouds broke, precipitating a darkness rent with forked lightning and the twinkling of our patent lamps which defied any hurricane, but were often smothered under the weight of insect life which took refuge in them. Jones and I had made a bargain by which I slew anything under three inches in length, while he dealt with such "animals"—they really couldn't be called insects—as giant locusts and the squelchy red-brown things with the bodies of monstrous worms, bees' furry heads and beetle wings.

At five o'clock I roused the aching caravan and hurried it through the hills towards Gondar. After two hours the first of the old Portuguese ruins appeared on a hill sprinkled with churches. Woldo Gorgis exclaimed, apparently surprised, "that was in the same place last time I came here," as if the seventeenth-century fortresses had a habit of hopping around the country.

"What about your short cut?" asked Jones, looking at his watch as if it were a calendar.

"Well, it's gained us half a day and lots of experience."

"Dear at the price. Our clothes and our tempers are both in rags."

"Lace puttees and boots with ventilated soles may not be the fashion," I retorted, "but in any case they're cool!"

So, on the thirtieth day from Addis Ababa and the sixty-first from Dire Dawa, after a total trek of 873 miles, we reached Gondar.

Under the walls of Fasil's palaces we passed, below the two great sycamores, one the tree of Justice, the other the scaffold from whose branches used to hang human fruit.

"I've found a splendid place for a camp. Inside here! Through the arch," shouted Jones, and we rode into what must once have been the main court of the twin palaces on the hill.

"What luck to camp right against your background," continued Jones, stiffness and swollen thorn scars forgotten as he seized his camera and clambered to the nearest point of vantage.

Aesthetically, Gondar was delightful. It was a world of ruins, half veiled in sugar cane and flowering shrubs. Out of a maze of fallen walls, with towers, pillars and broken domes scattered about them, rose the two massive Moorish castles. They were pale golden, from their cupolas and the ramparts which ran along their roofs between arches, carved and exquisite, to the great flights of steps, curving up to the first stories, where the windows were like the entrances to cathedral aisles. The similar portals below were walled up, and loopholed so that the ground-floor halls provide shelter in case of brigand raids. A few years ago, when the local *Dejezmatch* was routed by a robber chief, so powerful that he was called King of the Mountains, most of the townsfolk took refuge in the palaces of Fasil and made terms with the brigand from behind their four-foot masonry. The three-hundred-year-old buildings are constructed from the rough stone with which the hills are covered, set in irregular plaster of a hard and durable nature, sometimes reinforced with pebbles. The arches of windows and doors are made of mud bricks. The main gateway is approached by a curved bridge over a sunken track, which may have been a moat, and is flanked by domed towers, between which one passes into the first of the square castles.

King Fasil of Shoa, descendant of Solomon, enlisted the aid of five hundred Portuguese in his wars against the Moslems and, when his battles were ended in 1640, these warriors turned their swords, not into plough-shares, but into the tools of mason and plasterer. They built the famous twin palaces and, for the ladies of their patron's court, the adjoining "house of many loves," with its beautiful gatehouse composed of quadruple arches under a parapet like carved lace. To them also are due the church which is in better repair than the castles of a once great king, the tomb of Fasil's favorite horse, Zeboul, and, near it, Usquam, the house of pleasure, where the lord of Gondar amused himself in secret ways. The whole hillside is covered with the traces of their industry, and the huge forts, with their miles of once crenelated walls, the high domed towers, the gates and bridges, cisterns and bastions, contrast strangely with the huts, which sprawl in untidy clusters round the feet of so much ancient stateliness.

A smaller castle set lonely on a ridge belongs to a later date, but other Portuguese workmen are responsible for it, as for the bridge over which we crossed the Blue Nile on our way to Debra Tabor and for other masonry, whose remains are seen on hillside and in river bed in Northwest Abyssinia. From 1490, when Pedro de Covilhao was sent on a mission to the Negus Alexander at Tegulet, the Portuguese had much influence in Ethiopia, for a series of their most gallant soldiers of fortune vowed their arms to the help of Christian Abyssinia in her struggle against the inroads of Islam, which ended in 1643 with the defeat of Mohammed Grav, the tyrant Emir of Harrar. Jesuit missions followed in the wake of these gentlemen adventurers, and to Portugal Abyssinia owes not only the architecture which made Gondar splendid in the days of her rule, but the best of her religious literature.

Our camp was a place of dreams, for surely the ghosts of those alien warriors who ventured so far in defence of the Cross must haunt the courts and halls built by their followers. There was no moon that night, but, between cloud rifts, the stars lit the parapets and ramparts of the one almost perfect fortress which lies below the double palace. Any moment a troop of soldiers might ride out from the towered gatehouse, a herald appear with his trumpet in the gallery, or a woman lean out of a Moorish window, with the shadow of a veil or mask across her face. All the ghosts would be cavaliers from Portugal or Moors, from whose prodigal waste of masonry the architects of Gondar stole their massive magnificence. The Abyssinians are a ruling race, but not a romantic one, so, illogically, I could not picture a shaven or woolly-curled ghost among the golden towers of Fasil's capital!

Practically, Gondar was unsatisfactory. Whenever our caravan had eaten more of our sugar, coffee or rice than it was possible to explain the loss of, they assured us there was an Indian in Gondar from whom I could buy everything. With this Jones and I had comforted ourselves when, owing to the retinue's passion for any-thing sweet, we had to limit our sugar to an almost invisible pinch in each cup, but of course the Indian was as imaginary as those so elastic distances. The Italian consul supplied us with the luxury of bread, for the last of our biscuits had been distributed to ease one of the famines due to the improvidence of our trustful escort, who always hoped the next Chum[3] would be at home, or, as Hassen put it, "Mary would send bread."

The only things we could buy were the local mixture of coffee and strong spices, honey, onions, and bitter native flour. To pay for these, when our salts and bullets were finished, Woldo Gorgis offered me some mysterious little bundles which he kept tied up in rags in his pocket. They contained fragments of incense, a square inch of *kehol*, and a few dozen large seeds, from which women grind oil for their hair, but their purchasing power was immense. As soon as it was known I possessed such aid to beauty, the camp was surrounded by "pretty ladies" offering chickens and eggs in exchange for the temporary renewal of their charms. These were not very obvious, for the women had a cowed expression unusual in an African daughter of joy. Perhaps their surliness was typi-cal of their Northern blood, for it seemed to me that, as the race became less diluted by alien intermarriage, its less agreeable char-acteristics intensified. The people of the North were arrogantly independent, casual, voluble and indifferent. There was no hint of servility among them. The great men were hospitable and courte-ous, but without the spontaneous charm of the Southerners. The

---

3 Headman.

little men were avaricious, yet too independent to earn the bak-sheesh they craved. A governor or headman would send a guide with us and the man after half a day would get tired or bored and leave us with a bow, despite the prospect of a week's pay for an hour or two more of effort. Yet the same man would sit for half the night opposite our tents and ask for everything from a new *chamma* to matches. They are proud beggars, who give lip service to their masters and the constant flexing of supple back muscles, yet contrive to remain an unsubdued, resilient folk, as ready to rebel against one lord as to acclaim another. "I fight for him, but I am not his slave," said an unwilling guide, sent by a *Feterari*, but determined for no price to travel beyond the next mountain.

The morning we left Gondar there were so many and such complicated quarrels between our caravan and the townsfolk, that we had difficulty in starting at all. The Italian had assured us that it was fifteen or sixteen days' march to Adua, on account of the bad tracks. I insisted that none could be worse than the spiked switchbacks from Lalibela, and that nine marches must suffice us, for we were getting near the time limit for the development of the films. Jones was beginning anxiously to count the days since the first exposures at Dire Dawa and I had to repeat a dozen times exactly how long it would take us by land and sea to reach civilization, by which he meant a dark room and miles of hypo tanks.

At eight AM the caravan seemed inextricably confused with shouting men and screaming women. I rescued Atto Daiwitu from a crowd who wanted to sell him a mule for three times its value and buy one of his weary beasts for nine shillings, and the groom from a couple of rogues who offered fourteen shillings a piece for our three horses, on the ground that we should not be able to use them in the mountains. Shrill above the clamor rose the falsetto of Balaina. A matron of large proportions and equal strength of lung was trying to drag him from his saddle, while another, youthful but quite as stalwart, had seized Gabra Gorgis's bridle. Exasperated, for the loaded mules were wandering loose among the ruins, I was going to leave them to their fate, convinced that their crimes had for once found them out. Next moment I saw the flour I had bought for the *zabaniers*[4] wrenched from a pack-saddle and poured into a *chamma* torn equally violently from the shoulders of our cook. The form of my intervention was fortunately altered by Hassen's explanation that, though I had paid for the flour, Gabra Gorgis had stolen the sack!

At last we got rid of the spoilers and, I sadly suspected, the spoiled. Amidst explanations and accusations, with an occasional scornful "that is the Abyssinian way" from Hassen, we trailed across the hills. Usquam, like a beautiful solitary minaret, emerged for a moment from its grove, then faded among the trees, but, hours later, looking back as the guide waved his farewell: "Thank you. God keep you, Gondar!" I saw the two proud castles sentinel and lonely on their hill.

It was a day of glimpses. Tsana, the lake of opal, appeared like rainbow wrack on the horizon. Antelope flashed between the thickets. The guide saw a brigand!

How he recognized him as such I do not know, but he hastily removed his sandals and looked to see that a strip of paper was carefully folded in each.

"What are these?" I asked Hassen.

"Charms written by a priest. He think they stop stones hurting his feet and keep him on the head road, so he never lose the way."

"But are they going to help him fight the brigands as well?"

Hassen looked doubtful. "I think more likely as they in his shoes they help him run away!"

---

4 Unofficial policemen.

1928

A Woman with the Legion—South of the Atlas, Morocco

Chapter from *Women Called Wild* (1935)

A Woman with the Legion—
South of the Atlas, Morocco

SOUTH OF THE ATLAS and the Sirocco had begun to blow!
As long as it lasted everyone would be—according to the
Arabs—"a little mad." With my head down, I rode along
the wadi, but the palms offered no shelter. They looked like agi-
tated feather brooms with their stems tucked into pink cotton-
wool. Behind me rose the towers of Bou Denib, with a froth of
almond petals breaking over the ramparts. Behind me, also, I
could hear the clinking of the Spahis' bridles. I envied the men
because they could hide their faces in the hoods of their scarlet
cloaks, whereas mine was exposed to the wind.

As a whisper it had come out of the South. Dust spirals whirled
in its path. Among the great dunes, it gathered force. Whipping
their crests into spray, it swept on across the desert, raging into
the valleys, where it scattered the blossom and broke down the
old mud walls, and flinging itself, at last, against the Atlas.

From Mauretania to Thibesti the palms lashed themselves to
fury and every traveller disappeared into his burnouse. Sand spun
up from the Hamada till the millions of curious grey fungi which

the natives call "cauliflowers of Bon Anané" looked as if they were covered with tomato sauce. But Sirocco was not satisfied. It shrieked into the camel's-hair shelters of the Bedouin, swung labouring caravans into circles, blinded the eyes of Tuaregs, inflamed the skins and tempers of the city dwellers.

At Bou Denib, where I had been staying with the Colonel commanding the district, it crept through the crevices of doors and windows, stimulating and exasperating. And in its wake it left a red mist of sand, intangible as the madness for which the Arabs waited.

I couldn't bear to sit inside a box of a house with Sirocco crashing against the walls, so I thought I'd ride to the fort where a squadron of the Legion were quartered. "It is folly," said my host, but he lent me a horse, which drooped and shivered under the driving sand, and I went as quickly as possible, feeling like a swimmer with the tide against me.

I remember as I approached the cliff, the whole landscape seemed to be changing shape. The only solid thing about it was the fort, clinging to the crest of one of those definitely shaped ridges which break the monotony of the Hamada. Mud-walled, desolate and menacing, it withstood the fury of Sirocco. Above it, the tricolour tore at the flagstaff like a thing possessed.

An officer forced his way across the yard. "What a day you have chosen!" he exclaimed. He was a small man in a stained linen coat and patched breeches. The crescent of the Spahis gleamed on his collar, and under a vast turban, his face showed mottled red and white. He put a hand on the neck of my disconsolate beast and talked to it while I dismounted. Then he led me across a square intersected by rows of earthen huts. Where the doors faced away from the wind, groups of men lounged against them, smoking, arguing and spitting. They wore faded khaki, or dingy blue slops, and nearly everyone had a dog. "That is the family of the Legionary," explained the little captain, proud of his squadron. "We have fifty-two dogs here. I encourage them. These men have neither family nor hearth, but they have their dogs and they sleep with them, and that reminds them a little of home."

"They look fairly cheerful," I remarked, as I followed the captain to his quarters, mud-built, in an embrasure of the wall, commanding a wide sweep of frontier between desert and mountains. "Yes, it goes well so long as they do not think. I have rabbits here, and pigs and sheep, beside the horses, a whole menagerie for them to look after. One must occupy them, for if they stay in one place more than a few months they get the 'cafard,'[1] and then God knows what it comes into their heads to do."

He stooped through a low door and I followed. Under an awning stretched over the rampart, some chickens and a kid with a tattered ear looked out of packing-cases. But Captain Dumont led me through another earthen doorway into a room like a tent. Moroccan carpets hung upon the walls and ceiling. Others covered the hard divan and served as curtains at the entrance to a sleeping place.

"It is comfortable, hein?" said Dumont. "Like this, I have a small interior which I take with me wherever I go." He invited me to sit on a particularly fine prayer-rug, and his servant, who looked like a Norse peasant, brought tea, very sweet and flavoured with mint.

"Have you any English here?" I asked, with a glass in my hand.

"There is but one, a brigadier,[2] who, yesterday, signed on for another five years. He is a type that, but he will not speak of himself. The others, they come at night and tell me of their affairs—over a mouthful of anisette, you understand?"

I could imagine the intimate, stuffy atmosphere of the room, the lamp shaded by one of those native scarves, and the captain,

---

1 The blues.

2 Non-commissioned rank comparative to a corporal.

with his collar undone, his face companionably red, his eyes very round and blue.

"There is one here, a German, who cut his wife into three pieces, but all the same he is a good fellow. A coup de tête, you will comprehend?"

"I don't know that I do," I remarked, wondering what had happened to the three pieces.

But the captain pointed out of the window to where the red earth blazed to the horizon. "In this country one must understand everything," he said and he began to roll a cigarette, slowly, between stained fingers. "See you, I have here a Colonel of the Imperial Russian Guard, and a Serbian decorated by Peter the First, and a banker who ran away with his caisse. That one wants to re-establish himself; but I made enquiries, and in his country there is no amnesty for crime with violence. One asks no questions with the Legion. That is understood, but, all the same, if one is sympathetic, one learns."

I put down my glass. Imagination filled in the background of the picture. So much trouble that grown men might not think and at the end of it all, after the building of roads and the fighting in the Atlas, or the Naboth's vineyard of Taffilelt, and the continuous movement, the "cafard" from whose bitterness there was no escape except by getting drunk on anisette in the native café.

"We had one here whom nobody could explain," continued Dumont, who had been transferred from a squadron of Spahis, because, in spite of his soft flesh and his reddened goggle eyes, he understood men and horses and could master them both. "Finally, one day, I said to him, 'Tell me then, my brave, what were you in the world?' And he replied to me, smiling, 'A priest.' Me, I was astonished, although I had noticed he seemed familiar with the mass, so I pushed my indiscretion so far as to ask why he had left his parish. Parbleu, he had humour, that one, for he answered,

'My captain, without a woman, which one of us men could have lost paradise?'"

"And the Englishman?" I asked, after a pause.

"Oh him. You shall see for yourself."

Towards evening, a lull suggested that Sirocco drew breath before renewing an assault which had already littered the yard with desert cauliflower. We went out. It seemed unnaturally quiet. A man leaned against the parapet where the cliff dropped into the wadi and watched a Belgian teaching his dog to walk on its hind-legs, with a cap on its head and a cigarette in its mouth.

"Hey, Robert, my friend, come here!"

The Legionary approached, bareheaded.

"I have told this lady you are English and she wishes to shake you the hand."

Embarrassed, we stood in front of each other. The captain's amiability enveloped us as a cloak, but we had nothing to say. "Are you English?" I asked at last.

"Yes."

"You like it here?"

"Yes."

"I came across the Atlas by Midelt, before snow closed the road. How different it is down here. . . ."

"Yes."

Then I realised I was still holding out my hand. The man hadn't touched it and I didn't know what to do with it. I looked up at him. He was thin, with grim lines dragging at his features, but he seemed to be amused. Hurriedly, I dropped my hand. "D'you know Erfoud and Wad Ziz?" I asked.

"Yes."

"I want to go there if the French will let me."

Another monosyllable and after that I gave it up. The Legionary saluted Dumont and went back to his companion, who had induced the dog to march, sentry-wise, upon the wall.

"What would you? Not communicative, hein?" commented my companion, and at that moment the sun sank behind the rim of the desert. A bugle called and the Captain of Spahis stiffened. From the top of the fort the tricolour came down. Scattered about the square, the troopers saluted. I wondered what they felt about it, if it had become a mechanical action, or if, standing there, on the edge of the world, exiles every one of them and nameless, they thought of their own countries while they saluted a foreign flag.

Slowly, I rode back across the wadi. The fires of sunset burned low. Sirocco battered against the cliffs and stripped great sheaves from the palms. With the hiss of sand and the grunt of indignant camels trampling in the yards, came the far clear note of bugles. I thought of the devil-ridden face of the English brigadier. There could be no doubt about his devils. Sometimes he fought them— his mouth had shrivelled into a line above the carelessly shaven chin. More often he gave way and his eyes bore witness to his defeats. I couldn't get his face out of my mind.

The following night, while my host strove with accounts, I went to what is familiarly known as the Legionaries' Café, with a young Frenchman, equally interested in local colour. Of the town I remember little, except a square with shabby trees along one side, and a crowd of Jews in the loveliest clothes I'd ever seen. At least, they seemed to me lovely, for they'd come straight out of Chaucer and the Middle Ages. The married women wore colossal velvet mitres on the top of coiffes. Their sleeves, their veils, their skirts were equally prodigious.

"They came here hundreds of years ago to escape some persecution—I don't remember which—and they haven't changed so much as a pin's head," explained my companion, and I appreciated his vagueness. I didn't want to know why those extraordinary people had chosen to walk out of *Pilgrims' Tales*. That they had done so was a miracle and as such should be left intact.

The café turned out to be a poor affair, huddled between blind houses in the Arab quarter. It was lit by oil-lamps. Their smoke had blackened the ceiling, from which most of the plaster had peeled. Across one end ran a bar, stained with a generation's slops. A blear-eyed Algerian half-caste leaned across it, listening to the gossip of some weedy Arabs without chins or foreheads. When we came in, most of the tables were unoccupied. A gramophone with a broken needle played five-year-old jazz.

We chose the least-battered chairs and asked for a bock and a syrup. It was no use specifying what kind of syrup, because though the colours varied from red and orange to a peculiarly livid green, they all tasted alike.

While my companion talked of Morocco and of the oases to the south, beyond the red Hamada, I looked at the walls, which were coveted with dirt and cracked from floor to ceiling. They appeared to be held together by garish cinema posters. "Tiens!" said the Frenchman, breaking off in the middle of a sentence. "Here is a habitué." Without interest, I glanced at the woman who had come quietly through a side entrance, and then I stared, for she was not all what I expected.

To begin with, she had no paint on her face. I doubted if it was even powdered. Her hat, a hard felt, thoroughly unsuited both to the climate and the circumstances, had obviously belonged to a man and it had come from a good shop. Beneath it, I could see a little hair, brown, with a hint of gold in it, very soft, curling gently at the ends. By the time I'd got over the first shock, the woman had crossed the room as if she didn't see it and seated herself in the corner furthest from the bar. Her feet were bare and thrust into sandals. She was so slight that she had scarcely any shape. Breasts and hips were lost under the faded cotton dress. A little coat that must have formed part of a well-cut flannel suit, hung open. With an untouched glass in front of her and her hands, thin, brown, very young, lying quietly on her knee, she looked at us. And I had a breathless moment when I imagined myself submerged in a tropical sea.

For her eyes were enormous and just that blue between indigo and cobalt which one sees on the Equator. But there was no more to her. I don't remember the brows. The lashes were long and straight, and from those amazing eyes the whole face fell away. It was tender, brown and nondescript, the nose too long, the mouth a trifle drooping. When she smiled at a kitten falling over itself in an attempt to induce a gigantic stag-beetle to play with it, her teeth showed small and white, but unevenly placed, so that they protruded one over the other.

"Who and what is that?" I asked the young Frenchman.

"I haven't the least idea who she is, but they call her Marie, and she comes, I believe, from Algiers. Rumour amuses itself with a father of the most respectable, a lawyer, or even a juge d'instruction. As for what she is, eh bien, tout court, if you permit it, Madame, she belongs to the English brigadier, whom she's followed from one sacré bougre to another for the last five years. Such a devotion! And it says nothing to the Englishman. He bores himself, that one."

The woman—oh, but she wasn't a woman at all, just a girl in the early twenties, if that—was still looking at the kitten. The tip of her nose hung over the unsatisfactory mouth. There was an undoubted rash upon her chin.

"But isn't she married?" I asked, for she looked as if she ought to have been supported by a perambulator as well as a wedding-ring.

"Not at all," returned the Frenchman.

At that moment a group of Legionaries pushed into the café. Simultaneously, the proprietor appeared at the bar and began to take down bottles from the shelves behind it. Familiar with the ways of the troopers, he knew they would satisfy their thirst and any feelings of conviviality they might have on his rank red wine. Later, when they started to get seriously drunk, they'd shout for anisette.

The Englishman sloped across to the table where Marie sat. She welcomed him gravely and when he flung himself on to a chair, she drew hers closer, leaning towards him and talking in a low voice.

Next to us a Belgian spoke to a man blackened by African service. Coat and shirt were open and a vast amount of tattooing showed upon his chest. "Come here, my old one! No cafard so long as there remain to us sous in our pockets." He tested the strength of a three-legged chair before settling himself astride it.

The man who'd been pointed out to me as a Colonel of the Russian Guard joined them, and soon they were all lapping up the raw wine, which might just as well have been vinegar. They drank with the careless haste of dogs, and the tattooed man, tipping his chair so that it leaned against the wall, smoked a quantity of black cigarettes, sticky as glue. The Russian embarked on the evidently familiar story of his escape, "Seven hundred miles I did on skis with the snow frozen, and only a flask of vodka to keep the soul in my body. . . ."

"What does it matter? What does anything matter?" retorted the African. He refilled his glass, but the liquor stank. "At this rate I shall vomit before I can get drunk," he said and shouted to the barman, who was spitting into a tumbler as a prelude to rubbing it with the hem of his soiled galabia. "A double anisette, and if I see thee putting methylated into it, I'll twist thy bastard neck!"

The Belgian had been waiting for an opportunity to interrupt the interminable reminiscences of the Slav. "Seest thou that

Klems has been condemned by court-martial," he broke in, speaking of a deserter who had joined the Riffs and used stolen French rifles against his own company.

"That is not the way to desert," said a Czech, dragging up a chair. "If one arranges it well, one can have two or three agreeable days at Casablanca before the police, who are, all the same, very good fellows, send one back to the regiment, and then one says it is a coup de tête, and if the officer is a decent sort, he lets one off with a reprimand." He leaned across the table, picked up a bottle and tilted the dregs down his throat.

The Belgian was sucking raw alcohol through a straw to ensure its maximum effect. An old soldier, he told with gusto of men who had deserted and disappeared, to re-enlist a few weeks later, under another name, in the other regiment. "My faith, one had all the fun of the Legion and two 'primes' as well. I assure you that second five hundred francs came in very useful."

They went on talking while the tattooed man emptied and refilled his glass till even the Russian expressed admiration, tinctured by surprise. "One sees that you have a head like a three weeks' old egg," he said, "but you must have blown the cash-box, hein?"

The African turned out his pockets and counted their contents. "Another anisette," he demanded, pushing forward a heap of small coins.

The Belgian ceased to take any part in the conversation. Red-faced, he sagged in his chair, an inert but good-tempered mass, while the Czech coolly twisted off one of his buttons. "That will make my affair," he explained. "I feared the two sides of my tunic would be altogether divorced."

At the next table, a German and a Swede cursed each other. Suddenly one of them seized an empty bottle and smashed the other over the head. The képi broke the blow and next moment the two were at each other's throats. The table went over and the Teuton, a spur caught in the wreckage, lost his footing and crashed on top of it, dragging his opponent with him. The other Legionaries exhibited a certain amount of interest. Bad form it might be to interfere in a strictly personal quarrel, but Sirocco had done its job and most of them were three-parts drunk.

Only the Englishman, making use of his corporal's authority, attempted to separate the combatants who were sprawling among broken glass and tobacco ash. He was, I noticed, dead sober, although he'd drunk enough to put a troop under the table. Deliberately and impartially, he kicked the two who were trying to tear out each other's windpipes. When this failed, he picked up a pepper castor and emptied the whole contents over their faces.

There was a second of thrilled silence. Then an explosion broke from the heap among the table legs. Choking and sneezing, with noses running and water pouring from their eyes, they stumbled to their feet and hurled themselves, blind, at the nearest enemy. The fight became general.

With a whoop of delight, a young trooper who found himself without anybody to hit, threw a bottle at one of the lamps swinging from the ceiling. It burst and the oil caught fire. In a moment some of the posters were ablaze and flames trickled along the floor. There were two doors and my companion acted with promptitude. Before I knew what had happened, he had thrust me through the nearest opening, and was following with something dragging and twisting behind him. "Voyons donc!" he exclaimed crossly, as we found ourselves in the square. "To what good do you wish to burn yourself too?"

Then I saw he'd got hold of Marie and was keeping a firm grip on her wrist, while she struggled with him, crying, "Let me go— let me go!" followed by an agonised, "Would you wish that I leave him to burn?"

The Frenchman held on till, with a sudden savagery, as awkward as it was inconsistent with her appearance, she bent and bit deep into his hand. Next moment she'd disappeared.

"Well, what d'you think of that?" remarked the young man ruefully.

"We must do something," I said, feebly.

"Agreed, but what?"

We looked at each other in a cloud of sand. "This wind of hell. . . ." began the Frenchman, and then the yard leading to the café filled. Troopers, with their tunics torn, poured out of one door, as the military police arrived by another. Marie, pitifully out of place, clung to the English brigadier and was, by him, thrust aside. The gesture was anxious rather than brutal, but the woman recoiled against a wall, staring, wide-eyed, at the scene. It was fantastic enough, with smoke and an occasional spurt of flame in the background, a blanketing of thick yellow fog rent by moonlight, and the clamour of half a dozen languages buffeted by the shrieks of Sirocco.

Ignoring the Frenchman, who murmured, "One has had enough of this, is it not so?" I pushed my way across the yard and told Marie to come with us. I didn't expect her to comply and I was immensely surprised when she followed me, soundless in her sandals.

In the square, with the Frenchman sardonic, for he felt nothing could be flatter than the repetition of a beau geste, I asked the woman where she lived. In the voice of a schoolgirl at her first communion, she answered, "Chez Mère Bonnard." And her eyes looked at me wonderingly. What a pose, I thought, but I knew quite well it was real.

With an occasional remark about the wind, received in dead silence, we attempted to enliven our progress across the "place" and down the blind streets. At the door of a whitewashed building, opening into the usual yard, we left our charge. She extended a limp hand and said, "Thank you thank you very much," while she regarded us gravely. Her enormous eyes wandered past us. She was not in the least interested.

Before turning the corner, we looked back. Marie still stood in the same position. It seemed to me she leaned against the wind. Her inadequate skirt flapped about her legs. I imagined her staring into the sand and pondering what she should do. Her brain worked slowly. One could feel it fumbling for an idea and examining it.

Next day I went west, towards Mauretania. I didn't get as far as I wanted, because the French considered me a responsibility, but I saw more of the Hamada desert and the wadis with their pill-box forts surrounded by barbed wire and even something of the Taffilelt, its independence threatened, as much by the nomad tribes on the south, as by the eagles of France on the north. When I returned to Bou Denib, this time to Mère Bonnard's, where one could get a room for a few francs a week, but no food except a cup of black coffee in the mornings, I met Captain Dumont. He rode soberly, his turban less effective than usual, his face unnaturally grave. Without any flourish, he greeted me, "Madame, there is bad news."

"What?" I asked, visualising a host of "dissidents" mustering in the mountains.

"It is the English brigadier. The man was ill. One saw that he suffered and the storm must have affected his nerves. It was a stroke, you understand, a coup de tête, for which no one can blame him. I only wish he had come to me."

"But what has happened?" I asked.

Sirocco still raged against the cliffs. Towers of sand whirled down the valley, but the force of the wind had spent itself. To-morrow or the next day would be still.

The Captain of Spahis hesitated. Then he spoke slowly, but, in spite of his distress, he couldn't help making the most of the tale. In the middle of the night, the brigadier had taken his rifle, which should have been locked up, and gone out into the yard. With "an exactitude of the most surprising" he had driven the butt into a heap of stones, wedging it at the requisite angle, which he must have measured as carefully as if it had been a fence at Longchamps. He had then retreated until he felt the wall behind him, opened his tunic and with a grimace, which he imagined a smile, run forward and thrown himself straight onto the bayonet.

The bugler who sounded the reveille found him spitted like a capon. For fully thirty seconds the boy had stared at the grim spectacle. Then dropping his instrument, for he was a lad fresh joined, "with all his past in front of him," he'd rushed to the nearest hut and shouted his tale to half-dressed men who were considering whether to wash.

This much the captain told in a vast number of words, so that the brigadier's suicide became sonorous and portentous as the death of Priam in the Iliad.

Then he changed his tone. "Madame," he said simply, "you must not blame the Legion. It is a good life for men who have nothing to regret. The loneliness of which they speak is not what they find in Africa, where there are good comrades and plenty of movement, but what they bring with them from the countries they've forfeited. We ask no questions and in return we expect loyal service, but we cannot stop men thinking. Enfin, if they are imaginative, they make comparisons, but here there is a chance of a career to take the place of a family. Half my sous-officiers are foreigners and these days any trooper can rise to command a company." The little man ceased his discourse as suddenly as he had begun it. "In the Legion, Madame, one must be simple. One cannot live in two worlds at once."

At Mère Bonnard's I asked for Marie and was told the number of her room. Like mine, it opened on to a mud porch which ran the whole length of the yard. A few plants struggled out of the sand. An almond tree leaned over the wall.

I wrote a letter and tore it up. There was nothing I could do, but I scribbled a few words and thrust them under the door, after which I avoided the porch. She should, at least, have privacy, but towards evening we met in the deserted corridor.

The woman's face hadn't changed. It was young, defenceless and dry-eyed. But every vestige of colour had left it. "I'm glad," she said. "Glad, d'you understand?" and then the fierceness died out of her. She drooped in front of me, with no more substance than a rag. I took her by the arm and led her into the porch. I pushed her into a chair and offered her a cigarette.

"No," she said. "I don't smoke."

Then she told me about the car which had come over the Atlas a few days ago. She hadn't seen it, so she drew freely on her imagination and since this was limited, what she would have made splendid, became pathetically commonplace. The car had contained a man "of the utmost importance," and a woman "no doubt beautiful," but she'd been heavily veiled, so nobody had seen her face. They'd asked for the Englishman by a name which no one recognised. After some misunderstanding, they found him and took him away on the road to the mountains. When he came back, he wouldn't say a word.

Robbed of the atmosphere which Marie contrived, in spite of her poor command of language, the tale was reduced to the fact that an old man and a woman, veiled against the dust, had arrived in a big car and taken the brigadier for a drive, after which he'd been rather more surly than usual.

"But," said Captain Dumont, discussing the incident later that evening, "I spoke with them myself. Without doubt they were most distinguished people."

The Spahi had come to Mère Bonnard's on the excuse of offering me a mount while I remained in Bou Denib, but really to tell me of his argument with the colonel. For the little captain had determined to bury his brigadier with full military honours and the commanding officer had protested, "D'you want to encourage suicides?"

Dumont's face grew rounder and redder as he gave me his version of the conversation. "Did I not say to the colonel straight out, à l'Anglais, 'Mon Commandant, do not mention that word to me, for, with my own eyes, I saw how the poor fellow had fallen over his rifle while he attended to a horse. . . .' You will understand there was no horse, but me, I was prepared to support one good lie with many bad ones. Enfin, the colonel, who is a brave man, gave way. 'It is your affair, but one cannot say it is a good example.'"

By this time, the cavalryman was damp, hot and scarlet, for his collar throttled him, and in mending the seam of his right boot, the local cobbler had made it unpleasantly tight, but he finished the story triumphantly. "'Enfin, Mon Commandant,' I said, 'the poor fellow did not find such paradise in Africa that we need deny him the chance of one upstairs.'"

"Quite right," I agreed, wondering if the brigadier would have been amused and how it would strike his mistress. She was a most unexpected person.

With Marie, I went to the funeral. She took it for granted that I would come. She just said, "It'll be very early. Will you wake, or shall I knock at your window?" I offered her a sedative and suggested I should do the knocking, but she wouldn't hear of it.

Before sunrise we went across the wadi. I had put on an old black suit. My companion showed no signs of mourning. Her legs were a lovely brown between the gay stripes of her skirt and those lamentable sandals. Her face was empty, like the face of a child who has cried itself dumb, and like a child she didn't expect anything from the world of grown-ups.

In silence we watched the procession file out of the fort. The coffin, covered with the flag for which the brigadier had fought, was carried by six troopers. Behind came the dead man's horse and his dog, a brown-and-white mongrel with setter blood. The squadron followed. Beside the unwalled cemetery, swept by the blast of Sirocco, they formed a hollow square.

A bugle called. The air was very clear and drenched in that green light which precedes the dawn. Slowly, the coffin disappeared. Round the open grave, the Legionaries stood at attention, their rifles reversed, while Dumont, his sincerity struggling with his sense of drama, addressed the dead. "Mon camarade," he said. "Whatever crime thou has committed in life, thou hast not the right to deprive a mother of the privilege of mourning her son. We do not ask thy secrets. Rest thou in peace and in the gratitude of France, but let thy grave be the object of a family's reverence and grief." False sentiment, I thought, for nobody knew the brigadier's name, so how could anyone weep upon his tomb—except Marie, of course. I looked at her and saw, for the first and only time in my life, I think, a sorrow irreconcilable with tears.

Dumont made rapid use of his handkerchief. I saw, or imagined, moisture in the eyes of troopers, wind-scarred and sun-blackened, waifs from war-wrecked Central Europe, fugitives from her prisons, blond adventurers from the north. But the woman beside me, with head held high, looked as if she didn't know where she was, or what it was all about.

Silence followed the captain's peroration. Then, to the surprise of everybody, a Legionary stepped from the ranks. Dragging a book from his pocket, he said with shy simplicity, "My Captain, I am a Lutheran pastor and I have here my office. Will you permit that I read it over our comrade?"

Dumont nodded, and the man, who looked as if he should have been wielding a rake in Swiss meadows, stood bare-headed by the grave. He was no longer a trooper, ill at ease and stiff, but a minister of his faith. The prayers rolled grandly from his lips. He turned the tattered pages, but did not look at them. There was no limit to his assurance, no compromise of any sort. The ambassador of a Supreme Power spoke to a subject who had served the throne.

Unconsciously, heads went up. I no longer wanted to cry.

The squadron marched back to the fort with the fair-haired Teuton, who, for a few moments, had been in possession of a kingdom, slouching in the last rank, conscious perhaps of a blistered heel and the enmity of the new corporal.

Later in the day, I asked Marie what she was going to do. "I don't know," she said, not stupidly, but as if it didn't matter.

"Haven't you any family?"

"Oh no, not now."

We were sitting on the mud verandah. I'd sent a non-descript youth for coffee and any food he could find, because I thought Marie had omitted to lunch. Somehow, I must approach the question of money, but it was difficult.

We'd been talking desultorily about the Legion, with which the woman was familiar, since she'd followed it from post to post throughout Algeria and Morocco. "Is it really so hard a life?" I asked, by way of distracting her thoughts.

"For one who wishes to work, it is all right," she said, "but heaven protect the vaux rien!"

"There are such foolish tales about it," I continued.

"Ah bas! Cela sont des cochonneries! But for the English, it is hard because they want too much. Beside the brigadier, I have known two, three, five English...." She counted them on thin fingers. "They grumbled because they could not learn the language and so they had nobody to talk to, and because they wanted comfort, un confort inouïe!"

She spread small surprised hands, with the nails bitten. I noticed the down on them, like pollen, and the same impalpable hairs gilded her temples. I wanted to know how she came to be a camp-follower, but she told me very little. I don't think she meant to tell me anything at all, but I gathered, from a chance phrase here and there, that she'd run away from a family where, as a fifth daughter, she was most certainly not wanted, to a man who would never acknowledge his need of her. And she'd stuck to him as closely as he would allow. She'd been everything that he chose to make her. She'd listened to him at his worst and played the harlot when he couldn't bear anything else. And always she'd loved him.

"Why did he want to get away from the Legion?"

"He wanted to get away from himself," returned Marie. She turned her small grave face to me and said, "He was always like that. He hated himself and so, perhaps, he hated me. . . ." I understood then the strength of the bond which had made these two, so dissidently, one.

The talk swung back to the Legion. "What you have seen here is an exception," insisted Marie. "For the most part, they are good fellows with no pasts and no more education than is necessary. They want a little adventure and to boast, in their villages, that they have been Légionaires."

A fund of common sense lay behind that wondering manner. I imagined the brigadier had told her most of what he knew. Perhaps she liked repeating his words. "Brutality, no. Bullying, yes. Where is there not bullying when men are together like schoolboys? The officers are good and they take a pride in their men, but if a sergeant has a grudge against you, it may go hard with you. And for those few who are too intelligent, it is a peine to live always with inferiors."

The shadows lengthened. Long-bodied insects crawled into the coffee-cups.

"How did you meet him?" I asked. That one thing I was determined to know. But it was very simple—a drunken Arab in Sidi-bel-abbès, where the father had business. A Legionary had interfered. They had walked together, and the Englishman's need had been sufficient to bring the girl to him. I wondered what his feelings had been.

"Have you any money?" I asked, abruptly, after having decided on a dozen better ways of putting the question.

"Not much," said Marie, as if it didn't matter at all.

"You must leave here, but where will you go?"

"I don't know."

I wondered if that indefinite mouth could be obstinate. The eyes dreamed. They held a constant, gentle surprise.

Before we went to bed, I'd forced some notes into her unwilling hands and arranged to take her to Algeria. There happened to be a spare seat in the ramshackle car I'd hired from an Arab.

But when the day of departure arrived and the driver, unshaved, his shirt fastened with string, was making a great fuss about my luggage, Marie could not be found. Madame Bonnard threw up her hands and eyes. Her breasts shook under the greasy bodice. Mademoiselle had paid her bill. That was certain. One had only to look at her room to be assured of its emptiness.

I went north alone.

A year later my francs were returned to me with two words in a widely looped writing.

I never saw Marie again, unless, well unless.... For not long ago, I lunched at the Negresco Hotel in Nice. To me it is like a railway station, confused with the furniture department of a modern store. There was, as usual, too much of everything, including food, scent and the dullest people. But at the next table a family party, immersed in black, applied themselves determinedly to their meal. They were pleasant to look at, partly because they were so thoroughly enjoying themselves. Prosperous bourgeois, I thought, celebrating the will of a rich relation. Maman was portly, with chin supported on a cutlet frill and a wide good-tempered smile dividing her face into half moons. Papa's moustache became entangled in the lobster and he licked it with relish. He wore a ring on his tie and another, larger, on a square and sensible hand. The children were charming. They whispered to each other, very serious. Black bows flared all over them. It was only when they got up and sorted themselves to leave the room, that I noticed the governess. She must have been the governess. The smallest girl, with the head of a medieval page and a chessboard of a frock, took her hand familiarly and smiled at her. There was a murmur of "Mademoiselle, this—Mademoiselle, that. . . ." To which a careless voice answered, "Yes, Madame, I have it. No, Madame, one left it in the car."

For a moment, I looked into eyes that held the blue of the Equator and a gentle, still bewilderment. "You! My dear. . . ." I exclaimed, half upsetting my chair, but the woman showed no sign of recognition. Bending to the children, arranging a bow with a pollen-covered hand and the suggestion that she didn't quite know what she was doing and it didn't matter any way, she passed out of the restaurant. Could it have been Marie?

1931

Interlude in Turkey, Iraq, and Persia

From Chapters II, VII, X, XI, and XXIV of
Conflict: Angora to Afghanistan (1931)

Veiled and Unveiled Women
of the Middle East

TURKEY HAS SUFFERED a female revolution and come out of it unscathed, except that, nowadays, the average pretty young Constantinopolitan would probably rather marry a foreigner than one of her own compatriots. For masculine human nature is hard to change, whether it be Western or Eastern, and the ordinary Turk grudges "this freedom" which the Ghazi[1] has bestowed upon women. He clings to his old authority and is surprised at the enthusiasm with which his wife acclaims the new régime. Yet, in this intermediate generation, between the harem and the polling-booth, freedom to most Eastern women means no more than the possibility of a good education.

Before the War, the inmates of the sophisticated harems in Stamboul spoke half a dozen languages and studied the literature of as many different countries. Today their daughters crowd the universities, but they consider intensive education as an end in itself rather than as the first step to a career.

---

1 Mustafa Kemal Atatürk, founder of the Republic of Turkey—Ed.

"What are you going to do after you leave college?" I asked a young woman of twenty-two, who had recently taken a degree.

"I don't know," she replied; and urged to consider the matter further, concluded: "well, I'm ambitious, so I suppose, if I get a good offer, I shall marry."

Next day I met the only woman lawyer in Angora.[2] She works on the *Conseil d'Etat*, which may perhaps be translated as the Privy Council, so, presumably she is well on the way towards the top of her profession, yet, when she accepted a cocktail from our mutual host, her father frowned at her. "Put it down. It is not good for you," he ordered in an undertone. His intellectual daughter, who is considered one of the personalities of the capital, obeyed at once.

"Tell me," I said to her when we found ourselves secluded on a sofa, "do the majority of Turkish girls hanker after a career, or is a husband still their main objective?"

For a while the dark-browed young woman hesitated. Then she said frankly: "I think most girls want a husband and a house of their own, but they would like to have a good education first."

But, a few days later, I was talking to another young woman, twenty-three and with no special prospects. "No; I don't want to marry," she said. "I am much freer as I am. Now I only have to obey my father, and whenever I ask him if I can do something he always says 'yes'; but if I were married, I should have to obey a husband who might not be so indulgent."

Yet the Turkish woman has progressed far beyond her neighbors in Syria and Palestine. She has the European code, which gives her equal rights of divorce, together with complete control of her person and her property; whereas by the *Sheria* law of Damascus, Jerusalem and Baghdad, a man may divorce his wife

---

2 Ankara—Ed.

after twelve hours, providing he repays her dowry. Many a man has ended his honeymoon and his marriage at the same time and sent a disillusioned child of sixteen or seventeen back to her parents, for no other reason than that, when he first saw her after the wedding-ceremony, driving away to his house, complete strangers, yet man and wife by law, he found she was not quite as pretty as his mother—who chose her—had led him to suppose.

To realize the magnitude of Turkey's evolution, one must compare the position of the educated women in Constantinople and Angora, whom one sees dancing at the foreign Legations or attending lectures at the university, with that of their neighboring contemporaries. In Syria, for instance, the only career open to women is that of a teacher in the elementary schools. True, five *veiled* girls are working in one corner of the men's class in the medical school at Damascus, but they will practice only on children and on their own sex.

In Syria, a woman must go to the courts for a divorce, but a man can still dismiss his wife the morning after he has married her.

The streets are crowded with slow-moving black figures, unrecognizable under a veil which ranges from a single thickness of black crêpe de Chine to three solid layers of a denser stuff, through which it is impossible to see more than a vague outline.

Beyrout has recently instituted a BA degree for women, but otherwise life in Syria is much the same as it was twenty and fifty years ago. There are shuttered compartments for women on trams and trains. Cinemas and theaters have special women's nights when no "man over eight years old" is admitted. At the chief restaurants there is a woman's section carefully screened from the rest of the room, and when I called on a comparatively emancipated friend, the crone who admitted me wouldn't even mention her name before the men smoking water-pipes in the hall until H.E. the Pasha should signify his readiness to receive them.

When I did get upstairs by divers and sufficiently secret ways, I found a committee in progress. A dozen women in long, dark coats, which have taken the place of the all-enveloping and entirely shapeless cloak (the habbara) of the last generation, their veils thrown back, were discussing, with the aid of Turkish coffee and the tiniest possible cigarettes, the formation of a national girls' school, for which they had already collected £800. "We are very proud because it has all been contributed by women," said my friend, "and you know how poor Syria is at this moment. We've given up most of our pleasures and all our vanities to get together the money, because the French don't encourage feminine education and we want a school of our own, where our daughters will be taught patriotism and politics as well as domestic economy." A brave ambition!

In Syria, each sex says the other is not sufficiently advanced to justify unveiling, but feeling has changed since the days when in the open bazaars, an Imam spat in an Englishwoman's face because he did not approve of its being shown in public, or even since 1920 when, by order of the Pasha, the police were armed with huge scissors with which they slashed the *habbara* of any woman lax enough to show an ankle or a wrist under the stifling drapery which collected the dust of the street and attracted innumerable flies.

But, even today, the only women employed in Damascan offices or shops are Jewesses, for the old-fashioned Christian families seclude their daughters almost as rigidly as their Moslem neighbors, whereas in Angora the number of girl typists, clerks and secretaries is increasing every year.

The typists' ball at Constantinople provided a scene which might have been staged in any Western capital, but a year earlier, for the long skirts have not yet come East. The Turkish typist still measures her modernity by the stiffness of her permanent waves and the small amount of material in her skirt. Though it is rumored that the standard of feminine beauty is to change, in obedience to Turkey's insistence on Westernization, the Constantinopolitan, whether typist or *grande dame* is still addicted to curves. She has lovely eyes, deeply fringed and much painted; thick legs and ankles; very often a beautiful mouth to make up for an indefinite profile; but she does not take enough exercise to acquire a naturally good complexion, and Eastern cosmetics are crude as the colors on a Noah's ark.

In the harem there was leisure to cultivate the charm of good manners, and the Turkish hostess has not lost the art of making each guest feel the object of her particular attention. In this she is unrivaled, for she has the natural grace of the woman who is never hurried; but it is rare to find her interested in affairs outside her own house and her own friends. Turkish men do not generally talk politics or business with the women they meet—still a trifle constrainedly—at dinners and dances. They pay them many compliments, but when flattery is exhausted, the sexes drift apart and each group is suddenly more animated. I remember a "raki" party at Angora, given by Rouf Bey, the Iraq Minister. It began at six-thirty and continued till the early hours of the morning. The guests sat on carpeted divans and drank innumerable glasses of araki. Water-pipes were handed round; the air grew thick with smoke. But long before dinner was announced to a company who by that time were impervious to anything but habit, two groups had formed. The men, gathered round the low table on which a regiment of bottles guarded olives and cheese, discussed Ismet Pasha's finance bill. The women, relieved for once of the necessity for sitting upright on rows of chairs, were comfortably installed in a corner where they tucked their feet under them, and heads close together, chattered happily about their families.

It is just as impossible to generalize about the women of the Middle East as about any other section of humanity, but it seemed to me that many Turkish wives regretted the leisure of the harem. In their minds the financial stringency of the post-war years is inevitably connected with the freedom bestowed upon them by Mustafa Kemal. "In the old days everything was easy. There was plenty of money. Now it is all so difficult," was the plaint of the bewildered women I met in the old wooden houses, condemned by a provident municipality as flammable.

The middle-aged Turkish woman has had to adjust herself to an evolution which has done away with so much more than the restrictions on her personal freedom. All the crises of Europe are creeping into Constantinople. Today there is a housing prob-lem, because young couples will no longer live in the intimacy of the husband's family. They want flats of their own. There is a servant problem, for the old retainers who were slaves are disap-pearing. There is a cultural one identical all over the Balkans and the Middle East, for the new generation is being educated beyond the possibility of finding suitable work. What are all these girls and boys, who come out of the American college with excellent degrees, going to do with their knowledge? There are few open-ings in a country intent on self-preservation by means of a rigor-ous isolation from all foreign contact. There are women guides in Stamboul and women sweepers in the streets, but it is difficult for the graduate of Roberts College to find salaried work of a kind suited to her attainments.

The first effervescence has subsided. The unveiled woman no longer throws herself, first into a succession of love-affairs and then into the Bosphorous, but she is up against the problem of the labor-market. In Turkey, as in every other country, she will find employment in those conditions where she can undercut the opposite sex; but the majority of administrative posts are likely to remain closed to her, simply because Turkey has not sufficient employment for her young men. A period of friction is inevitable, for women want more than men can afford to give. Turkey cannot employ more than a certain number of doctors, lawyers, technicians and so on. For each vacant post there are anywhere from twenty to a hundred applicants. Consequently, girls, whatever their qualifications, are forced back into the ranks of elementary teachers, stenographers, secretaries, employees in shops and banks. There are seven women lawyers who are employed largely by their own sex. The institution of a new alphabet has eliminated the ancients, who wrote the letters of an illiterate public with pens as fine as stippling brushes, and filled their places with girls. Commerce and industry have been quick to take advantage of the fact that the newly emancipated young woman is more adaptable than her brothers. She will work longer hours for less wages. But competition is keen and each year it is likely to increase.

In Europe youth has created, or is on its way to creating, an original relationship between the sexes, based on a variety of common purposes; but in Turkey friendship between men and women is still at a discount. Co-educated students share their work, but not their play. It is still comparatively rare to see a man and a woman lunching, driving or walking together.

"We really had much more freedom in the old days," said a perverse Constantinopolitan. "Nobody knew what we were doing. We could go where we liked. The yasmak reduced us all to the same pattern. Under her haik, every woman was in a world of her own and nobody could question her." But serious-minded youth, intent on education, would not agree with her. It seemed to me that the girls were taking life hard. Singularly defenseless, for to the average Turk the unveiling of women is no less superficial a gesture than the substitution of a bowler for a fez, they are earnestly seeking the freedom which the West is almost ready to discard.

Turkish women have been deprived simultaneously of custom, tradition and creed. A few of them, like Halidé Khanoum Edib, have been able to substitute an intensive nationalism for the cult of domesticity to which their mothers and grandmothers were dedicated. But, on the whole, I imagine the unveiled Turkish woman, in the whirlpool of transitory conditions, is as aware of frustration as of opportunity.

Long ago I asked Halidé Khanoum, then a leading spirit of the revolutionary Committee of Union and Progress, whether she worked for Turkey or for Islam. At that moment she replied: "I do not really know. I must think it out"; and later: "no, it is not religion—it is, quite definitely, for my country."

A few months ago, eating rose-leaf jam in one of the very new houses of Angora, I asked my hostess if the claims of nationalism had effectively routed those of Islam in the new capital. "Among the men, yes," she said; and I remembered a most delightful and amusing member of the National Assembly who had represented Turkey at the Meccan Moslem Conference in a bowler hat and a tweed suit, less concerned with the Koran than with the possibility of getting apoplexy in a climate which he stigmatized as "possibly holy, but certainly uncivilized."

"And what about the women?" I asked; realizing how effectively the middle-aged Turkish lady maintains the reserve with which the harem tradition has endowed her. "For us, it is different," said my hostess, whose three daughters were respectively a lawyer, an author and a doctor. "This freedom is taking our children from us, and we must rely on another life for what we lose in this."

One of the daughters was in the room, a brooding young creature with a frown between her heavy brows. "There must be something in religion," she interpolated; "but we are too busy with all we've got to do for Turkey to trouble much about the future; there may be time later. . . ."

This freedom, so momentous to the youth of the city and pro-ductive of so much conflict between class, generation and sex, has left the peasant woman unchanged. She still works all day in the fields and most of the night in her one-roomed mud-built house, for in the Anatolian plains sleep is reduced to a minimum. Like her husband, she is unmoved by the disestablishment of the Church for there is no God but Allah and He is great. Like him, she is a firm believer in the polygamy which long ago, went out of fashion in the towns, for, without it, how would she get any rest at all?

"Don't you mind your husband re-marrying?" I asked an elderly peasant, whose three sons had been killed in the war.

"How should I mind? I chose the girl myself. She is fourteen and very docile. She will be like a sister in the house and she will do much of the work. It is time that I sat still a little, for my joints are stiff; but this girl is strong and *Inshallah*, she will have sons, so that there will be someone to work for our old age, else how should we exist?"

Iraq and the Holy Cities
of Shia Islam

FROM PALESTINE AND SYRIA I motored across the desert to Baghdad.

When Nairn first established his service, transport by it was something of an adventure. There were no sign-posts and no tracks. The Bedouins who were persuaded to act as guides generally lost their heads and their sense of direction at the same time. They were not accustomed to going so fast and they found that the desert, familiar enough from the back of a camel, looked quite different when it was flying past a six-cylinder car at forty miles an hour.

I remember the first time I crossed with Nairn; the largest pistol I had ever seen hung conveniently on the windscreen and the driver enlivened the journey with tales of convoys "shot up," before remarking in a cheerful voice that his weapon was unloaded and the ammunition somewhere in the baggage van. Of course, nothing happened, but the pistol reminded us of the chances Nairn took when he set out to make a high road across Arabia. In those days, if anybody wanted to sleep, he rolled himself in a blanket and stretched out on the sand for an hour or two before dawn and if it happened to be winter he froze so that even the hot breakfast sausages, eaten at sunrise, failed to cheer him. But today, the desert between Damascus and Baghdad is much less adventurous than Michigan Boulevard in Chicago.

The tracks are clearly marked by an army corps of mechanical transport running Eastward, hustling Eastward, bearing the labels of civilization and all the doubtful blessings of modernity to peoples who don't yet know what to make of them.

The route is patroled by armored cars, French and British. Half-way across there is a hotel disguised as a fort, wherein there is electric light and I rather think electric fans. The food is not even tinned and the "romantic" Bedouin encampments which surround the post are built of petrol cans! Fortunately the post is garrisoned by Iraq levies who wear scarlet cloaks, and if it happens to be spring all along the route, scarred by wheels and signposted with empty tins, there will be herds of camels, with long-legged youngsters looking as if some joint had been omitted by mistake. As likely as not, beside the black tents from which bearded nomads have watched the disappearance of the ghazu (raiding party) and the gradual evolution of the road, there will be a patrol drinking coffee, while its maxims provide topic of conversation for half-naked children with amulets tied to their top-knots.

In one direction a lorry full of pilgrims, bearing the scars of last Muharram, may be bound for the Holy Cities where life is changeless and progress a synonym for evil, and in the other a six-wheel Pullman coach be carrying American tourists in a row of armchairs and the most illogical luxury to join a Mediterranean cruise.

During the same night, we passed a convoy of motor-trucks bound for the Persian oil-fields, a super-charged and superupholstered saloon ordered by the Shah of Persia, an airplane which had come down and was waiting for a spare part, and a camel caravan laden with corpses for burial in the Holy City, but on this road there is no conflict between East and West. The laws of the nomads still prevail and the camel amiably pulls the lorry out of the mud, or the convoy provides the caravan with much-needed water.

It seemed to me, however, that if there could be no clearer indication of the manner in which the West is gradually impinging on the East than this trans-desert highway, certainly nothing could better express the conflict which results from the attempted imposition of one set of habits, ambitions and traditional points of view upon another, equally deep-rooted but utterly divergent, than conditions in Mesopotamia today.

Iraq, I imagine, must now regard herself and be regarded by the rest of the world as the most successful solution of a Mandate, the term which has given rise to more conflict in the Middle East than any other coined at Versailles, except perhaps Wilson's "self-determination." But in Baghdad just before the Treaty of Alliance was signed, the nationalists were saying: "Show us one place where England has established herself and which she has subsequently left," and the most popular proverb in the country to describe a guest who had outstayed his welcome was, "He lingers like English colonization."

Six months previously, a Prime Minister, Abdul Muhsin Bey, who was unique in that he probably possessed the confidence of nine-tenths of the population, had shot himself because he could not reconcile the claims of the extremists with the more conservative policy he believed essential for the country.

The explanation lies in the importance of Iraq to any European government intent on establishing and safeguarding communications with the East. Iraq is as much a key to Asia as was the Suez Canal to India, and it is as essential to British Imperialism as Clapham Junction to the railways of which it is the center.

We are entering upon an epoch when the air will be as vital to the maintenance of peace as was the sea. Iraq lies across the main air route to India and the East.

Moreover, the Shatt-el-Arab is the channel by which the Anglo-Persian Oil products are shipped to the outer world and it is controlled by Basra.

Kirkuk in the province of Mosul is the center of another oil region to be developed by the Iraq Petroleum Company, but before the wells can be opened, some five hundred miles of pipe-line must be laid to a port in Palestine, probably Haifa.

If the grain-growing provinces are to export their wheat direct to the Mediterranean, a railway should accompany the pipe-line, in which case Iraq will become the main route to Asia and India by land as well as by air. At the present moment, if the capital were forthcoming to complete the hundred and fifty miles of line between Nisaibin and Mosul, the Taurus express would reach Baghdad seventy hours after leaving the shores of the Bosphorus.

It will be seen, therefore, that Iraq only needs capital to consolidate her position as the nucleus of some of the world's biggest oil interests, as the junction of air and land routes all over Central Asia and as the distributing center of goods going East or West. But Iraq is the key to the politics of the Middle East as well as to its commerce, and three of her neighbors, Turkey, Persia and Arabia, are ruled by dictators.

Hence the necessity of a strong and stable state holding the land between the rivers so that it may form a barrier between the nomads of Central Arabia, the militarism of Turkey and the acquisitiveness of Persia, who has already occupied the province of Arabistan, as Arab in speech, tradition and origin as it is in name.

Iraq, therefore, if she can develop her resources by the help of foreign capital, is likely to play a considerable part in any redistribution of power in the Middle East, but at present she is suffering from the usual financial crisis, which, owing to over-production and the fall in the cost of raw material, is becoming ubiquitous throughout Asia. During the last few years the Iraqis, always optimistic, suddenly realized the possibilities of irrigation, so they rushed to the nearest towns and bought numbers of pumps on credit, hoping to pay for them out of the subsequent crops. But no man had calculated the cost of upkeep, nor could he foresee that the price of grain would slump. Five years ago wheat was selling for two hundred rupees a ton. By 1930 it had dropped to thirty-seven. Consequently a deficit in the budget is inevitable and the landowners who had increased the area under cultivation by forty per cent are disillusioned. There is a huge reserve of grain, destined to remain unsold, partly because Russia has come back into the market and is selling at cut-throat prices, and partly because the Iraqi still mixes a certain amount of dirt with his wheat, hoping thereby to increase the weight.

In the North, the Christian and other Minorities are anxiously watching the situation. To put it baldly, they cannot believe that England, on whom they imagine they depend for continued security, intends to abide by a Treaty even if she has signed one.

The Kurds, suffering on one side the pressure of Turkish nationalism, and on the other from the misunderstandings and mismanagement difficult to avoid when there are two governments in one country, are agitating for an independent state, comprising the three separate provinces now ruled respectively by Angora, Tehran and Baghdad.

The Basra Sheikhs, who control large tribal sections and who represent one of the few wealthy elements in Iraq, are inclined to welcome the termination of the Mandate, feeling that they are quite strong enough to evade taxation by an independent Government.

A further problem is represented by the many young Englishmen who accepted posts in Iraq at the end of the War, believing that under the aegis of Whitehall, they were going to create a second Sudan. They had every reason to regard themselves as settled, with a hard task, but one which would repay a lifetime's inconspicuous and uncomplaining labor. The majority of these are now going to be on the unemployed list, because after the rebellion of 1921, the British Government discarded their first interpretation of the word Mandate, which for all practical purposes amounted to colonial administration, and instituted the dual régime. Owing to the tact displayed by H.M. King Feisul and by a series of able High Commissioners, this curious system has functioned with comparative success, but by the recent Treaty of Alliance between Iraq and England, it is to end in 1932 when the independent Arab state will be recommended for entry into the League of Nations. Thereafter Britain will be present in Iraq only to safeguard the communications which are essential to her imperial entity.

In order that Iraq should be ready for the independence she has obtained by means of years of active negotiations, it was necessary that the system of local government instituted when Mesopotamia had perhaps less claim to national entity than any other portion of Arabia should be modified. For instance, during what may be called "Mandatory Interpretation 2," wherever there was a Mutasarif, there was also an English official, so that the former had no urgent reason for learning his job. He need not take any responsibility so long as there was an Englishman whom he could consult. If he happened to be indolent, the Englishman did the work and covered the mistakes of the Iraqi. Such a system shielded the incompetent and did not give the capable a chance. Sooner or later, the local officials have got to learn to govern and it was felt among the more intelligent nationalists that in order to force them to shoulder the responsibility for their own acts, the Englishmen should gradually be concentrated in the central offices and should make tours of inspection when necessary.

Re-organization on these lines was already beginning in the spring of 1930, and since the Treaty has been signed the majority of British employees are leaving at the end of their contracts, while some, whose posts can already be filled by Iraqis, are being dismissed with compensation. In fact, the individual Englishman who, in the majority of cases, has done splendid work for the country, in whose progress he felt himself personally concerned, is paying with the loss of his job for the changes rung by Whitehall.

Perhaps the sentiments of a country faced with so many problems, racial and religious, political, agricultural and financial, a country which outside the educated classes of three of four towns, is devoid of national unity, are best summarized in the words of the King: "The Iraqi is gradually becoming much less conservative, but his enterprise is limited by political expediency. If suspicion of England could be eradicated, he would get on twice as fast. When the Treaty of Alliance is signed, there will be no more powder for the magazines of our young agitators and they will set to work with agricultural treatises instead of studying the press for signs of Whitehall's intent to colonize!" It seemed to me that His Majesty, who, during a number of difficult years has attempted to reconcile the interests of Iraq and England, realized that for several decades, his country would need the services of foreign experts, but since these, in the past, have not always been well-chosen, he wished them to be selected and employed by the Iraq rather than the British Government.

Such were the general outlines of the situation in Baghdad, when I set out with a young nationalist, whose spirit was by way of being as Occidental as his clothes, to visit the holy cities of Southern Iraq. My companion was a nephew of Doctor Shahbender, and with his long-suffering uncle, he had been first imprisoned and then banished for the part he played in the movement for Syrian independence. Naturally, he was less interested in the

desert, inhabited by a horde of most engaging creatures of the liz-
ard tribe, but so large and fat that, scuttling out of the way of the
car, they reminded me of Eryops, the Mud Puppy, than he was in
the problematical progress of a united Arabia.

Bumping frantically against the roof and ricochetting from
side to side till we found ourselves in an ungainly heap upon the
floor, we indulged in spasmodic politics, interspersed with frantic
prayers to the driver who suffered from a convenient deafness. By
the time the first oasis blurred the horizon with palm trees which
stood waist-deep in mirage, I had been informed that in the combined products of Americanized education and nationalist principles represented by my fluent and elegant companion, East and
West had met, irrevocably and for the obvious benefit of Arabia.
An hour later, we were stumbling through a street which would
have shocked the eugenic principles of Haroun el Rashid. I did
not mind the dirt or the sores, or the fanatical hatred of the ultra-
religious, because the setting was so picturesque, but my companion held a handkerchief across his mouth and nose. From behind
it, he muttered in genuine distress: "Oh, God! And these people
believe they are fit to govern themselves!"

For the Shias, Kerbela and Najaf take the place of Mecca and
Medina. A pilgrimage to these desert towns, known as Zyaret, the
Visit, is as meritorious in the eyes of Persian Islam as the longer
and more difficult journey to the Hedjaz. The annual number of
pilgrims varies between a hundred-and-fifty thousand and two
hundred thousand, and in a prosperous year it may rise to something like three hundred thousand.

Each group has a leader who carries a flag stamped with a
text from the Koran, or the names of the twelve Imams, descen-
dants of Ali, the son-in-law of the Prophet, Mohammed. Having purified themselves by the prescribed ablutions, the pilgrims
present themselves at the shrine of Husayn, and after begging

the Saint's permission to approach, they circle the grave three times and then prostrate themselves to the accompaniment of prayers and lamentations. For, to them, Husayn represents all that was most gallant in the young warrior, Islam. He was the son of Fatima, the famous daughter of the Prophet, and Persian legend attributes to him a bride of the Royal Sassanian House, last of the great dynasties to rule in Fars, and thus insuring him a double claim to the veneration of loyal Persians. Invited by the Kufans to proclaim himself Commander of the Faithful in place of the brilliant intriguer, Moawiya, who had already founded the Omeyad Caliphate in Damascus, Husayn marched across the deserts from Mecca with thirty horse and forty foot, including women and children. In the plain of Kerbela he was met by the hosts of his rival, and deserted by the Kufans, was massacred with every male in his party. It is in memory of this wholesale martyrdom that the Shias keep the first ten days of Moharram as a period of lamentation.

Where Husayn pitched his camp in Kerbela there is now a small mosque approached between a double row of dwarf arches supposed to represent the tents of the butchered warriors. From here the mourners start their annual procession. Armed with axes and other sharp instruments with which they strike themselves on heads and shoulders, they advance, sometimes linked together, intoning a frenzied lament for the death of their Saint.

It is said that the richest treasure in Islam lies under the great golden dome of Husayn's mosque, but, alas, the bazaar huddles so closely round its walls that all the infidel can see of this most famous shrine is a blaze of mosaic through one of the four great doors which open straight into the *suqs*.

Like Gertrude Bell, I climbed on to the roof of a neighboring house. In the glare and dust of a desert noon, I looked across a wilderness of mud walls to the splendor of Husayn's dome, covered with beaten gold, between minarets of the same precious material, and I remembered her appreciation:

> It was the sense of having reached these regions which saw the founding of imperial Islam, regions which remained for many centuries the seat of the paramount ruler, the Commander of the Faithful. Within the compass of a two days' journey lay the battlefield of Kadisiyah, where Khalid ibn u'l Walid overthrew at once and forever the Sassanian power. Chosroes with his hosts, his satraps, his Arab allies—those princes of the house of Mundhir, whose capital was one of the first cradles of Arab culture—at his coming stepped back into the shadowy past; their cities and palaces faded and disappeared, Kirah, Khawarnak, Ctesiphon and many another of which the very site is forgotten; all the pomp and valor of an earlier time fell together like an army of dreams at the first trumpet blast of those armies of the Faith which hold the land unto this hour.[1]

But there is another aspect of Kerbela which must affect the stranger coming from the more progressive towns of Iraq bent on modernization and a place in the League of Nations. Kerbela today is exactly as it was six hundred years ago and so it is likely to remain, for harassed officials assured me that, with the exception of the late Mayor—who was particularly successful in dealing with the obstinate, avaricious and narrow-minded Sayeds claiming descent from Ali and unable to think about anything else— nobody has been able to compete with the intensive holiness of this isolated district for more than a year at a time.

---

1 Reprinted from *Amurath to Amurath*, by Gertrude Bell, by kind permission of the publishers, Messrs. Macmillan & Co.

"The virtuous are excessively difficult to argue with," remarked a doctor whose life was made intolerable by the knowledge that in the center of each beautifully tiled court, round which are built the harem rooms, there is a pool where the water is never renewed, though everything human, animal and culinary is dipped into it in turn.

The high-roofed bazaars of Kerbela are as Persian as its houses; and the slim, hollow-chested figures crouched behind their wares in open-fronted booths are of that Persian type which has the Jewish nose and a smooth, pale, hairless face. There are Persian tiles in the cafés, where Bedouins in checked black-and-white cotton kufiyas, Indians in gold-embroidered caps, Sayeds with rolls of green round their fezzes, and the subjects of Reza Shah, forced much against their common-sense to wear the Pahlavi hat, an atrocity rather like a railway porter's cap, but excessively stiffened and high-crowned with the peak pointing skywards, drink Persian tea instead of Arab coffee.

There are frescoes representing old Persian stories, on every convenient wall and between the honeycombed booths—heaped with oranges and sweet lemons, with pistachio nuts and the heads of roses, with plaques of sacred earth on which the believer presses his head in prayer, with shrouds stamped with texts from the Koran, with sharp-pronged instruments representing the hand of Fatima with which the faithful tear and stab themselves in their frenzy of lamentation—walk Persian ladies under tents of black silk, or cotton, with a wire visor protruding just above the eyes so that, perhaps, they can catch a glimpse of the way they would go.

The Arab women show one eye, and the Indians, distinguished by their brilliant silk coverings, grass-green, purple or red, have an inch or two of thick meshing like a grid over the eyes, but they all look like perambulating tents, for nowhere is Islam more repressive to feminine aspiration. In Najaf there are no schools for girls and the *Mujtahids* forbid that any woman should learn to read or write, yet, in both these sacred towns "mutta"—temporary—marriages can be arranged for a night or a month according to the taste of the pilgrim. The "wife" is paid according to the duration of the marriage, which is celebrated by a formal ritual in the presence of witnesses who sign the contract, but no divorce is necessary.

At Najaf, Ali, cousin and son-in-law of the Prophet, is buried under another golden dome, and one of the attendant minarets, slightly out of the straight, is said to have salaamed in honor of Mohammed, and to have remained pointing reverently in the direction of Meshed, holy city of Persia.

Najaf is the burial-ground of the Shias, and thither, all the year round, are brought the corpses of the faithful in cars, and on camels, horses and donkeys; in baskets, boxes and rolls of reeds, covered with a red cloth; on men's backs and in their luggage, for the Government roused a storm of protest by forbidding the import of "wet" corpses, *i.e.* those which had been dead less than a year. Consequently, the faithful are obliged to smuggle the uncomplaining dead, with apples sewn in their shrouds to hide the odor of decay; but for "dry" corpses there are no restrictions and it may be that a man will converse with you in the desert with the remains of his long-dead relative very obviously sticking out of the bundle on his back.

The whole of Najaf lives on the burial trade and as tombs in the holy area are a vested territorial right, families sell space in them for anything from five to a thousand rupees, according to their proximity to the mosque. There is a parking ground for unburied corpses which is always crowded, while the relatives drink tea and smoke water-pipes on acres of narrow wooden couches arranged round a huge earthen stove laden with gaudy china from the Midlands.

The Turkish Government used to charge nine shillings import duty on a corpse and the price of burial was then £40 at Ruwaq in Najaf and only £6 at Samarra, but the *Mujtahids*, known collectively as the *Aatabir*, the Threshold, who have great influence (in spite of the fact that they number over two thousand, only forty-one of whom substantiated their claim in the face of Ottoman inquiry) used to insist on additional fees for their services.

For half an hour's walk outside the walled city of Najaf, which is treeless and set suddenly in the middle of the desert without any cultivation at all, the ground is holy. It is strewn with tombs of every size, the largest adorned with beautiful blue domes, to which the townsfolk refer as the house of so-and-so. In fact they live so habitually among the departed that in the course of the average conversation you never know if your companion is referring to the living or the dead, or whether the dwelling which he enthusiastically describes is somebody's new house or a tomb which, with forethought, a prosperous citizen is preparing for his own, or somebody else's end.

The most interesting thing in Najaf, apart from the distracting glimpses of the mosque obtained from bazaars so narrow that two cannot walk abreast between the shops, is the subterranean city which, during the torrid summer months, houses the whole population.

If the brogue of an infidel happens to impinge upon the first paving-stone of the great, mosaiced gateway by which the court of Ali's mosque is approached, a sullen murmur swells among the crowd. Pale faces crowd round the trespasser and there is age-old hatred in eyes which look as if they were drowned in opium, but the fanatical citizens become quite amiable when asked to show their underground retreats.

Preceded by a lantern, I went down an old well shaft into what appeared to be the heart of the earth, and there were great columned apartments, still warm from the sun-baked streets. Further down we went and the chambers were cooler and low-roofed, some with tiled or frescoed walls, and then down again till we were five stories under the earth and in a temperate climate.

From one house to another stretch the suites of underground rooms, with here and there a cavern or an ancient well, called "the home of a wind," up which a breeze blows strong and cold. With the first summer heat, carpets, tea things and water-pipes are brought down to the subterranean houses, with bedding for those storm-swept nights when the flying sand makes sleep on the roofs impossible. And, as the temperature increases in the desert leaguered town, the people of Najaf merely move one story deeper into the earth.

Interlude in the Anderun

I HAD MEANT TO drive straight from Sultanabad to Tehran, for between the Manchester of Persia and the capital, the road is good. Also I was curious to see what manner of men were responsible for the change which goes deeper than the dressing-up of a people for a brief act on a Western stage. The passing of religion, the adoption of a Western standard of education, the growth of security and a network of new communications, may well foster in the average Persian a feeling of self-importance unknown when his ignorance was at the mercy of the Mullah and his goods subject to the depredations of government officials as well as of brigands, but it seemed to me from the first moment I entered Persia-beyond-the-oil-fields that the whole fabric of modernization depended on the capital. So I would have hurried across the scarlet desert, the Western edge of the Dasht-i-Kavir, whose saline desolation occupies the whole of the interior of Persia. But when I reached Qum I was fascinated by its gold and blue. It happened that I had an introduction to a merchant who spoke some Arabic and who insisted on taking me round the bazaars, famous for their shoesmiths and their armorers, for melons, long-necked water-jars and a host of objects which reproduce in pottery the blue of the domed imamzadés.

From Qum half the roads of Persia radiate to towns which were once dynastic or commercial capitals, but the holy city is only interested in her pilgrims, who, after they catch sight of the great golden dome blazing out of the polychrome sands, must dismount for prayer.

Like all Persian towns, Qum has known little but war and destruction. Timour sacked it and the Afghan invasion completed its ruin, but later it became the burial place of the Safavi and Kajar Shahs. The famous Fath Ali Shah swore that if he achieved the throne he would so enrich the shrine that it would make Imam Reza (buried at Meshed) jealous of his sister Fatima, who is supposed to have fled from Baghdad to escape the persecution of the Caliph. He fulfilled his vow by replacing the blue tiles, which would now have been priceless, by a dome of beaten gold and by erecting a college for a hundred students. Moreover, he always approached the city on foot, with the result that now from all the new roads which bear modern lorries to the trading centers of Kazvin, Tehran and Isfahan, wild men with matted hair and sheepskin coats, amulets sewn into the flesh of their naked chests, come barefoot through the heat of the desert and the snows of distant mountains to the Safavi Mecca.

After our tour of the bazaars, my friend fed me on manna (gez) which in its original condition is a white, glutinous substance found on the branches of tamarisks, willows, thorns and oak. Some say it falls from heaven, and some that it is deposited by insects, or exuded by the bark, but whatever it is, the Persians regard it as a special delicacy. In the early morning they shake or scrape it off the boughs into flat baskets, and mixing it with chopped almonds and pistachios, let it harden into a paste not unlike a stiffer form of Turkish delight.

The merchant then presented me with a bowl of rose leaves and took me to the house of a singularly religious friend who did not believe in the emancipation of women. We drank tea and we gazed at piles of delicious-looking sponge-cakes which were apparently only used as ornaments or as indication of a most generous hospitality to follow. After the third cup, my host voiced his feelings: "Never, never shall it be decent for any woman to read or write!" he thundered, and everyone listened respectfully because he was a *Mujtahid*, famed for so much learning and holiness, that pilgrims visiting the sacred city considered his blessing almost as important as a journey to the tomb of Fatima the Immaculate.

He was an old man with a gray beard, hennaed in deference to the wishes of his youngest wife, a long, white robe not unlike a nightshirt, and a turban of the vivid emerald green which signifies that the wearer has made the pilgrimage to Mecca. He had consented to entertain me in deference to the wishes of the merchant whose house overflowed with wedding guests, but after satisfying his instinct for hospitality by providing me with what he called "an unworthy and inadequate meal," consisting of one sheep, two lambs, five chickens, a sack of rice, several mountains of vegetables and a veritable sea of sour buffalo milk, he voiced his horror of modern woman. Subsequently, unable to mention the anderun[1] or its occupants before the other wiseacres whom he had invited to drink sweet Persian tea and smoke water-pipes, while an invisible lute challenged the nightingales in a thicket of white roses, he pushed me, without any explanation, through a door which I had not previously observed.

It shut firmly behind me and I found myself in what might well have been an entirely separate house. A wide veranda ran round four sides of a court in which there was a sunken tank surrounded by pomegranates in flower, orange trees and flaming scarlet creepers. The stars were just coming out in the square of sky that could be seen. Carpets were spread on the tiled floor and a group of

---

1 Anderun is the Persian for harem.

women of all ages sat cross-legged upon them or leaned against the hard, Eastern bolsters which always seem to have been stuffed with young potatoes.

My hostess rose awkwardly and gave my hand an uncertain shake. She was probably quite young and she must have been beautiful for she had the green eyes of a Circassian set in a pale face, finely modeled, with straight features, but her hair hung in crimson wisps. Kohl was smeared down to her cheekbones. Her fingers had been dipped in paste made of marigolds and henna, and the palms of her hands, her toes and the lobes of her ears were dyed the same fierce orange. Unfortunately, she could only talk Turkish and a few words of Persian, so we were unable to do more than gesture our interest in each other. For some minutes we sat in silence, while the lady of the house sucked at the amber mouthpiece of a kalyan, in which the rose-water bubbled. The usual glasses of strong tea were brought to me, with a saucer of rose-leaf jam and some long, loosely-rolled Persian cigarettes. Then a girl in a very short cotton frock with bobbed brown hair spoke to me in halting Arabic. It transpired that her mother came from Iraq and that both regarded the life of the fanatical city wherein they now lived much as a co-educated collegiate might consider "Slocum-in-the-Mud."

She translated for me and I learned that the painted lady was the mother of my host's three sons and therefore secure in her position. A few years ago she had selected from among her friends another wife for a husband whose attentions had become too exigent, but as the girl proved delicate, she had been supplanted by a mere child, apple-cheeked and plump, grand-niece of a Persian Shah. So now there were three wives. My self-appointed interpreter pointed them out.

The middle one wore black trousers, immensely wide to the knee and tight as stockings from there to the ankle, with a white silk dress tucked into the top of them, under the habitual chudda, the all-enveloping black mantle which transforms the Persian lady into a sable tent when she walks in the street.

The youngest was splendid in a flowered muslin robe worn under a long coat of sapphire and gold brocade. She tinkled with heavy gold jewelry and her smooth dark head was surmounted by a turban tasseled and decorated with gold coins.

Most of the other women were visitors, still wrapped in their chuddas, with the quaint little black horsehair visors under which they look out at a narrow strip of life, pushed up on to their foreheads. They were all very polite and pressed upon me all sorts of things to eat, from melon seeds, whose regular cracking made an accompaniment to their speech, to sherbet which is a sort of fruit squash. Servants leaned against the wall, or sat on their haunches and stared at me, joining in the conversation whenever it pleased them.

At last a number of opium pipes were brought and a girl kneaded the sticky brown pellets above a fragment of charcoal in a wire sieve which she swung about in the air to induce a glow. The pipes had round china bowls, pierced with a single small hole, above which the pellet is balanced, and a wooden stem about a foot long.

The first one was offered to me, and stimulated by curiosity and a little fear, I accepted it. At first the smoke stuck in my throat and I choked. The women laughed at me and showed me how I must inhale deeply and slowly. They indulged in two or three pipes before their skins became more thickly opaque and their eyes acquired a peculiar glaze. I contented myself with one pipe, and as a result, felt no more than a mild benignity. I was no longer bored with the interminable repetition of question and answer, punctuated by long silences. I did not care whether I slept or not. Life was quite agreeable, though bereft of past and future.

While we smoked, the servants had been spreading thick viv-idly-covered quilts on the flat roof, surrounded by a wall which ensured privacy. When I had reached a stage in which I was not conscious of existing separately from the floor on which I sat and the bolster against which I leaned, there was a stir among the women. Some slipped away through a passage which led even-tually to the street—black formless shadows among blind walls. The others climbed by means of ladder-like steps, each one a couple of feet high, on to the roof, where my hostess offered me a choice of quilts. I selected a violet one with a royal purple bol-ster and wondered vaguely how much clothing I was expected to remove. The women settled the question by tucking them-selves, fully dressed, between their wadded coverings, which they drew well over their heads in spite of the intense heat, so that soon the roof looked as if large, brilliantly-colored cocoons had been dropped all over it. A servant went among the sleepers with a silver censer which she thrust under each quilt in turn, so that its strongly perfumed smoke eddied among my dreams and added to their confusion.

Sunrise stirred the anderun roof to reluctant activity. Strained white faces yawned upon unyielding pillows. One by one the women dragged themselves from the cocoons of scarlet, orange, and petu-nia. Children whom I had not noticed the previous night emerged from what was now a litter of exotic bedding. They were seized by their mothers, shaken and patted into comparative tidiness.

I felt that only a cold bath would save me. The girl in the European cotton frock had gone home to an anderun with brass beds, muslin frills and pink bows, Germanic illustrations of Shakespeare on the walls, and on a chenille fringed tablecloth the Eastern equivalent of an aspidistra. But when I expressed my desire for a large basin and much water—in Persia this gen-erally produces the family baking-tin, which serves admirably as a bath—a servant whose eyebrows had been plucked and a black streak substituted right across the forehead from one ear to another, led me to a tank sunk in the tiled floor. There was a good deal of rustling up above and it occurred to me that the whole of the household proposed to watch my ablutions. The water was dark and turgid, but the servant encouraged me to undress and to lower myself, gingerly, into unplumbed depths. Clutching the stone rim, I stretched out a cautious foot. Lower and lower went my inquiring toes till they touched a substance soft and squelchy. The squeal with which I leaped out of the tank startled my companion. Explanations followed, but I could not understand them. Finally, with many comforting gestures, the girl produced a pole with which she fished out the body of a very dead cat. Smiling cheerfully, she then invited me to proceed with my bath.

Unwashed, I continued my journey to Tehran. It began to rain. Within the city gates the car skidded from one pothole to another, while trams glided with derisive smoothness as if suggesting that the hummocks only existed in the Buick's imagination.

The capital keeps the secrets of its beauty behind miles and miles of garden walls. There are walls of every kind, of plaster, brick and mud, for when a Persian buys property, the first thing he does is to build a wall round it. Then he makes an imposing gateway, but very often he doesn't bother about a house. He plants a garden with lots of fruit trees and flowering bushes. Water he must have, and beside his sunken pool, fed by a canal from the city main, he grows roses, the single yellow, white, and orange varieties sung by Iranian poets. There is never any grass, and generally the flowers grow wild among the trees, but there may be a small pavilion or a tent from which, on what the philosopher considers a really fine day, he can watch the rain feeding his precious garden, wrenched at the expense of hard labor from the surrounding desert.

On the day I came to Tehran I saw nothing but dripping sun-blinds, striped orange and white, which gave the town a Continental expression. Behind the convex blinds were rows and rows of shops, most of them open-fronted, from which the goods escaped on to the side-walk, so that pedestrians picked their way between anything from furniture to teapots. The long, straight streets were lined with planes and acacias, the latter heavy with white bloom. There were scarlet buses, and policemen in pale blue raised on tribunes which looked like small pagodas. Victorias rattled by, the hoods lined with scarlet and the horses splendid in silver-studded harness, but their reign is almost terminated. American cars are taking their place.

In the main square a number of public buildings were being constructed after the unimaginative fashion sacred to municipalities all over a civilized but unaesthetic world. The Imperial Bank was moving—with the times—from an old house studded with tiles to a construction which would find favor in the Middle West.

It was said that the new prison, built to accommodate foreigners after the withdrawal of the Capitulations, was more comfortable than the hotel, but most of the garages let rooms after the fashion of the caravansaries which harbored camels on the ground floor and their owners up above.

My first impression of Tehran was slightly Hollywoodesque, for the new streets looked as if they had not quite settled where they were going, and the rows of new houses, one-room deep, were all frontage. They seemed to have no backs at all and they ended suddenly in space as if they were part of an unfinished set which would never be used in filmland. A profusion of notices in a variety of languages indicated emporiums of Levantine aspect, which just escaped the restrictions of a bazaar without achieving separate entity, since a passing glance failed to reveal where one ended and the next began.

In front of much commerce, accentuated by signboards as a face by too heavy brows, passed a stream of pedestrians at approximately one mile per hour. There were a few hats among the visors which make gratings in the Persian chudda, revelatory or not, according to the angle at which the wearer adjusts them, but they belonged chiefly to foreigners. The hat is not yet a usual form of headgear among the ladies of Tehran, though subsequently, I met a number of charming models perched on equally attractive heads, whose owners spoke French and thought after the manner of their speech.

The next day it had stopped raining and I saw the vaulted bazaars tunneling into dead centuries, but the booths under the arches had been Europeanized. They sold high-heeled shoes and modern jewelry, but there was an old man sitting cross-legged beside a tray of sour green plums and a stall whereon the bottles of milk and dogh were arranged like the pipes of an organ. There was a whole street of brass wherein the hammers imitated a jazz orchestra, and I found a lovely cook-shop where everything mysteriously edible was sizzling on a dozen braziers. Sweetmeats tempted equally the Pahlavi hat, the chudda, and the plus-fours, while their vendor sang a little song all about sugar.

I was taken to the American college and told there were eight hundred and fifty students drawn chiefly from the upper and lower classes, representing from different angles the land, for the middle class, absorbed in individual trade, does not contribute in proportion to its numbers. We studied the list of books taken that day from the library and found that with the exception of five novels (including a Dostoievsky and an Anatole France), and one volume of the Arabian Nights, it consisted of works of science, philosophy, and religion.

The Persian is easily interested in literature, for he likes the sound of the words and the swing of poetry, but he is also learning baseball and he gets up at five AM to practice it.

There are fourteen American teachers and the total courses, elementary, secondary, and collegiate, spread over sixteen years. Students can specialize in literature, science or commerce. The second includes geology and chemistry, while book-keeping, accountancy, shorthand, typing and economics are comprised in the third. There is also a pre-medical course to prepare students for the training given at the American college in Beyrout. Here then is one side of Persia, a-religious, for no difference is made between Moslem or Zoroastrian, Jew, free-thinker or Christian, a side which will eventually, one hopes, find expression in industry and scientific agriculture, rather than in politics as represented by government employment, hitherto the Mecca of educated youth.

Later that day, in a garden where pine-trees and roses were reflected in a marble tank, I talked with a young Persian who must have been earning a couple of thousand a year in Persian oil. His energy was remarkable and unusual. He had even acquired the European habit of saying what he meant, whereas, for the majority of his countrymen, the only purpose of words is to disguise thought. I asked him whether the whole structure of modernization, represented by the American and Church Missionary Society colleges, and the new high roads with their efficient policing, by Western dress and the "*nolo-me-tangere*" attitude of mind encouraged by politicians, depended on the life of the Shah.

He replied that nationalism in Persia was not new, and he gave me its history thus:—Seyed Jamal ed Din, known as the Afghan, but really from a village near Hamadan, started the national movement more or less simultaneously in Persia, Turkey, and Egypt. That was about seventy-five years ago. One of his strongest supporters was Malkam Khan, for a long time Persian Minister in London, who was against the theory of absolute monarchy and in favor of general education, whereas with Jamal ed Din, it was primarily a Pan-Islamic movement, which he induced the Sultan Abdul Hamid to foster. The younger generation of Mullahs tended to divert the Sayed's policy towards an independent nationalism, for the Shias were never, in practice, Pan-Islamic.

Between 1907 and 1914, Persia was dominated by the Russo-English agreement which divided the country into two spheres of influence. The first constitution was exacted from Muzaffer ed Din, whose father, Nasr el Din Shah, had been killed in 1896 by a disciple of Jamal ed Din, but an absolute monarchy was re-established by his successor, Mohammed Ali. The latter was followed by his son Ahmed, a boy of 13, during whose minority the constitution was restored. The long struggle represented by these alternate victories and defeats, not only consolidated a definite national party, but gave rise to an anti-foreign feeling which was justified by Lord Curzon's attempt to impose a virtual protectorate upon post-war Persia. From this she was saved first by Russia and then by Reza Shah, for in 1920, the British policy veered from what my young Persian termed "one of those useful synonyms for colonization in which your language abounds," to a cry of "Hands off Persia." The reason being that with the Russian occupation of the Caucasus, Lord Curzon knew that if Britain attempted a protectorate, Russia would advance and, if necessary, enforce an equal claim.

The "Hands off Persia" policy gave the nationalists their chance, and Reza Khan, then a colonel of Cossacks, took it with both hands. Within six years he had established himself by means of a military occupation and the stepping-stones of Prime Ministry and Presidency, as Shah of what is practically his own invention, for the original conception of Sayed Jemal was utterly different from Reza's Persia, isolated equally from East and West, standing on its own merits and resources, under a national banner which pays no tribute to Islam.

It was this Persia that I set forth to see, and because lorries, bearing carpets and asafetida to India, pilgrims to the Holy City of Meshed, cotton to Turkestan and sugar from Russia to all parts of Azerbaijan or Khorasan, have taken the place of mule caravans, it was by motor-truck that I traveled some five thousand miles round a land which is at present balanced between the conflicting claims of centuries far apart.

There is amazing progress in the towns. There is safety from one boundary to another. Except in the blank spaces represented by the vast central deserts, the Sea of Salt (Dasht-i-Kavir) and the Sea of Sand (Dasht-i-Lut), communications are spreading all over the kingdom. But in the country districts, civilization is no more than a symbol, such as the Pahlavi hat, and nowhere is the conflict between old and new more clearly registered than on the three-quarter-ton lorries or two-and-a-half-ton trucks which cross anything from three hundred to seven hundred miles of desert, laden with European goods. On the top of these, packed like locusts, crowd veiled women with hennaed finger-tips, and peasants with Pahlavi hats balanced on top of their turbans.

The majority of the drivers are Armenians, with a sprinkling of Russians, Turks, Afghans, Baluchis and Sikhs, but the passengers are Persians, whether they be neatly tweeded or wrapped in diverse folds. They talk politics and business, or smoke an opium pipe. They descend at intervals to pray, or to help change the tires, but whatever their costume and creed, at certain moments they are completely united. That is when they drink tea. In fact, on those five thousand miles I found but one fundamental unity and it was expressed in the tea-khané, shortly no doubt to be interpreted by a thermos flask.

From Isfahan to Shiraz
by Motor-Truck

IN THE DAYS of its glory Isfahan was the capital of Shah
Abbas. It had a population of nearly a million. Its circumfer-
ence was twenty-four miles; 1,500 villages flourished in the
neighborhood and its proud inhabitants boasted that "Isfahan is
half the world."

Today, its dim, vaulted bazaars and its gardens, which keep their
secrets behind twenty-foot mud walls, are strewn over a third of
the original space, and the polo ground of Shah Abbas, 560 yards
long, is to be converted into a public park.

With a very modern young Persian, who had married a grand-
daughter of Shah Nasr-ed-Din, I wandered round a city of sudden contrasts.

"The Isfahanis are very mean," said my companion. "It's in the
air. If a Tehrani comes here, he catches the infection. It is hard
to do business, though an Isfahani will sell anything, his own or
somebody else's—at a price. I know a very rich man who tests
every egg bought by his cook with a curtain ring. If the egg is
small enough to pass through the ring, it is promptly returned to

the bazaar. When the late Shah visited Isfahan, he halted at a village outside and said to his courtiers, 'If you want anything from me, ask for it now, but be silent when we reach the city.'"

Within sight of the Masjid-i-Shah, wherein is preserved the blood-stained shirt of Husayn, and from whose tall minarets no *azzan* was allowed to sound for fear the *muezzins* might see too much of the royal harem, we visited the largest modern factory in Persia. Here three hundred workers are employed, including two German mechanics, and an average of three hundred yards of cloth is turned out every day. Half of the material is khaki for the army, but the rest supplies the rather loosely woven fancy suitings of young Persia at approximately eleven shillings a yard, double width. In this factory seventy women are employed sorting the raw sheep's wool into piles of different colors and spinning it into a rough preliminary yarn on hand looms. They work and eat in a large harem room, which no man may enter and they earn fourpence to eightpence a day, while the men's wages vary from one shilling to five shillings in the case of expert mechanics.

Beside the Ali Kapi gate, from whose colored roof in 1660 Shah Abbas used to watch the slaughter of his enemies, or the arrival of a foreign embassy, and which still offers "bast" (refuge) to anyone who can establish himself under a great chain cluttered with votive rags, there is a humble sort of factory. Here, in a cellar which is cool and high, there are a dozen eighteen-foot looms whereon, for eleven hours a day, small, chubby infants, aged four or five, make fine carpets with 1,600 knots to the square inch. They earn twopence a day, and having timed the mite who was supposed to be most expert, we found he could do twenty knots a minute with fingers that looked more suited to a bottle or a woolly toy. Meanwhile, a foreman was chanting the pattern in a sort of rhyme and this particular work is hereditary in certain families.

With the same efficient guide, I motored out of Isfahan, whose population is now estimated at eighty thousand. The majority of these are engaged in the crafts for which the erstwhile capital was famous: copying old designs in silver and brass, or in inlaid and painted wood. We passed the blue-domed madrasseh of Shah Husayn, built two hundred years ago as a dervish monastery, with its huge silver-plated doors and the marks of the Afghan invasion still apparent in its battered roofs, and crossed the finest bridge in old Persia, 380 yards long, with a double arcade on either side, the gift of Ali Verdi Khan, the most successful general of the great Shah Abbas.

"Most of my contemporaries are free-thinkers," said my companion, glancing back at the city which knew so many martyrdoms in the name of religion. "They have no time to study any faith. They do not even know the names of our great poets. They have no time for the philosophy which delighted our parents. Everybody must make money because the standard of living has increased with this new desire to imitate Europe. We must have motors, and our wives must have crêpe de Chine, but, with the new tax on cars (approximately £2 a month, irrespective of horsepower) it will be cheaper to put away our motors and take an extra wife!"

I learned that the necessity for economy was enforcing monogamy among the upper-class Persians. "And we marry much later, not till we are twenty-six or thirty," explained my companion, who had been allowed to catch a glimpse of his wife in a mirror before he became engaged to her.

But still the hospitals of the Church Missionary Society, which does excellent work in Southern Persia, are full of children of twelve or thirteen suffering from the effects of premature marriage. In the poorer classes the mothers sell their daughters to any man who can feed them, for Persia is passing through a financial crisis. The merchants are paralyzed by the edict forbidding the purchase of foreign sterling. The import of raw material has stopped, so the small hand factories are closing and unemployment is rife.

"The modern spirit has affected the peasants," said my companion when we reached his eight-thousand-acre estate on which the largest village has a population of five thousand. "In the old days, the landlords had their own prisons and they could beat the peasants as they chose, but now if the laborer refuses to pay us our share of the crop, we can do nothing but be polite and go to court about it and justice is often delayed for two or three years."

Amused at the seigneurial idea of "the good old days," I inquired further and learned that the value of Persian land depends on the density of its population, for labor is bought with the estate. The peasant cultivates his landlord's acres and pays him from one-third to two-thirds of the crop, according to whether the land is irrigated or not and to who provides seed and implements. As the peasant is invariably in debt to his landlord, he cannot leave the estate, but with the new creed that each man is as good as his neighbor and better than the foreigner, it is becoming more and more difficult to collect the landowner's share of the crop.

"The Persian is the best liar in the world," said my companion, who was engagingly frank. "He thinks it is stupid to tell the truth and he prides himself on evading it as far as possible."

With this remark in mind, I was not surprised when the driver of the motor-truck, which was to take me to Shiraz, arrived three hours late with a host of such ingenious excuses that it was impossible to blame him.

On the top of huge bales of cotton, sprawled the half-dozen passengers, among whom were an Arab with a sense of humor and a veiled Persian woman who smoked steadily for seven hours.

As we left Isfahan the sun was slanting over the red desert. The hills were sudden outbursts of sharp red rock. Kumisheh, a great city before the Afghan invasion, with its miles of broken walls and its great round pigeon-towers, provided welcome relief to the monotony. In a large cemetery cheerful groups had spread carpets over the family graves and were having tea-parties with the dead.

It was dark when, averaging twelve-and-a-half miles an hour, the overloaded truck jolted into Yezdikhast, which means "God willed it." This amazing village consists of tiers of mud-built hovels projecting from either side of a boat-shaped rock some hundred and fifty feet high, which stands in the middle of a ravine, once the boundary between Fars and Iraq. It is a gash in the earth, perhaps a hundred feet deep and two hundred and fifty yards across. Entrance to the houses which hung like bird-cages far above our heads, is obtained by a bridge of rafters from the "mainland." This can be drawn up at night and it admits to a single tunnel-like street, between the crazy houses, which are rapidly falling down, and off which, in a high wind, children are continually blown. From the pointed end of the rock, in 1779, Zeki Khan caused eighteen villagers to be thrown because they refused to pay the exorbitant taxation imposed upon them. The last victim happened to be a Sayed, whose death so incensed the Khan's own soldiers that they cut the ropes of his tent while he was asleep and the villagers stabbed him to death as he struggled under the canvas.

In this most unsuitable spot, the driver, by this time wild-eyed and stammering, proposed to spend the night. "There are robbers on the road," he said without the slightest truth, but his miserable passengers rebelled.

"He wants to smoke opium," explained the Arab, and even the Persian lady burst into speech. For protection against the imaginary robbers, three soldiers were piled on top of the heaped mass within the wire grid which enclosed the truck at sides and back. The driver, forced from his "dreams of a soul's disentanglement," flung himself on to the seat beside me, and with a screech of gears we bumped into the night.

Bruised and breathless, I held on with both hands while we charged what appeared to be an endless series of walls and ditches, for, owing to the weight of the lorries which transport all goods from the Persian Gulf inland, the roads are little more than a miscellany of holes interspersed with rocks.

At intervals, the Arab murmured information, "All drivers on the southern roads take opium or cocaine. Otherwise their nerve would break. On the Shiraz-Bushire road, which is the worst in the world, there is one pass called 'the old woman,' with a hundred and thirty-two (hairpin) turns in eight miles, and at each turn a lorry must back ten or eleven times to get round."

After this I no longer wondered at the driver's nerves. By the time we reached Abadeh, the little man was in a state of frenzy. He crashed on his brakes in the middle of what appeared to be a rubbish-heap and left us for the nearest hovel where he could get a pipe. It was midnight. The village was deserted. We could hardly distinguish the outline of the mushroom-domed booths wherein are made carved sherbet spoons of pear and boxwood, the bowls as transparent as paper. The Arab however proved invaluable. With his help the Persian lady and I found refuge in the telegraph-khané, where we were regaled with "dogh," made of curdled sheep's milk, and where the jackals kept us awake with their pressing attentions.

Next day we were supposed to reach Shiraz by sunset, but it took some time to find the driver and more to rouse him from his poppy dreams. We jolted forth about eight AM and since the overloaded truck had to be refreshed with water every half-hour and Jehu would have gone mad had he been refused his midday pipe, sunset found us no further than Persepolis.

The palaces of Darius and Xerxes loomed above the plain. In the hall of a hundred columns, Alexander feasted his successful generals after the conquest of the known world. And on the lowest step of the great double flight, below the porch with the winged bulls derived from Nineveh, which lead to the "Great Kings'" hall of audience, sat a dervish. With his knife he tried to open a soda-water bottle for me and the result was a deep cut along his wrist. We all saw it. The blood dripped on to the bottle and stained the label. Then the dervish pressed his thumb along the cut and it disappeared. In its place there was a faint purple mark. "That is common work," said the Arab. "These men are holy and can control the flowing of their blood." Well, if it was a trick it was a good one, for the bottle was still smeared with red.

The first sight of Shiraz from the Teng Allahu Akbar Pass is supposed to elicit the exclamation, "God is Great!" from the lips of the grateful traveler who, after three hundred and fifteen miles of desert, looks down on the gardens of the poets' city.

> The Kazvinis steal our hearts, the Tabrizis have lips
>   like sugar
> Beautiful are the Isfahanis, but I am the slave of
>   Shiraz.

Sadi and Hafiz, best loved of Persian philosophic poets, are buried, each in a garden court where, under pomegranates, cypress and orange trees, their admirers drink tea and smoke their water-pipes.

Sadi, Sheikh Maslah ed Din, was born in 1193 and lived to be ninety-eight or a hundred. He led a varied existence, for he made no fewer than fourteen pilgrimages to Mecca, was at one time captured by Crusaders in Palestine and during extended travels in the East he adopted the religion of Vishnu. Later he is supposed to have reverted to Islam and became a Sunni, with the result that a particularly fanatical *Mujtahid* once destroyed his tombstone. Sadi's best known poems are "The Rose Garden" (Gulestan), "The Fruit Garden" (Bostan) and his Diwan.

Hafiz, or Mohammed Shems ed Din, died at Shiraz in 1388. Of the two he is probably the more popular poet, for though he praised wine, women, music and love, his work has the mystical undercurrent so necessary to the Persian mentality, which is always blaming the cruelty of unresponsive heaven and asking it for reasons. If any word could be found inscribed on a Persian heart it would be the question: "WHY?"

Shiraz is called Dar el Ulm (Seat of Learning) but its people are famous for their convivial habits. All the business of the town, export of tobacco, wine, opium and dried fruits, import of groceries, hardware and piece-goods, is done by strangers. Commerce is in the hands of Jews and of Babis or Bahais, who since the Pahlavi Government wisely removed all restrictions from this much persecuted philosophical sect, represent one of the most progressive elements in Persia. The Zoroastrians of Yezd and Kirman are their only rivals in the way of education and a business ability founded on tolerance.

The native Shirazi loathes work and loves a philosophical argument. As soon as he has made a few krans (fourpence), he borrows some more and, leaving the flat-roofed city, dominated by the domes of three imamzadés shaped like the tips of vast asparagus, their blue tiles hoary with grass—a city which knew the mercy of Genghis Khan and the brutality of Tamerlane—he sets forth to some walled garden where, as long as his money lasts, he will sit beside pulsing water under the shadow of fruit-trees, drink, smoke, play the lute and recite poetry with his friends.

In such a setting, I had a two-hour conversation with the General commanding at Shiraz. It is the avowed intention of the present government "to eliminate Russian influence in the North and British in the South." With the latter object in view the first order of this particularly keen soldier was that none of his officers should hold any communication with foreigners. "For three thousand years we have been lords of Persia," he said; "but during the last century the Persian has been intimidated by foreigners. Only by encouraging a certain arrogance, can we make him realize that he is the heir to a mighty past. Now we are in a halfway stage which is unpleasant, but it is necessary if the Persian, who is gentle by nature, is to be sure of himself. Civilization is different for every country. For us it must mean a hardening of the national character and a temporary isolation which will make us self-sufficient."

Concerning the Chauvinism of Tehran, the *Amir-el-Ashkar* fenced with typical Persian adroitness: "Madame, I am but a simple soldier"; but when, at the end of our verbal battle, I asked him if he had visited the tomb of Hafiz, his whole face changed. "How could I fail to do that?" he exclaimed, and the poet leaped to life in the soldier. So it is with the older generation of Persians, but, among the younger, the talk is generally of money. It is exceedingly expensive to turn the East into the West and the Pahlavi Government is determined to do it in one generation.

But the native Shirazi, remembering the days when "Shiraz was Shiraz and Cairo one of its suburbs," is less interested in economies and the introduction of civilization by means of a standardized dress, than he is in wine, women and song. Since the days when a conqueror demanded two hundred maunds[1] weight of eyes as punishment for the town's defiance, and the women of Shiraz had to give themselves to his soldiers to save their sight, they have been reputed exceedingly free in their morals. In this pleasure-loving town, the chudda is very short, flesh silk stockings are at a premium, small feet are thrust into the highest heeled shoes and the ruband (a long, white veil) is so cleverly manipulated that it suggests an invitation.

---

1 A maund weighs thirteen-and-a-half pounds.

Through the Mountains of Kurdistan

W HEN THE TIME came for me to leave Kurdistan, I determined to do so by the new road which will eventually link Tabriz with Mosul. This route, when completed, may prove to be one of the most profitable highways in Central Asia. For Persia it will probably mean freedom from the Russian market, because direct communication with Iraq will enable her to import the machinery necessary for the agricultural development of her fertile northern provinces from any European port she chooses, whereas at present she is obliged to purchase inferior implements at exorbitant prices from Soviet Russia.

The railways and the northern cities of Iraq will benefit because of the increase in goods and passenger traffic, and if the road is properly kept up—at an estimated cost of half a lac of rupees a year until the bitumen sealing is completed, after which a fifth of that sum will suffice—it should be the pilgrim route between the Holy cities of the Hedjaz and the whole of Western Persia.

To Iraq and to her energetic neighbor the strategic value of a road which opens the heart of Kurdistan must be incalculable, for both countries have suffered from the war-like propensities of the mountaineers who, fortified among their hitherto impregnable passes seven thousand feet high, by winter snows and summer drought, have raided whichever side of the frontier offered best hope of plunder.

During the last six years British influence and the presence of the redoubtable Assyrian levies on their frontier have done much to quell the turbulence of a race which regards raiding as the finest possible sport. Aziz Agha, headman of Busserini, through whose incredible gorge, hitherto unpenetrated except by an exiguous and very dangerous mule-track, the new road is already pushing its way, explained with naïve amazement, "It is strange. Before the coming of the British I could never come down from the mountain without an armed force. The village was deserted and the fields untilled. Now, I see men working among their crops with no rifles on their backs and the sight is curious."

But the Kurd is still unconquered among his rocks. He pays unwilling tribute to the Iraq Government, which he regards as alien and inferior because, barring the stalwart Assyrian Christian, he is the finest fighter on the Asiatic border, and equally unwilling homage to the British who defeated him on his own ground. In theory, he would like an independent Kurdistan, united as far as any tribal community can ever be, but there is no love lost between the leaders of the various clans situated on Persian, Turkish and Iraqi soil. A measure of civilization may come to them with the trade which will flow along the new road, but until their standard of living is raised by the opportunity to barter their agricultural produce, their hides, wool and felts for the European goods passing between Mosul and Azerbaijan, they will remain a threat to the peace of three countries. For the only merchandise in which at present they are interested is expanding bullets, and during the ten days I wandered south from Mount Ararat towards the road-camps in South-west Persia and Northern Iraq, the only pegs on which I could hang my discarded clothes at night were the triggers of rifles slung on mud walls, or the center poles of tents.

The Persian Colonel commanding at Urumeya had been kind enough to inform the sergeant in charge at Nagadieh of my imminent arrival. It happened that I was a fortnight late and it seems that time in modern Persia means considerably more than it did under the old régime, for a soldier stationed outside the village to watch the only track by which anyone could approach, greeted me with approximately these words: "Here have I been sitting on this mound for fourteen days and three hours. It pleases me that you did not delay any further, or the saddles would have worn into the backs of the horses which have so long awaited you."

The influence of the new road begins at Nagadieh from where Kurdish transport now crosses the barrier range in three or four marches. Here I hired a couple of stalwart mountain ponies with a guide attired in vast goat's-hair garments, belted with twenty yards of sash, in which he stuck all the necessities of his existence, tobacco, a couple of murderous knives, an odd coil of rope, a very dirty handkerchief with some coins tied in one corner, and a supply of local bread. The Persian Army supplied me with an excellent riding-horse and a charming companion in the person of Sergeant-Major Hussein Khan. Unfortunately we couldn't speak a word of each other's language, but both he and the two troopers who accompanied him were exceedingly efficient in dealing with the minor difficulties of the situation.

We started forth at three PM with the optimistic intention of reaching the frontier post of Khané, about thirty-two miles away, that night, but we'd reckoned without the baggage which strewed itself over the plain whenever the charvadar (muleteer) urged his animals out of a walk. Consequently, when we reached

Galvan, a small Kurdish village set on a hummock in the plain, the sun was setting and we were glad to accept the headman's hospitality. His house consisted of one large mud room, the further half raised some three feet as if it were a platform and protected from the animals and chickens, which huddled among a miscellany of vivid quilts below, by an eighteen-inch wall. This portion was carpeted and surrounded by rolls of well-stuffed bedding against which we leaned while we ate saucers of cherry jam and drank equally sweet tea. The walls were hung with rifles, embroidered saddle-cloths, and the ribbed brown felt waistcoats worn by the Turko-Persian Kurds. After a lengthy conversation conducted chiefly by signs, a huge tray of sheep's cheese, "mast" (a junket made of curdled buffalo-milk), onions, cucumbers and the sheet-bread which is thin as newspaper, was brought in and when the soldiers had withdrawn, it was followed by my host's wife. She was immensely ponderous, with neat black hair and a rolling gait. Her waves of flesh were immersed in yards and yards of spotted white cotton, and once she had sunk on to the floor she appeared incapable of movement.

Other women came in, strong-featured and sunburned. They wore red and black striped turbans set at a rakish angle, with a chin-strap fastened above each ear by a tasseled ornament. Their short velvet jackets, brilliant green or violet, were embroidered with gold and worn above a straight black robe, which in its turn was lost in unnumbered yards of striped cotton skirt, the whole being surmounted by a floppy red and white sheet which had no visible fastening.

It was very late when I was led through the dim mud streets, splashed with moonlight and thick with dust. Gone was modern Persia and the Pahlavi hat. On the flat roofs, a few mightily turbaned figures were engaged in the last of the day's five prayers. Goats were spread round the houses like a thick, dark carpet.

Boys, perched on the backs of dust-gray water-buffalos, sang odd little songs to encourage their unwieldy steeds.

My camp-bed had been erected in a hermetically sealed hut, in which it was obvious that the Sergeant-Major, who evidently regarded me as a beefeater holding the keys of the Jewel Tower, was also determined to sleep. My Persian was sufficient to acquire "a large basin," *i.e.* the family baking-tin in which to wash, but quite inadequate to dislodge the self-appointed Cerberus. As soon as he saw me laid upon the camp-bed and already involved in warfare with a homemade mosquito net, he stretched himself on a straw mat across the door, placed his sword under his head and his revolver at full cock beside him. I hoped he would not have a nightmare.

It was not a peaceful night. By twelve o'clock the vocal duel between the village dogs and the jackals who defied them was at operatic pitch. A dust storm scattered bits of the mud and thatched roof over our unprotected persons. At frequent intervals the troopers held what they imagined to be whispered conversation with the Sergeant-Major. Between whiles they sang in minor thirds. At four AM someone shook me and said it was after six.

However it was a cool morning, and after more unleavened bread, flavored this time with a bowl of sour milk mixed with chopped herbs, we started off across a band of hills glued as if for ornament along the edges of a plain. Desert Persia, burned a reddish brown and scarred with salt of the Kavir, was banished once for all. Here was grain for mile after scented mile and the barley, wheat and millet were interspersed with masses of single hollyhocks. There were splashes of petunia, blue and yellow painted across the downlands which were velveted with short, fine turf like the horns of a stag.

All travelers were armed, and some of the women carried a rifle on their shoulders and a baby slung below it. Monstrous wagons,

mounted on solid wooden circles, creaked behind teams of buf-
falos with large and splendid young men, huge-girthed and fair-
haired, lying across their rifles, asleep, but always one strode
watchfully in front.

Kurdish villages appeared like mud terraces, the roof of one
hovel forming a platform in front of the door of another, so that
seen from above, the hillsides looked as if they had been terraced
for sowing. Among the crops, men worked with their striped, bal-
loon-like trousers tucked into felt leggings and the six or eight-
feet sleeves of their white cotton garments turned up as cuffs and
then tied above the elbow.

This time we left the baggage to look after itself and ambled
at an excruciating pace, neither walk nor canter, to Khané at the
foot of the frontier range, up which Persia is rapidly pushing her
end of the new road. Here the gradients are easy. There are no
rocks to blast, no gorges to manipulate, no river to bridge, and
the tents of her engineers are climbing steadily towards the watershed. By the end of 1931, it is hoped to reach the frontier of Iraqi
Kurdistan, and when this happens Persia will be able to congratu-
late herself on a success justly due to native enterprise and energy.

At Khané there is a small customs post like a clay bandbox
dropped in the middle of a plain. There is also a detachment
of frontier guards under the Nayib Dedache Khan, who kindly
offered me his mud hut, seven feet by four, but I elected to pitch
my bed among the ankle-deep grass beside a stream clear and ice-
cold from the mountains. From there I could watch an exception-
ally interesting scene, for it happened that Hadji Garani Agha,
Amir of the Ashahiri tribe, had just returned from the pilgrimage
to Mecca and more than five hundred horsemen had assembled
to kiss his hand, or his garments, as he crossed the frontier.

A crop of tents grew up like mushrooms. The plain was alive
with horses, whose tails, swishing a continual protest against

hordes of insects, were like wind-driven grass. As for the warriors, they were splendid beyond description and as the spines of a hedgehog so were the arms with which they bristled.

The great among them joined the Agha in a huge tent and their rifles were stacked outside. A row of large brass samovars provided relays of tea. Gaily colored pots, probably from Moscow or Kharkoff, steamed on the top of metal funnels, and servants carrying glasses half filled with sugar passed in and out under the flaps. The Agha's son, a boy of twelve, wore his gigantic width of trousers stuffed into cavalry boots. His fringed turban was four times the size of his head and he told me with pride that there were forty yards of material in his intricately knotted sash. Among his companions, there were some overalls of lime-yellow cloth immensely wide in leg and blouse, surmounted by wasp-striped waistcoats and turbans in which black and yellow predominated. Other tribesmen wore emerald velvet jackets and such an amount of sash that when they rode at full gallop from one tent to another or indulged in wild races, ending in a mounted wrestling match, a tug-of-war which was only decided when one competitor lost his seat, or a powder display in which rifles were fired with a careless abandon that ended in several being wounded, they looked like a couple of balloons surmounted by a life-belt, with a proportionately small torso emerging for just that amount of space between the chest and another gigantic balloon in the shape of a turban.

Darkness put an end to the racing, in which each vainglorious chieftain "matched" his horse and so many tomans against another that he coveted. If he won, the rival mount was handed over to him. If he lost, his steed as well as the money with which he had backed its prowess went to his antagonist. The evening prayers were a gorgeous spectacle, when, after ablutions in the stream from which everyone simultaneously drank, the tribesmen ranged themselves behind the newly returned pilgrim and thundered their worship toward the Meccan Ka-aba, over whose exact position there had been considerable argument.

I had hardly arranged my inadequate defenses against the plague of mosquitoes, when a storm arose and with the suddenness habitual to Central Asia, blew me head over heels into a crop of corn. My bed went with me, and we bowled merrily into a group of Kurds who had lingered over a starlit meal of bread, chopped onions and sour goat's milk. They arrested my progress, picked my pillow out of a bowl of "dogh" and kindly offered me a share of their tent. With gratitude I accepted, and as portions of my bedding had gone astray in the dust which belched out of the plain as if a funnel were on fire, I lay between quilts provided by my hosts and was devoured by every form of bug. Nevertheless, towards the dawn, I slept and was roused by what I imagined an earthquake. Actually, it was an unknown Kurd vigorously shaking my shoulders and repeating: "Must I travel to Mosul alone? The mountains are dangerous, and you have soldiers with you. Wake them—it is not good to sleep so much—and we will ride together."

An hour later, we were climbing up the frontier slopes, watching the new road sketched above and below us. A horde of laborers, Persians and Assyrians, Turks, Kurds and Armenians, with a considerable number of Russian refugees and a few odd Turkoman, Indians and Levantines worked on its ever-growing tentacle, the indication of a great ideal which must develop into an international highway bearing the commerce and the civilization of peace into a mountain-land which has lived only by war.

For twelve or fourteen miles between the frontier posts of Persia and Iraq, the aggressive peaks, streaked with snow and smooth as metal, offer insecure refuge to outlaws who own no nationality. This no-man's-land used to be a haunt of the redoubtable Simko who, during the War, murdered under his own roof, the last Mar Shimun, head of the Nestorian Church. Having been outlawed by Iraq, Turkey and Persia, he raided the three frontiers in turn, until a few weeks after my uneventful passage, he was surprised and killed by a Persian patrol.

Between gray limestone and barren shale, we climbed slowly, driving the baggage in front of us in spite of the protests of the guide, whom we had mounted on a mule of noble appearance and vile temper. After four hours' ride we reached the summit and saw the flattened roofs of Rayat promising food and a change of horses, for our small Arab stallions, grass-fed, had done two fairly long marches and having worked themselves into unbridled frenzy at the approach of any rival, with accompanying plunges, bucks and whinnies, they were now feeling the heat.

The hospitable Effendi in charge of the Iraq Customs fed us on the best "mast" (sour junket) I'd yet tasted, and sent me down the pass with an escort of the Iraq Mounted Police, large, fair, sunburned men, exceedingly smart and soldierly. Their horses were well groomed, their saddlery and equipment splendidly kept, and they looked like a British outpost, than which no higher compliment can be paid.

Within the next two years, the Government of Iraq will doubtless have completed the road which, with commendable foresight, it is making from Erbil in the plains east of Mosul to the Persian frontier, where it will join the new route to Azerbaijan. Seventy-five out of the projected hundred and sixteen miles have already been completed, though the surfacing is not yet finished. Innumerable difficulties have been surmounted, for the portion of the road already constructed passes through the Rowanduz Gorge, where previously there wasn't even a camel track, and where walls of rock rise a sheer five hundred feet out of the rapids of a river which is a tributary of the greater Zab. During last summer, five hundred men were employed between Rowanduz and the Busserini Gorge, where the road halts forty-five miles from the frontier. The average laborer was paid one rupee a day, skilled drillers two rupees, eight annas, and tradesmen up to four rupees. Already, five metal bridges had been thrown across a river which used only to be spanned by swaying structures of withes or branches, three feet wide, slung between protruding rocks sixty feet above the torrent.

The annual budget of Iraq is only six hundred lacs, yet realizing the importance of a highway which will bring her the trade of Western Persia and allow her to export her own and European goods straight into her neighbor's richest provinces, she has wisely authorized an expenditure of twenty-seven lacs of rupees on what will eventually be one of the main arteries of Central Asia. Ten and a half lacs have already been spent, and the Iraq Government is to be congratulated on a remarkable engineering feat, for Erbil, the southern terminus of the new road, has an altitude of a thousand feet above sea level, whereas the pass of Rayat rises in a series of precipitous limestone crags, showing the complete range of oil-bearing strata, to five thousand five hundred feet. The maximum gradient of the road will be one in twenty, but the mule track down which I rode from Rayat on a blistering July day, with the mercury soaring over 107° Fahrenheit, showed a gradient of one in five. It reveled in sudden descents where the path was the width of a wrist-watch strap, sloping outwards so that it seemed as if no animal could possibly avoid slipping into the chasm below.

For four hours we rode into the blaze of the westering sun. The animal I bestrode was an army horse. Without a martingale, it held its head on a level with my own. Whenever the track ceased to exist, it leaped forward in a series of bounds which covered considerable horizontal and little vertical space. The upcurved cantle of the army saddle came into violent contact with flesh already raw from Kurdish pommels. The rifle in its leather bucket flogged my heel whenever my mount skipped more vigorously than usual.

The heat was refracted from igneous rocks, and even the scenery, as magnificent between the scrub oak fringing the stream and the mighty peaks, iron gray or blinding white, as any out of the Himalayas, was insufficient to comfort me for the unending slither of a descent which prophesied at every moment a fall on to the boulders hundreds of feet below.

At last we turned aside and climbed the overthrust mass of rock, last spur of the Persian plateau, on which is plastered the village of Gellala. Each house looks down from a separate hillock on to the roof of its neighbor, and for this crag-guarded ravine, the sun sets in mid-summer shortly after five.

A little doubtfully, the clean-shaven Iraqi policeman suggested I might sleep in the Mudir's office. It was littered with cigarette ends and unsatisfied suppliants, each feeling that the only thing which mattered in the world was his own particular case. Large and squelchy tarantulas decorated the walls.

I protested, and the sound of a feminine voice roused the Mudir from his afternoon's rest. Satisfying his hospitable instincts, he hurried me up a low-roofed, twisting stair, each step a separate mountain, through an apartment crowded with humanity and cooking-pots, and so into the usual Eastern room, mud-walled, with cucumber skins and ashes littering the earthen floor between the carpets, traveling chests and bundles of clothing which flanked the walls. But, to me at least, there was nothing usual about the three women smoking long native cigarettes in a corner by a tiny window. They were Kurds, like everyone else in the village, and sisters, but they came of a great family and they might have stepped out of the pages of a medieval Missal. Dulac would have painted nothing else for the rest of his life. The most beautiful was the wife of the Mudir. She was tall and very pale, with thin, closely shut lips. The bones of her face were perfect and her eyes deep-set between the molded cheek-bones and an exquisite brow, so that their darkness brooded mysteriously under a thicket of lashes. Her hair was the soft black, tip-tilted at the end, as all the best Bond Street bobs, and it fell to just the right length below her ears. She moved slowly, with a strange and supple dignity. Her hands were long and very fine, and there was the individuality of a Medici in the way she held a cigarette. But it was her clothes— the clothes of all three of them—that made me incoherent for the rest of the evening.

The Mudir's wife wore long tight-fitting trousers and I suspect a wadded petticoat to her ankles, but they were disguised by a flowing robe of semi-transparent apricot muslin powdered with mist-blue flowers. Over this was a royal garment, a long brocaded coat of sapphire and gold with tight sleeves. It was stiffened and lined with cramoisie, so that it stood out like the court dresses of the Renaissance. Round her shoulders was a scarf, a web of blue woven with gold, the ends crossed in front and tied behind her back. A gold chain bearing amulet cases of the same precious metal hung below her waist, and on her head the lady who should have been a medieval queen, wore a cap sewn with golden coins, from which depended strings of coral, other larger coins and small satin-covered sachets containing amulets. A gold chin-strap hung with tiny ornaments held the cap in place and round the edge of it was swathed yards and yards of fine black silk bordered with round tassels which stuck up or out anywhere like expect-ant blackbirds. The ends of this scarf were tied behind the head and hung to the knees in a cascade of tassels, and the whole thing was held in place by two strings of gold and uncut stones which depended from the cap and were looped back over the scarf in a glittering, faintly tinkling fringe. This exquisite being made me lie down on the best carpet, fanned me as I gasped in the dry heat, refused me more than half a bucketful of water, fed me on rice steeped in sour milk and mixed with powdered herbs. Finally

when it was night, she led me up on to the roof, which was surrounded by a stockade of dried branches inadequately shielding
it from the police post on a still higher ledge, where she bade me
take my choice of the gaily colored bedding. I chose a fuchsia colored quilt and a violet pillow, and then asked hopefully for water.

A chased silver ewer was brought and a trickle poured over my
finger-tips. Firmly I seized the jug and removed the fretted cover
from a bowl the size of a breakfast cup. At least a dozen women
gathered round to see what I would do. Old rose, marigold yellow and the blue of midnight skies, their brocaded robes made a
wall around me. Only their faces and their finger-tips were visible amidst the splendor of their garments. My courage failed me.
Removing my riding boots, I crept unwashed beneath the quilts.
My hostess sighed with relief and discarding her turban, established herself comfortably beside me.

I remembered another night, during which I had slept in the
house of an Assyrian peasant in the Turko-Kurdish mountains.
The same rows of quilts, shabbier but quite as thick, were laid
side by side on a mud platform in the yard, where chickens, goats
and a couple of dogs wandered at will. I chose the end place, and
was afterwards much relieved, for men and women undressed
beneath the coverings, and having nonchalantly stacked their garments under their heads, went to sleep naked as they were born.

We started late next morning because sunrise did not reach
the roofs of Gellala till the plains had baked for hours. Down
we went, on foot where the track was no more than a cascade of
rocks, on mules where it widened slightly between crags of shale.
The Kurdish headman of Rowanduz, a tall, fair young man with
turban and mustaches waving in the wind and a whole range of
saddle cloths, petunia and mustard yellow, rode with us on an
unbroken three-year-old, because he was carrying money under
his sash. We passed one village flattened on the edge of the river,

so that its roofs looked like three terraces prepared for sowing. The inhabitants were all lying under trees round a samovar, from which they gave us tea. After this we climbed steadily till, in spite of the protests of the Assyrian police who had accompanied me from Gellala, I insisted on leaving the track to visit the Kurdish village of Dergela. Here we were most hospitably received by the headman, Mohammed Emin Beg. During the worst heat we sat round a tank sunk under an arbor of vines and drank sour goat's milk out of beautifully carved wooden ladles with wide handles, thin as paper, and bowls four inches deep.

We learned that eighty Assyrian families, fugitives from Russia, had passed through Azerbaijan and crossed the Persian frontier, but had been refused admittance into Iraq, so that, without food or shelter, they were now stranded in the bleak no-man's-land near the Khanishu Pass. Such treatment of a people who were our allies during the Great War and who, after giving up their homes and lands in the mountains near Julamerk in the extreme south-eastern corner of Turkish Kurdistan, in order to fight on our side against the invaders of Persia, asked nothing at the Peace Conference except that their old territory should be included in a British protectorate, reflects little credit on our own authorities. It is also exceedingly short-sighted policy on the part of the Baghdad Government, for it would be greatly to their advantage to settle numbers of Assyrian Christians along the turbulent Kurdish frontier.

Under the Turks, the Kurdish mountaineers paid, in theory, the equivalent of one anna per head of sheep or cattle. In practice it was rarely collected. Since the inception of an Arab Iraq, their taxes have been increased six-fold, and with the aid of British officials, backed by the Air Force and by the Assyrian Levies, the only native troops capable of standing up to the Kurds during Sheikh Mahmoud's rebellion of 1923, they have been regularly collected.

Since the British inspectors from the Ministry of the Interior have been removed from this area, the Kurds complain of the exactions of Iraqi officials, who are biased in favor of their Arab dependents, and in accordance with a tradition which it will take generations of training to eradicate, prepared to enrich themselves inordinately during their terms of office.

If the Air Force is removed from Mosul, it is easy to prophesy that no more Kurdish taxes will be paid. The Iraq army would have no chance of coping with the mountaineers on their own ground unless backed by the wholehearted support of the Christian minorities, all of whom, Armenians, Chaldeans, Assyrians, Baptists, should be encouraged to form a settled barrier between the Arabs of the Mesopotamian plains and their hereditary enemies in the passes of Kurdistan.

After leaving Dergela, four hours' ride along the Rowanduz river, sometimes a thousand feet above it, sometimes level with its rapids, brought us to the scene of road-making. Before fording a gorge where drills had already been at work, we saw the line of the road scarred across the opposite cliffs. Part of a bridge was suspended in mid-air and on the end of it, a man sat casually regarding eternity. Air compressors were driving the twenty-foot tubes filled with gelignite into overhanging crags and the roar of blasting shook the pass. But the noise stopped with the sunset and when we reached the coolie camp at Jinjaan, a hundred fires twinkled in front of the tents. Every kind of cooking pot steamed with the evening meal. All sorts and conditions of men were strewn in various stages of undress amidst bright colored bedding. In the semi-darkness, the scene resembled an ancient color-print of a shipwreck, for the men were stripped like castaways and they were of all types. Momentarily exhausted, they had flung themselves down amidst what might well be salvage. One, flat on his back, wore dungarees and a felt hat. Beside him was a dervish in scarlet loin-cloth and turban. Here a fair-haired youth, sun-burned so that his skin looked darker than his khaki shirt, pillowed his head on an outflung arm, while his companion, with shaven bullet head and a hirsute torso, revealed by his torn Russian blouse, stirred the rations in an Australian "billy." There a Persian tribesman with black, curling beard shared a quilt with a red-headed lout from the coast. In all tongues they greeted us, their god the road and their only interest, "How far has it gone on the other side of the frontier?"

An hour later, we reached the headquarters of the first Assyrian Battalion of the Iraq Levies, the frontier post of three peoples, where the British flag flies over a sentry-box that looks as if it had come out of Noah's Ark. Here, since the formation of this extremely efficient Christian force, which keeps peace on a Moslem border, the village of Diana has grown up with a population of three or four hundred Nestorian families all engaged in agriculture. Out of the raw material represented by exiled mountaineers, part of that tragic exodus of 1917 which left twenty-five thousand dead among the passes of Azerbaijan, and which, encumbered with women and children, harried by Persian and Turk, fought its way south to the refugee camps of the Tigris, have been created troops of which Iraq has every reason to be proud.

The tents which cluster under the crumpled Kurdish hills above the gorge of Rowanduz, with its five openings sprawled among the cliffs like the tentacles of an octopus, are to be replaced by hutments made of mud bricks. On this work, a whole company was apparently engaged and these stalwart soldiers, smart as any British unit, with scarlet ospreys in their khaki felts, were turning out sun-baked bricks at a pace which would disturb the average Trade Union laborer. The neatness of their lines was so insistent that I thought of the villages on the Urumeyan plain or in the highlands of Julamerk, from which the Assyrians came.

From a distance the orderliness of the camp was that of a child's playthings neatly arranged in the wilderness. And in the intervals of patrolling an armed frontier, the NCO's attended elementary classes held by their priest in a school which they have built themselves. But the childishness of Diana ends with the primers and with the Noah's Ark aspect of the camp. Westwards the plains are scarred and cracked by a temperature of 112° to 125° Fahrenheit. The surrounding mountains are a chaos of rocks, the highest ranges seamed with glaciers. They shelter the lawlessness and the treachery of the Kurd, for whom the Arab villager is a natural prey. If justification be needed for British colonization, alternately ridiculed and maligned since every inchoate collection of tribes has been united, spasmodically and uneasily, by the will o' the wisp of self-determination, it may be found in such places as Diana, where the work of the individual Englishman means the security of a frontier.

Beyond Diana the new road runs through a gorge which was the limit of the Russian advance in 1915, and thereafter climbs successive ridges till it fords the Greater Zab and passes into the plain of Mosul with Nineveh as its goal. Along it, or within range of it, are settled most of the Minorities which engage the attention of Leagues and Conferences. Here are Mandaeans and Manichaeans, Sabaeans who call themselves Christians of St. John, the devil-worshiping Yezidis and a dozen sects of Protestants and Catholics, not to mention the survivors of the ancient cults of the Moon and the Fish, Zoroastrians, Chaldeans and Nestorians.

When I came down the road in July, the conditions of the Anglo-Iraq treaty had just been published in the local papers, and at every village between Erbil and Jebel Sinjar, where the heroic rais of the Yezidis protected three thousand Armenian fugitives during the War, I was asked: "What guarantee of safety have we if the British leave Iraq?"

Merchants and cultivators were already considering a premature emigration into Syria, so it would appear that the first duty of independent Iraq must be the reassurance of the Christian and other Minorities on whom depends the stability and to a large extent the commercial prosperity of the North.

The test of any civilization is its treatment of minorities, racial, religious and political. If the Iraq of the future is to be a stabilizing factor in the region which has always been a bridge between East and West, she must conquer what appears to be the natural impulse of all new states to ignore or repress the voices of minorities. The road through Kurdistan will be an important addition to the trade arteries of Arabia and Asia, but its value will be lost unless it runs through peaceful country whose tradesmen and agriculturalists, whatever their origin or creed, have full confidence in the government, from whom as law-abiding subjects they are entitled to the fullest possible consideration.

1937

From Kabul to Samarkand

From Chapters XI, XII, XVII, XVIII, XX, XXI, and
XLIII of *Forbidden Road: Kabul to Samarkand*
(1937)

The Nomads' Road to Kabul

ROM THE KHYBER to Kabul, I saw the road as a moving string of camels. The nomads, who had spent the six months of winter in India wandering as far south as Calcutta and the ports of the Western Ocean, were returning to their mountains. The great serai at Dakhr could not hold a tenth part of the animals laden with merchandise, tents, and bedding. Huge, shaggy beasts, with tassels hanging among the folds of fur, filled the lane between rows of tea-booths. They looked as if they wore stockings and mufflers. I suppose they had put on their thickest coats for the journey, but the material was beginning to wear thin. Hip-bones and shoulders protruded from the woolly coverings. They were proud beggars, those camels, with their magnificent fur in tatters.

As shaggy and as loosely covered were the huge men in pushtins who mingled with them on the most intimate terms. Or perhaps they were quite small inside their colossal leather coats, the raw hide embroidered with orange and lined with sheep's fleece, the unused sleeves standing out in peaks. Each pushtin had the appearance of walking about by itself. The owners had wine-dark faces with the boldly curved noses of Jew or Roman and though they wore all sorts of haphazard headgear, from hateful little woollen caps, mass-woven somewhere in a sweated civilisation, to turbans biblical in volume, there was enough red and blue about their persons to maintain the illusion of Asia.

The women had the same arrogant noses and a flush of red under their brown. They were covered with silver. It was sewn on to their sleeves and spread in a breastplate of coins upon their bosoms. It hung in fringes on their foreheads and made fans below their ears. It imprisoned their ankles, sheathed their arms from wrists to elbows. Each woman was a banking-account, recording her husband's prosperity. And some of them were beautiful as well, with a sun-ripened, fruit-like beauty, and hair wrought into many plaits.

I admired those women. They were bold and active, prodigal of movement. They were like Joseph, in coats of many colours. Their skirts blazed with bands of red and yellow set upon black, and they walked all in a piece without movement of hip or shoulder. They never looked at the ground. With their shoes upon their heads they trod sublimely, bare-footed over sand and rock.

The camels looped upon an unending string. The men sat on the shelves of the tea cupboards, their legs tucked under them, their lips moist and drooping, bowls of pale green liquid in their hands, water-pipes beside them. The women shouted as they strove with the camels. Their children and the young of other species, kids, lambs, and puppies, were piled high above the humps, from which they looked as if they must immediately fall.

My lorry, loaded with benzene, from Peshawar to the frontier no more than a cheap means of conveyance, became a red Bucephalus. Simultaneously, it was one of those small, stalwart horses, thick of neck and coat, astride which the proud lords of Persia fought the invading Tartars, or the Moghuls hewed their way to the rape of India. It charged among the camels and its driver waxed mightily indignant. His father had been in the Sind Horse, but he, an Afridi, loved machinery. Gesturing splendidly among the turmoil of beasts he had no hands left to drive. The women shrieked and strained against the lumbering towers of camel. Ropes broke. The engine over-heated. Boxes of tea and bales originating in Japan, became intimately involved with our benzene barrels. Tails went up, loads were shed. Bucephalus bucked forward. And this went on for two days.

No doubt at intervals the road was clear. I remember one evening, a well-dressed man in brown praying all alone in the middle of a desert. There was no village within sight, yet he remained unhurried and imperturbable. As he knelt upon the sand, he contrived to interpose his state of mind as a barrier to protect him from his own and everyone else's activities. I thought of him at the time as a pilgrim who had discarded for a space the habiliments and the countenance he usually wore.

At another time, the road ran rough between a waste of stones, the graves of the third Afghan war. The driver shivered as we passed. "There are too many dead. The earth is restless. It moves—" He became a politician, as is the habit of India. "This is what you have done and now you want friendship after one hundred years of blood. You hope the young will forget, but in the schools they are saying that it was the tribes who fought you. It was with them you had a quarrel, yet you left the mountains unpunished and destroyed the towns." With the last words he put a hand on his breast, and the terrible humility of India overcame him. "I am a poor man. I understand nothing of these things."

The plain broke into villages. All of them had mighty walls. They looked strong and prosperous. Yellow mustard gilded the land. There was no sign of the intrusive poverty in which an Indian village heaps together its dust and sores, its dogs, children, and the remnants of its hovels. Those villages were defiant and completely self-sufficient. "The richer the peasants, the poorer the Government," said a man who had asked for a lift. After that he talked a great deal. He said, "The Afghan has only one vice and it is hospitality. If he has fattened a chicken for weeks to eat it with his family at some little celebration, he will kill it, without a thought, for a guest. He is the friendliest and the most suspicious of men. His obstinacy is only equalled by his desire to serve his friends and destroy his enemies. The Afghan—well I am an Afghan."

He might have added, "and the citizen of no mean country."

On the second day we left what I had imagined were the mountains and came to the real mountains. Bucephalus misbehaved. It was the camels who passed us with their scornful heads averted and that staccato gait, so detached from the earth, that suggests tortoises on stilts. The lorry made intractable noises, while we all gathered snow and packed it under the bonnet. We threw handfuls of snow at the radiator and forced more into it. I don't know what this effected, but with the help of amused peasants who emerged, earth-coloured out of the earth, we incited Bucephalus to movement and leaped hopefully into our places. After a few hundred yards we stopped again among a host of donkeys whose patchwork loads made a quilt upon the road. More snow. More help from camel-men and tent-dwellers.

Occasionally a nomad in an immense quantity of coats hailed us with a greeting originally Australian. If he had not himself acquired it selling camels or rugs in the Southern hemisphere, he had no doubt inherited it from a parent. "All Afghan carpet merchants marry Australians," explained the driver. Pressed as to the accuracy of his statement he modified it. There had been, he said an Abdul Wahid, known some thousand miles further south as Mr. Wade. There had also been a fierce red-headed woman called Kate, who had ruled a tribe with her tongue. She swore louder and with greater variations than anyone else in the country, but this was long ago. Perhaps such marriages did not happen nowadays. He added that the price of wives was falling.

For interminable hours we laboured up a road that deserved better of us, for it was well made and not too rough. We exchanged compliments and condolences with other red lorries quiescent in peculiar positions. We helped to push. We were ourselves most generously pushed. At one moment we made a forward rush, result of much snow poulticed over the more feverered portions of the engine, and at the next, most of the floor fell out. The hands of strangers replaced it. The barrels were re-arranged, and the owners of the hands ensured further disaster by adding themselves to our load. And all this among the same slow turmoil of beast and driver. So that the road moved with us and in the end we became part of the caravan with which at the moment we were confused.

Kabul

ABUL HAS A beauty like nothing else on earth. The Afghans do not appreciate their capital because it is not sufficiently modern. They long for the traffic of London, the buildings of Paris, and the inconveniences of every American "burg." With an infinity of charm they explain that Kabul is only beginning and they are so sad about it, and at the same time so proud, that one dare not draw their attention to the mountain setting or tell them that Kabul has only one rival—Santiago in the Andes.

"We are building schools and hospitals—" they say, and it is true. There are a number of modern buildings, simple in design and well placed beside the river or at the end of long avenues. In fact the new Kabul, clean, quiet, spacious, has a good deal to recommend it. There is a Nordic air about the canals, the shorn white trees in winter, the unbroken line of the walls, the white paint or the grey, and the orderly restraint which applies to the demeanour of the people as well as to the style of their architecture. But this is an acquired effect. It is not yet Afghanistan.

The country is so individual that it merits more original expression in its capital and this it finds in the great walls which fling themselves over the hills above the fortress of Bala Hissar.

In the contrast between the plain where Kabul lies, an earth-coloured city splashed by the new white buildings, the new grey roofs of barracks, palaces, and colleges, and the mountain ramparts so much more brilliantly white which enclose it, in this sharp insistence on change where for thousands of years men have dwelt too near the earth to need anything else, lies the challenge which contemporary Afghans fling at Afghanistan.

The plain holds a lake delicately blue. It is shadowed with a mist of poplars. In Spring, the villages, each surrounded with smooth splendid walls, stand deep in fruit blossom. It is a flood of red and rose-colour spreading over the earth. Only the watch towers rise out of it, and the broken bastions from which the last rebel, Bacha i Saqan, shelled the town. Around the plain there are mountains and they are not feather-smooth like the Sierra near Granada, which reminded Osbert Sitwell of the "wings of angry swans." They are rugged under the snow. Clouds add to their height and shadows deepen their ice blues and greens into the purples of a storm-driven sea. But on a clear day they are white, and I have never looked at them without surprise. They are nearer to the city than most mountains, and more final. The country needs no other defence and certainly no further justification.

The Afghans, perhaps, have ceased to see their mountains except as barriers to invasion, and to the mechanised civilisation they long to impose upon a land familiar to Alexander, Genghis Khan, and Akbar. But in moments of relaxation they play tribute to their orchards, to the foam and froth of blossom breaking against the poplars.

The bazaars present a more difficult problem. They may be dirty. They are certainly old-fashioned if the term can suitably be applied to Abraham or Mohammed. But they are, as surely, beautiful although the Afghans who know Paris or London refuse to acknowledge it. Instead of an ancient tapestry in which each figure has its value, they see tribesmen who will insist on wearing too many garments and all of them the wrong shape. They see townsmen who will sit on their feet instead of on chairs. Instead of a diapason of sunshine falling through torn roofs upon the street of carpets, they see beams out of alignment and walls reaching for mutual support. They talk of poverty and age as if no beauty could be found in them, yet the bazaars of Kabul satisfy every sense.

They are full of smells, strange exciting smells, whose origin I long to know. They echo with an amusing—and for that matter most modern—cacophony of sound—but the singing of birds predominates. For in every cupboard shop, with the merchant tucked away on a shelf among his canes of sugar wrapped in brilliant paper, his furs, knives, striped rugs, long-necked bottles, fat stomached pots, his books of large squiggly lettering, his silver bracelets and gold-embroidered caps, there is a cage or half a dozen cages full of the smallest imaginable birds. And they all sing. They never stop singing.

But the place where I can never refrain from that quick intake of breath which means delight, and an always-surprised delight as well, is that very street of carpets with the broken roof. One comes to it from the dimness of the covered bazaars, from the raw scarlet of silk and chemists' labels. The sun is spilled between the beams so that there is a lovely pattern of light and shade. The shops are heaped one upon another, each warm and rich with colours that have come from Merv, Isfahan, Samarkand, the legendary towns where men went to their looms as an artist to his easel. Dust turns to gold in the streams and spears of light that fall all ways across the darkness and the calm faces of the merchants, leaf-brown, leather-brown, framed in beard and turban, acquire a distinction that is in itself an emotion, like the sudden discovery of a new effect in a familiar masterpiece. I shall never forget that street. I shall never be able to describe it.

In Kandahar

IN KANDAHAR, I stayed in an old Afghan house. It belonged to an Indian and it consisted of several yards leading one into another, with rooms opening round them and screens blocking any direct entrance so that it seemed as if one walked a long way before reaching the central court. Here there were cypresses, a huge mulberry tree, and many zinnias in pots. Pigeons and a fighting partridge sunned themselves on the flat roofs which commanded an excellent view of the city. Towards evening a clamorous host of starlings went to bed in the cypresses.

Part of the court was screened for the use of my host's wife and four daughters. Here and in the small rooms beyond, the mother, an old woman at 48, was happy enough "to rest after the bearing of ten children" and "to occupy herself with her books and her prayers." But the eldest of the daughters was sixteen. She was pretty, with the eyes of a faun and the smoothest golden-brown skin. She could speak some English and had been to one of the big Indian schools. I wondered how she occupied herself in the seclusion forced upon her by wars that have bred hatred between neighbours sharing language and religion. For the court of cypresses was always empty. No Afghan would extend hospitality or receive it from one who served the British.

In that great town, my Indian friends, intelligent, charming, and widely travelled, knew no one. When they went out they smothered themselves in the chadour with its cruel mesh across the eyes. For the rest of the day and the rest of the year, the five of them inhabited a few square yards of space, imprisoned as securely by the doubts and suspicions of their fellows as by the walls which shut out everything but a patch of sky.

Here, I thought, while we discussed the marriage of daughters and the contrariness of peas which refused to grow familiarly with a tortoise, an apricot tree, and a clothes-line, was another and more drastic "life of the interior."

Outside the house of cypresses, the wide and tree-lined streets spread splendidly between government buildings. When they reached the bazaars, they made themselves into a cross and ran straight out towards the horizon, leaving behind them, in their determination to reach Kabul, Herat, Chamman, and Baluchistan, all the little shops, stuffed with silk and sheepskins, silver, pottery, copper, and water-pipes, that clung to their beginnings. I liked the bazaar, white-walled and filled with the white clothes and turbans of men from Northern India and Southern Asia. Dust added to the general whiteness. Donkeys and camels were coated with it. Dark skins became grey under it. Eyelashes and lips showed a furring of soft dim-colour.

But Westwards, beyond Kandahar, the new houses are in a wealth of green. I had not realised how incomparably superior to any other colour this silken green of grain growing and leaves budding could be, till I came to it after so many miles of brown. I had thought the blossom lovely when it flared above mud walls in the plain of Kabul, but here the orchards of plum, apricot, almond, and pomegranate, all of them in flower, rose out of wheat fields riotously green and spread their rich red and white to the foot of mountains no longer-snow-covered, but carved like old jewels and set, hard, and precious, against the pallor of a desert sky.

It was the most surprising contrast, for a mile away on the other side of the town a harsh earth littered with stones erupted into rows and rows of termite houses, round-shelled because there is no wood for beams or posts, and beyond them the same earth heaped itself against the desert wall of India.

In the late evening I drove out to Chel Zerin. Having climbed the forty steps, so much too high for modern gait, to Babar's arch of victory, I sat upon the narrow rock with the headless lions behind me, and looked down on the oasis of Kandahar. Delicious domed villages appeared to have tumbled into the middle of the fruit-trees. I could see the black and red of nomad caravans camped for the night, and imagine the piles of gaudy bedding, the skirts like carnival balloons, and the children's caps of proud purple ornamented with silver.

Tongas rattled along the road. Lorries trailed a funnel of dust behind them. Camels ignored the presence of donkeys, who, however, went faster and a great deal more companionably towards their goal.

The sun sank and light too clear to have any colour at all was poured over field and orchard. The blossom took the colours of wine. It spilled from a jade-green cup and then, quite suddenly the whole earth was in shadow with the peaks standing up like thrones of kings or, maybe, since Afghanistan is more faithful to her Mullahs than her princes, like the altars of a surrealist deity.

Beside me the only occupant of the rock cast off his shoes and flung himself on his face. A moment later, oblivious of his sores and rags, he was intoning with the arrogance that has never known doubt. "There is no God but God and Mohammed is his Prophet."

Travelling with Afghans

To travel with Afghans is a pleasure and something of a humiliation. I am referring to lorry travel, which is a test of manners and character. Unfortunately, few Europeans can do more than remain patient and polite after a dozen hours jolting over a bad road and a good many more doctoring a recalcitrant carburetter or tying on chains that slip with every skid. But the Afghan regards all these matters as the concomitants of an ordinary existence and, unlike the Westerners he admires and distrusts, he has no quarrel with life.

Arabs are equally kind to their fellow-travellers and their courtesy is equal to the most outrageous demands, but they haven't the Afghan sense of humour which turns adverse circumstance into a joke and thus defeats it.

Persians are charmingly whimsical over the difficulties of, say, a seventy-two-hour journey across a desert, the tyres stuffed with sacking or dry bush and the radiator leaking, but eventually they become exhausted and then they seek solace in opium. But the Afghan seems to thrive on foodless days and sleepless nights. If, piled upon a leaning tower of luggage on the top of a two-ton truck, he is thrown into the mud, he carries it off as if it were a trick performed for the delight of an audience. If, crushed among the top layer of those within the lorry, he hits the roof with a crack that would split an ordinary skull, he congratulates himself on having put on his thickest caraculi hat and announces—perhaps—that his brother who lives in a town has always told him his head isn't hard enough to deal with the village moneylender.

It was my good fortune to return from Kandahar to Kabul with seventeen Afghans on the post lorry. Now the southbound journey had been without incident, unless the revelations of Monsieur X could count as such, but since then it had rained, and forty miles out of Kandahar the road became a morass. We had started, of course, three hours after the scheduled time, but the gay and gallant little driver, his filbert-brown face at once gentle and determined, assured us all that he had mended the lights and would reach Mukur "before the moon."

Unfortunately there is little metalling on that particular road and in the wet clay, the lorry proceeded in a series of graceful curves that took us first into a ditch, and then within a few inches of the drop into a river bed. The Afghans remained unmoved. When the vehicle shuddered as if with distaste at its narrow escape and scrambled sideways in a succession of remarkable skids, they laughed and suggested that we might do better backwards. It was I who begged for chains, and immediately the whole company descended into the rain. During subsequent hours most of them kneeled, crawled or lay in a foot of mud, regardless of their clothes, while they attempted first to fasten the chains in normal fashion and then, when it was discovered that nobody knew how the hooks worked, to tie them on with a mass of wire and string. After I too had lain in the mud underneath the lorry because I felt that I alone must by superior intelligence know at once how a hook that looked like an intestinal accident should close, someone suggested that it would be altogether simpler if we jacked up the lorry. While a dozen still amiable people did this and subsequently regarded the problem from a new, but no less disturbing angle, I went for a walk. When I returned, it was raining harder than ever and the best dressed of the passengers, his coat laid aside, his admirable trousers harmonising with shirt, socks, and tie of agreeably assorted blues was bending over a small, artificial pool which a friend had just created for him with stones and water scooped up in his hat. Noticing the surprise I was not quick enough to hide, the young man smiled and said in the most natural way—English—"I am just praying to God."

"Oh yes, of course," I replied, looking at the skies which registered I thought no normal hour for devotion.

Later, with the lorry bucking over ruts and making a great fuss whenever her tail swung sideways in a soft slither of mud, I wondered why civilisation insists on shirts being worn inside and tempers outside. A terrific bump landed me full on the thigh of the enchanting Afghan who had squeezed himself into a third of his rightful space on the front seat in order that I might be more comfortable. He bowed and made a gesture indicating that, if anything, I had added to the distraction and comfort of his journey. He even refrained from rubbing his leg which must have been momentarily paralysed. I looked over my shoulder and from the dark interior where turbans, feet, and bodies were peculiarly confused, I garnered thirteen smiles. The other two were presumably on the floor, where their owners strove among the feet, the luggage and the water-pipes of their friends.

Hastily I relegated civilisation to the waste-paper basket and I marveled the more that even the youngest and most brilliant intellectuals, ambitious to place their country on a pedestal composed of machines, electricity, concrete, macadam, and tweeds, can so overlook the basic qualities of character in which Afghanistan is so rich in favour of the general anaemia of morals, manners, and tempers which constitute the European empyrean.

Meanwhile I was having great difficulty in remaining on the plunging truck, for the door would not stay shut. In vain my fellow passengers had tied it up with string filched from their parcels and handkerchiefs which should have been holding fresh almonds bought in Kandahar. As soon as I was thrown against it, the door triumphantly opened. At last the driver, who had had nothing to eat all day, sighed, smiled, shook his faun-like head, and got out into the rain. From the back leaped also one Aziz Ullah, whose name, literally translated, means Beauty of God. He was our last and most effective resort in all trouble. Did the lorry show signs of rolling backwards on a hill, Aziz Ullah flung himself from the tailboard and wedged stones under the back wheels. Did the engines make sounds indicative of a volcano about to erupt, Aziz Ullah fled for the nearest liquid and poured it, clay and all, into the protesting radiator. Now, caked with mud, scarred by various missiles flung from the back wheels, he approached my door, and on an impulse that would have done credit to Raleigh, he removed his belt. A three-inch strip of sound leather, would, he felt, put an end to that door's power of making a nuisance of itself, but unfortunately nothing was left to hold up his trousers. With a beautiful completeness, they fell down. The lorry rocked with the delight of its occupants. The joke was the better because Beauty of God stood ankle deep in slime. The driver laughed. So did my neighbour, but loudest and longest laughed Aziz Ullah.

Towards midnight we arrived at Mukur and the whole company saw me into the rest-house before they would consent to find beds and food for themselves. While I stood in the middle of a comfortable room, with hot water and a fine, new bed waiting for me, most of them returned to ask if I wanted tea, or a bath, or somebody's coat as an extra blanket. My neighbour, whose name and business I never knew, came last of all and murmured in German, "You perhaps bathroom paper have not. I bring—so." Thrusting the sheets into my hand, he departed, stiff, unshaved and a great gentleman.

Next day the rain stopped and engine trouble began. Three times the driver and Aziz Ullah took the entire carburetter to pieces and removed from it birds' nest substances. With the utmost patience and good temper they sat in the mud with a cold wind blowing, surrounded by more and more engine, while all the ordinary lorries which had started hours later from Mukur gathered like flies round a honeypot. Their occupants offered every kind of help, and when this was refused because not more than twenty people could operate on one carburetter, they hunched themselves into bundles under the shelter of their enormous sheepskin cloaks and sucked their water-pipes, or lay upon their backs heedless of the amount of earth that would adhere to them, or prayed with a strip of shawl spread towards Mecca.

The heaviest loaded of all the lorries halted in front of me. I counted eleven passengers balanced upon a leaning tower of luggage that swayed from the roof like a skyscraper in a gale. Inside cheerful travelers were compressed into the substance of prune mould. They could not stir. Each urged the others to make the first essential movement that would relieve the mass. Finally there was a general upheaval and from it men were ejected into the road. They laughed, stretched and shook themselves. One said it was a great thing to travel. He wished he had brought his son. The boy had seen nothing of the world.

After an hour or so we proceeded on our journey, and in that glow of satisfaction that unites all proper travelers after a difficulty surmounted, we conversed fluently in Pushtu which I didn't understand, English incomprehensible to both my companions, twenty oddly assorted words of German garnered in Kabul by my neighbour, as much Persian of which I was inordinately proud, and a language unknown to any of us which the driver said was "Belgis." By this time we were all so much aware of each other's thoughts that it didn't really much matter what we talked. In fact, when my neighbor told a grim tale of having been upset on the road from Mazar to the capital, in a lorry which had turned over no less than three times on its way down a cliff, his gestures were so descriptive that he needn't have used any words at all. The only detail I was unable to discover was the date of the accident. I don't know if it happened last week, or five years ago, but nevertheless I felt as if I had been present when the first skid sent an overloaded truck to the edge of eternity, a second gave it brief respite and the last sent it hurtling over until it landed, piecemeal, a surprising number of feet below.

That day we lunched in the middle of Ghazni street under the lovely long walls of her fortress, because everyone felt he must keep in touch with the lorry. The cook-shops were urged to a speed that left them disorganised for hours. Still masticating, the passengers climbed into their places. With a disheartening amount of gulps, the lorry forced her way through a crowd who were, I hoped, pleased by the pantomime of haste we provided for them. At me, they gazed with interest, appreciation and mirth. The driver disapproved. "All this men is fool," he said, surprisingly in English.

Five minutes later, we were seated, this time in snow, while we took to pieces whatever came handiest under the bonnet. Unruffled, those passengers for whom no loose portions of engine were available, conversed about the excellent progress we were making, and how, soon, there would be no camels left. A very old man, who spoke to me in fragmentary Arabic, ventured most courteously to interpolate amidst the general appreciation of the new security and speed of life, the remark that with a donkey one had the certainty of arriving and also the knowledge at what hour one would arrive. The others thought this was an excellent joke and after a while the old man agreed.

After a third and still longer breakdown, during which the carburetter had yielded a variety of interesting objects with which it should have had no relation, we halted, in darkness and a gale, to drop some mail at an isolated tower. Snow had drifted against it. There was not a tree within sight. We had had no food for eight hours, and were half frozen by sleet and wind. Yet no sooner had the lorry stopped than men flowed from the back, and the stream-effect was heightened by the fact that the carpets and pieces of clothing they carried blew out interminably behind them. With one accord they cast the stuffs upon the ground and knelt swiftly, bowing as one person towards an invisible kibla. The very smart young man in selected blues made room on his rug or coat for the old man bundled up in a mass of white draperies who had spoken of donkeys. Together in the most complete unison they performed the swift doublings and undoublings that automatically accompany the Moslem prayers. Presented with the sudden accentuation of their posteriors, I admired for the hundredth time the utter lack of self-consciousness which the Afghan brings to his devotions and wondered why he cannot introduce a little of it into his daily life, during which he is a martyr to his own fear of criticism.

As soon as the last genuflection had been made, the passengers remembered, perhaps, their empty stomachs and their aching joints. Stiffly, they hurried towards the lorry. We started and in splendid fashion—brakes and lights both doubtful—we charged down the further side of the pass. Kabul was within sight, five miles, four, three. We could walk it now, I thought.

The lorry gasped before coming to a precipitate halt. With the expression of a small child that has been refused an unreasonable request, an expression that did not even protest, the driver descended and began at once to dismember the carburetter. "In a few time, I starting—" he assured me.

Two hours later we reached Kabul. The passengers descended. They embraced each other, or repetitively shook hands, self-congratulatory after such an excellent journey. "Allah be praised for this good day," said the old man, and I found myself suddenly agreeing with him. It had been a good day. I had enjoyed it.

Bamyan, Valley of the Giant Buddhas

THROUGHOUT THE AGES there has been a route from China across the legendary Oxus, now the Amu Darya, "Mother of rivers," into Afghanistan and India. But the old "Silk Road" through Balkh, where Alexander of Macedon camped, and Bamyan, whose giant Buddhas were defaced by Genghis Khan, circumvented the main ranges of the Hindu Kush. Only the Afghans, encouraged by Nadir Shah, have had sufficient enterprise to fling their new strategic road directly across the Shibhar Pass and to force it for some thirty-four miles through the cleft made by the Surkhab river, with at times scarcely more than a lorry's breadth between cliffs rising to several thousand feet.

The total length of the road between Kabul and Mazar-i-Sherif, the holy city of Afghanistan, is 382 miles. It is, of course, a fair-weather track, impassable during heavy snow. In places it degenerates into a couple of ruts running across the steppes of Ghori, or climbing between a succession of frozen red breakers over the Mazar Pass. But, given the spectacular difficulties of the terrain, it is a magnificent achievement. It is also the "forbidden way" to the Soviet Republics of Central Asia.

After leaving Kabul, we rolled down the "Skirt of the Hills" valley, from which came the brigand Batcha Saqai and his revolutionaries to the overthrow of Amanullah and the destruction of a good deal of his capital. Small tulips coloured the grass. Judas brushes made a purple flame. Kochis were strung along the road amidst a confusion of camels or donkeys. These gypsy folk were bundled in all manner of clothing and some of them carried fighting partridges in cages, or the breasts of their coats. The village of Serai Khaja might have been a bird market. Before every open-fronted shop, trailing its tea-couches into the mud, hung cages of singing birds. The roofs were lined with bright-coloured reed structures from which came a flutter of wings and song. It was raining, but the birds didn't mind. They went on singing above the clatter of tea-pots and cauldrons and the harsh speech of travellers sunk like tortoises into the shells made by their humped and wadded coats.

Kuli Khan wanted to buy a half a dozen green and red birds scarcely larger than his thumb. He said they would be companionable. But he was sternly repressed. With the three of us on the front seat amidst a litter of cameras, field-glasses, and sporting implements, and the other two crumpled into any odd space between the baggage and the roof of the lorry it seemed unnecessary to add to our impedimenta. But Kuli Khan left us in no doubt as to his disappointment. His long face drooped. Hollows deepened under his cheek-bones. The picture of misery, he leaned above us and commented on the state of the road.

It rained. It went on raining. And Kuli Khan looked as if he were going to cry.

Across the Pangshir river, Lord Curzon's "Singing Sands" were heaped against the hills. When the wind is in the right direction they shift across the rock face and a curious drumming echoes down the valley. The sound suggests a hive of monstrous and very impatient bees. According to the natives, "the sands walk," and in effect there is a certain amount of movement to account for the noise.

Our road, sunk deep in ruts, crossed a fertile plain where peasants were ploughing with instruments known to the book of Genesis. Fruit blossoms flushed the gardens. The houses were still of the square mud-built type, heavily walled, with here and there a watch-tower, but they scrambled together instead of standing proudly isolated as on the Indian frontier. In the distance we saw a village resembling a honeycomb. The buildings were cells, layered one on top of another.

At Charikar, the whole population seemed to be employed on the road, which had slipped into a morass. Every man had a spade which he used in the fashion that best suited him. I thought of a male chorus as I watched the elegant figures, draped in blankets, lingering in the mud.

Charikar is a new market. The shops are well built and modern. A rampart of them rose above the tide of camels couched among bales and saddlery. I thought of the markets familiar to Chinese travellers of the sixth and twelfth centuries. The form of the caravanseries has not changed, but the old "Silk Road" has given way to the petrol route by which caracul skins go in bulk to Russia and raw materials come South.

After leaving Charikar, with the Gorbund Valley rich in coal and lead, we came to the first gorges of the Kush. The road narrowed as it hung above the river. Two wheels appeared to be always on the verge of slipping over the edge. A chute of loose stones followed our passage. Kuli Khan breathed heavily and murmured that he had in his dreams visited the tomb of the sainted Ali at Mazar-i-Sherif, but saw no likelihood of doing so in the flesh.

George remained unmoved. So did the driver who believed in speed. At one moment he said, "If I go quick enough, I do not see."

To this principle he adhered until we began to climb the Shibhar Pass. At 10,000 feet the snow was thick, but frozen into breakers on either side of the track. The bleakest villages in the world lay under the crest. They seemed to have taken root in the snow. Their low walls, immensely solid, were a continuation of the drifts. There was no sign of life. Animals and human beings had taken refuge under the flat roofs weighted with stones. Above us, in a splendour of desolation, the Pass reared with the effect of a heavy bird, its wings spread for flight. On the other side, the valleys fell steeply, one on top of another. The road became a thread drawn between towering cliffs.

To the protest of brakes and an anxious monologue from Kuli Khan, we descended between winged pinnacles of rock. They were redder than anything I had ever imagined. In Kabul people had tried to describe to me this particular redness. They had used all available similes and I had been prepared for the colouring of Arizona, accentuated by a background of snow. But when we turned Westwards, off the new track, I found what I had supposed to be exaggeration was the mildest of understatements. For the cliffs were the violent red of flames, and, like them, etiolated. Where the stream we had followed poured into the Surkhab, which is part of the Oxus watershed, it was also red. And Zohak, that ancient and mighty fortress, now so much a part of the cliff on which it has stood for 800 years or so that the ramparts and towers are no longer distinguishable from the rock, is the culmination of this fantastic carmine.

The rain had turned to hail. Mist shifted across the road. It was ice-cold. In spite of sheepskin-lined coats and knee-boots, we froze behind the open wind-screen. But the approach to Bamyan became more and more spectacular. The ghosts of poplars shivered in the fog. The earth seemed to smoke. Through the climbing vapour, we saw the ruins of a village. Light struck through the gaping windows. The walls were cardboard, the towers a stage effect. Then the mist closed and we drove through blanketed whiteness.

Kuli Khan muttered about ghosts and I wondered myself if what we had just seen were real. For the few remaining inhabitants of Bamyan believe that Shahr-i-Gholgola, "the place of sorrow," is haunted by a race of wolf-men who are human by day and animal at night. They attribute the loss of their cattle to the predatory instincts of these creatures who were once warriors, prematurely slaughtered by Genghis Khan in revenge for the death of his grandson.

When the mist lifted, we found ourselves in a little valley. Furrows ran across it. The fields were bare and separated by streams. A few fortress farms each with four towers rose solidly—earth out of earth. But on the nearer side a rampart of red rock climbed sheer to the snowline. It was porous with caves and split by the niches of giant Buddhas. Strange flying formations rose above the honeycomb town and the proud colour was slashed with green, rust brown, and indigo.

So I first saw Bamyan, Valley of the Buddhas—a confusion of mist, snow and an overpowering blood-red—with a procession of small men, red-bearded, coming in and out of the cliffs. When the wind caught them their clothes were blown backwards, so that I thought of them as walking half naked in the gale with great swirls of drapery as a background. So many clothes they wore and so little use they seemed to be!

The driver, who rarely spoke, said, "These men are children—so small. Have they, perhaps, nothing to eat?" He was a practical person, interested in the multiple concerns of his engine and his own inside.

Through the Hindu Kush to Doab

I N AD 632, the celebrated Hiuan Tsang described Bamyan as a centre of art and commerce, a holy city of Buddhism, inhabited by thousands of monks and the goal of pilgrims from all parts of Asia. It was a market for the wares of China and India, and, after Balkh, the most important halting place on the "Silk Road" south of the Oxus.

A Byzantine traveller described the city of the valley destroyed by Genghis Khan, of which no traces now remain, as "standing proudly, like Rome, at the cross-roads of the world."

To-day a clutter of mud hovels, wind-swept and flayed by dust, lie at the feet of the biggest Buddha, 150 feet high. On the opposite cliff the Afghan Government have built a comfortable modern rest-house.

The sight of this square, white-washed building was comforting in view of the hail which had driven into the lorry till we felt battered and out of shape. The twentieth century has its advantages. There were stoves in the rest-house and a bathroom with a primitive heating apparatus. There were also a number of cell-like rooms from which one should have had a view of the rock city. The rest-house was far enough away to command the whole expanse of cliff, pitted with caves and still inhabited by a few half-troglodyte people who kept their goats in the lower caverns and lived like birds in the least accessible holes they could find. But every window was covered with a thick white stuff. Through it nothing could be seen and these curtains fitted so closely that it was impossible to contrive an aperture. So George and I spent the first half-hour taking them down, while Kuli Khan wandered in, asking, "Would you like mutton flan for dinner? There is no rice and I do not think a sheep has been killed."

We replied that we didn't mind what we ate provided it were hot. Kuli Khan drifted away. No other man could express such depths of foreboding. While we leaned upon the sills, enchanted by a spectacle sufficiently remarkable to be included among the seven or seventy wonders still left to us, Kuli Khan returned with the news that he couldn't cook. "You have taken all the wood for baths. There is no fire left. You will be very clean, but how can you eat?"

We begged him to show a little of that resource for which he was famous, but the situation was not sufficiently unsatisfactory. Kuli Khan had decided on tins, and nothing would deflect him from his purpose.

We spent the evening making up the fire, for the stove was voracious. It ate wood faster than we could provide it. In alternate spells of heat and cold we studied maps and decided upon the length of exposure suited to our various lenses, for Bamyan is difficult to photograph. Either the dark entrances of cells, passages and shrines are so confused with the organ-like structure of the cliffs that they disappear among a multitude of shadows, or, over-emphasised, they incline to the form of warts upon a tormented body.

While we yawned and smoked, Kuli Khan made his last appearance. He spoke of baths as if, like Moses, he had conjured them from the rock. A fearful steam came with him. Choking, we followed him along the passage. The bathroom seemed ablaze. We had to shout above the roaring of the heating apparatus. The water hissed and spat as it burst from the taps. There were other frantic noises. Kuli Khan looked delighted. He enjoyed havoc. "Perhaps something will burst," he said.

George did all that was possible to prevent catastrophe, and got very black in the process. "We'd better leave it to cool down," he suggested.

This was essential, for something had happened to the cold water. With infinite satisfaction Kuli Khan was able to announce that it would not work.

Eventually I got my bath, but the water was the colour of beetroot; a thick sediment coated the sides of the tub. Soap added the effect of cream on the best Bortsch. It occurred to me that bathing in champagne or asses' milk was cheap compared with such an extravagance of soap.

Next morning we found all the curtains in place again. As a race the Afghans are peculiarly afraid of criticism. They do not even ask like all South Americans, "What do you think of our country?" They don't want to know. They don't want the tourists whom other countries regard as manna from Heaven. They want to be left alone to go as far as they please, but no further. They have so much of which to be proud, but it is not enough. Behind closed curtains and a guarded frontier, they are safe from criticism.

What effect does it have on a man's nature to live without a view? The houses of Afghanistan have always been secretive. Within high walls and blind walls they keep themselves to themselves. They represent the antithesis of the Russian warrens, where flat-dwellers share everything that for a thousand years has been included in the Mohammedan religion of privacy.

After relays of eggs provided by a despairing Kuli Khan, we tramped across the valley. The wind was an iced razor-blade and the snows blue-white above the blazing cliffs. By daylight, Shahr-i-Gholgola was less ghostly. It was difficult to believe in the wolf-men. The small boy who trudged with us showed scepticism, but he told us the tale of the king's daughter who fell in love with Jelal-ed-Din at the inconvenient moment when, at the head of Genghis Khan's army, he was attacking the town. For his sake she betrayed her people, and she did it in a manner which proved her ingenuity. From a bow of exceptional size she shot an arrow into Jelal-ed-Din's camp. Attached to the shaft was a message explaining that if he cut off the city's water supply he and his men could creep in at night by the empty conduits. For this information she claimed a promise of marriage. Jelal-ed-Din gave it, but, according to legend, he killed the lady on their wedding night because "she who had been dangerous to many men might be even more dangerous to one."

For hours we climbed about the cliffs and at the most giddy moments I insisted on reading extracts from a leaflet written in French by an archeologist who was not a historian. Dutifully following his directions we found the circular cavern with its bas-relief of faces, some of them more like pigs than wolves. We clambered up behind the shoulders of the largest Buddha and stood upon his head under an arch of rock, while the wind did its best to dislodge us and fragments of peeling frescoes fell upon our heads. Pursuing the past, we went between recurrent light and darkness into the depths of what were once hermitages and temples. We found a good many of them inhabited by gnome-like men with thickets of fiery beard, and by thin, small women whose eyes had burned into their heads. Before our feet failed us we'd learned something of the extent of Bamyan and were willing to credit Hiuan Tsang's tale of pilgrims by the thousand hospitably entertained by Buddhist monks, but I could not imagine the city as it had been when it defied the Mongols. Since Bamyan held up the enemy advance, it must have been a fortified town like Balkh, whose ramparts are still imposing, but in all history there can never have been destruction more complete than that which was wrought at the foot of the indestructible Buddhas by the orders of Genghis Khan.

There is nothing left in the valley.

Between furrows and swollen streams we made our way back to the gorges of the Kush. Kuli Khan was comparatively cheerful. In his opinion it was impolite to linger on the way when at the end of it Sherif Ali waited. To the Moslem, whether Shia or Sunni, a tomb is a person and death no interruption to the continuance of a relationship. So Kuli Khan spoke cheerfully of going to see the son-in-law of the Prophet and made no mention of the Sherif's death. The hospitality of Ali would continue so long as there were Faithful to visit him.

"We must hurry," said Kuli Khan anxiously. He was not interested in the road. Chikar and the shooting of them he regarded as an interruption. But the driver and the greaser whom we called "Deadly Nightshade" were sportsmen. They saw partridges where there were only stones. When we passed a camel caravan, bound at a bare two miles an hour for the Southern bank of the Oxus, they asked eagerly after game. And the dark, bearded gypsy men who'd brought their merchandise from the ports of the Indian Ocean, kindly invented animals which they called "lions." After that we were in imminent danger of leaving the track for the river bed.

For 34 miles, between Bulda and Doab-i-Mezhari, the road crept between cliffs several thousand feet high. They were striped with the colours of old metal and showed traces of copper, lead, manganese and nickel. There was no trace of vegetation until, from the width of a few feet where the river and road together forced themselves through a cleft without sight of the sky, the gorge widened and forked to embrace a hill with an old fort on the crest.

Willows and fruit trees appeared at Jalmask, but Doab, where we spent the night, was sunk below a table-land of cliffs. The horizontal strata were of different colours and the whole formation looked like Edinburgh rock, but on a grand scale. The Hindu Kush has no fear of overdoing the effect. The rest-house at Doab was unfinished. Carpenters still worked on the roof. Pipes and other appurtenances of plumbing lay about in the mud. A shaggy mass of camels sheltered against the walls. Men as dark and ragged camped among their merchandise. They had come from the plains round Mazar, and they were Turkomans with the flat cheekbones and narrow eyes of their Mongol origin. From the few booths beside the road drifted an uncertain smoke. Having arranged the scattered beds and tables to suit our needs and sent a tall man in a magnificently flowered chapan to look for a receptacle in which to wash, we went out to buy meat.

By this time it was dusk. The camels were a dark tide lapping against the shore. The rest-house stood like a cliff above the movement of men and beasts.

We found the booths empty, so we turned up the road to stretch our legs. Down it came a succession of unkempt figures, worn and thin. They were the first tramps we'd seen. For, in Afghanistan, the village is a unit and the land divided between the members of a family. The code of Islam (Sheria) still prevails. By it and by traditional law, no man who has relations need fear starvation. Each of the feudal farms, as solid as a fortress within its walls, harbours three and even four generations and a number of hangers-on who work for their keep and clothes. No serfs or slaves are acknowledged in Afghanistan, but the children of retainers serve in the houses where they are born. Apart from the villages where every male contributes his share of labour, for Islam is one of the earliest forms of socialism, there are only the nomads, whose life is even more communal, or the shepherds, relations or henchmen of the flock-owners.

Outside the towns of Kandahar, Kabul and Herat, there is little hired labour. Each family looks after its own, and in the south there is little difference in wealth, for all depend on the land and what it produces. Only Amanullah attempted to build palaces out of keeping with the wealth of the country. Modern Afghans live nearly as simply as their forebears. They find their pleasures in sport, tea-drinking and chikar fighting; a lute, or, if some relative has travelled, an ancient gramophone, seem to occupy the leisure of the masses.

If there are no signs of luxury between the Khyber and the Oxus, there is also no indication of poverty. Villagers and towns-folk appear to be prosperous. In fact, the people are richer than the Government.

Until we reached the Kush, I saw no destitute, and beggars were conspicuous by their absence. But Mazar is a holy city and it was the season of the New Year pilgrimage. From every part of Asia, in wind-blown March, came pilgrims to the Shia Mecca.

Many of them apparently supported themselves on what the charitable offered. Like ghosts they slipped through the valleys of the Hindu Kush. They carried nothing but a stick. Their inadequate garments flapped behind them. Their sandals were split, or their rough felt leggings torn. Some of them looked as if they hadn't eaten for days. Where they slept I don't know. Limping and glassy-eyed they came from the dusk to disappear into the night. But one stopped us. He said there was a woman ill. We were foreigners. We must be doctors. We could give her medicine and she would be cured.

He led us to a mud shelter full of dung. It had been intended for goats. Two or three newly born kids huddled in a corner. In another crouched a tragic figure. It was shrivelled beyond sex or age. Its limbs were bent in a fashion suggesting paralysis or arthritis. But the youth who had brought us said it was a fever.

The woman did not speak. Her matted hair hung loose and mingled with the dirt. Her arms and legs were covered with mud. The boy whom we took to be her son treated her as if she were inanimate, moving her and straightening her limbs for our inspection. "She is tired, that is all," he said.

We gave him money for food and something that might relieve his mother's pain.

"She is not my mother. She's my wife," he said.

George, surprised into impulsive speech, exclaimed, "But she's so old!"

The lad shrugged his shoulders. "Yes. I hadn't enough money for anything better. But I'm going to Mazar of the Sherif. If I make money, I will buy a younger wife. You are right. She is too old, that one."

The Glory of Tamerlane

FROM THE GUR EMIR,[1] where, in peaceful surroundings, with the clean, colourless houses silent and a little remote, one can imagine the blue loveliness that must have astonished the fifteenth century, we drove down a slope, thick in dust, to the old town. And immediately, we became immersed in what might have been a London fog. For dust hung thick over the maze of alleys and half-fallen houses. Through the stinging substance, I had a glimpse of markets thronged with peasants who seemed much dirtier, shabbier and worse tempered than those with whom I had become familiar in Afghanistan. In Mazar-i-Sherif I had seen no women, but a great number of smiles. In the bazaars of Samarkand I saw lots of women, most of whom had come in from the country wearing black or coloured parandjas that covered them from head to foot, and the hideous horsehair veils thick with flies. But the men's faces were cheerless. The sense of brotherhood, familiar to Islam, had gone, and the insistent friendliness of eager socialism had not yet come. So there were no picturesque greetings, "Go in peace and safety," "Allah

---

1 In Samarkand—Ed.

make you strong," or "May your sons be an honour to you," and no embraces. Friends of long standing did little more than grunt when they met, and even in the tea-houses, whose carpet-covered couches spread wherever space offered, faces remained grim and men counted out the price of their drinks as it they were measuring the sands of life.

Such gloom, of course, may have been due to the wind, which raised dirt and dust like a blanket and flung it upon the shelterless people who bought and sold, drank thirstily, and stood in front of the cook-shops to eat meat impaled on sticks, their heads sunk tortoise-like into the collars of their drab and faded coats. That day, certainly, there was a blight upon the markets, and I was disappointed in the old town straying shaggily round the Registan.

In vain I told myself that this most famous square was surrounded by buildings fabulous even in the fifteenth century, that it was renowned as the centre of art and civilisation on the greatest caravan route of all time—the Silk Road between China and the West.

I saw only a three-sided square heaped with dust and three great buildings crumbling into decay. I stood on the heap of rubble, with shoddy tea-houses behind me, a tuneless gramophone blaring and a banner displaying an anti-religious slogan. I stared, with aching eyes, through a yellow haze, at the Tillah Kari medersa, "the thousand and second night," flanked on one side by Ulug Beg's mosque built in 1417, and on the other by the Shir Dar, which is an exact replica, except in the matter of mosaics, although it was constructed 200 years later.

So little do the present inhabitants of Samarkand know about the history of their town that the Professor cheerfully explained to me that the builder of the Shir Dar (in the seventeenth century) was obliged to erect the far more ancient Ulug Beg medersa opposite as a punishment for having decorated the façade of the first with lions' heads, forbidden to Islam with all portraiture of men or beasts.

In spite of the wind I insisted on sitting down upon my rubble-heap in order to consider the Registan. The Professor stood beside me, shifting from one foot to the other. Silently we gazed at the brownish yellow, the greens and blues of the great façades. Across the intervening space, a few figures in nondescript coloured coats, belted above the hips, were blown amidst a confusion of dust and litter. After a while we followed them into the Tillah Kari medersa. Once through the great arch flanked by a double row of cells, there was peace. To the left rose the immense iwan, the formal arch leading into the mosque, and in front of it were ranged a few pairs of shoes. In the centre of each wall was an alcove set in mosaics that still kept their fresh colouring, and on either side were the double galleries with pointed arches into which cells opened. Most of these seemed to be deserted, but in one three women, veil-less but wearing the parandja, were sewing, and in another an earnest man was cooking over a handful of charcoal.

In silence we climbed, by heaps of mud and fallen bricks, to the top of the Tillah Kari,[2] and from a windswept roof looked down on the twin mosques. The mosaics were, to a certain extent, restored by Viatkin, and a Soviet writer states that 65,000 roubles were spent in one year on the preservation of the Registan. But from the roof of the seventeenth century Tillah Kari, the famous square seems to be surrounded by ruins. The mosque of Ulug Beg is still magnificent because the iwan and the colossal square of walls which frame it are deeply blue, but the two minarets which flank the main arch have lost their tops. One of them leans slightly away from the main building. The domes which originally surrounded the roof have gone. The whole structure

---

2 Built in 1630.

now looks truncated, though it is only fair to admit that, on close inspection, I couldn't tell the difference between the old mosaics and the new tiles made in the same sort of oven and applied with careful delicacy by Viatkin's workmen. A good deal has also been done to restore the leaning minaret to its original position. By means of slow pressure exerted over a year and a half the structure has been forced approximately upright, and the ornamental brickwork has not suffered to any appreciable extent.

The Shir Dar still keeps one of its lovely ribbed domes set upon the round base peculiar to Central Asia and although the minarets have lost their conical tops, they are still vividly coloured. Three hundred years have mellowed the blue, green and yellow of Talank Toush's building, but they have not entirely destroyed the sunshine and sea-water effect.

When we came down from the roof of the medersa, we paused under the great façades of Shir Dar and looked up at the lions' heads which had caused such ferment of criticism among the true believers. Time had robbed them of suggestive outline. They fitted into the general effect of an autumn garden. In her delicious "Turkestan Solo," Ella Maillart quotes some of the phrases inlaid in Arabic characters upon the walls of Shir Dar: "The architect has built the arch of this portal with such perfection that the entire heavens gnaws its fingers in astonishment, thinking it sees the rising of some new moon." "Only the eagle of thought could presume to attain to the summit of this medersa," and "Never in all the centuries, will an acrobat's thoughts, even with the bow of phantasy, scale the forbidden heights of this minaret." There is another: "When thou goest on a journey, leave thy spirit on the path, else shalt thou not obtain full merit." In fact: "Partir, c'est mourir," because on every journey, one must leave some of oneself behind.

From the Registan we drove to Bibi Khanoum, which was once the largest mausoleum in the world. Built in five years, five memorable years of conquest while Tamerlane was away on his campaigns, the mosque was intended to be the burial place of his favourite wife, a Chinese princess—or was she a dancing girl? The work was completed in 1404, and it is said that just before his death Tamerlane had himself carried into the great court, three hundred feet long, so that he might for the last time approve the extent—and perhaps also the beauty—of his work. It is also said that Bibi Khanoum, as autocratic as her lord, had the Arab architect flung from the top of the building as soon as it was completed, either because he dared to love her, or—more probably— lest he should dare to erect another equally magnificent mausoleum for somebody else. It seems to have been a Mongol habit to reward the best artists with death and those of slightly less eminence with blindness.

To-day, all that remains of Bibi Khanoum's splendour is the main arch, eighty feet high and still ravishingly blue. We entered by the court, once paved, now grass-grown and shaded by acacias, through the new wall which surrounds the mass of ruins. A group of Mullahs in pale blue coats and white turbans, sitting cross-legged on a brilliant carpet, lent colour to the foreground. An iron bowl stood on a column. In the middle distance reared the white marble lectern which used to hold Caliph Osman's Koran. It was brought from Mongolia by the scientist, Ulug Beg, and under it, in the dawn, pregnant women used to crawl, fasting, in the hope that heaven would reward them with sons.

At the end of the grass and the trees, beyond the great heaps of fallen wall, rose the still lovely façade, centring on the iwan. Above it, the arch just held, and through it we could see the last fragment of the dome, but it looked as it the next storm must destroy both. I felt I must tread gently as I approached the aching blue of this cardboard façade that has no back at all. Scarcely daring to breathe I climbed among the broken bricks, turquoise, sapphire, and chrome yellow. With infinite precaution, I seated myself upon a slab of faience and I looked away from the remnants of minarets with their raised design in sea- and sky-coloured bricks. I saw the mighty heaps of mud that had been the reception chamber of the mosque, the pylons, reminiscent of gigantic ant-heaps, that were once the ramparts of an arrogant, although borrowed, Faith, and I saw also the market in the square and the dim, flat roofs of a city, mud-built, unchanged since the days of Tamerlane, or the Hegira.

As I clambered down from the roof of Bibi Khanoum's "Song of love in stone," a trickle of sound went with me. It was made by the falling mud. A sharper noise came from the bricks which my steps dislodged. I could imagine the first of them falling on the heads of the worshippers who had gathered to honour the completed mosque. For the Arab architect built too quickly. Without the Russian cannonade of 1868, time would have played its usual havoc with what was in effect a grandiose conception carried out in mud.

Beyond the slow, secret sounds of disintegration, I could hear the confusion of noise in the bazaars. Quite clearly, there came to me the succulent slap of breads plastered on the mud walls of an oven. Next to the bakery, there was a school, where noisy Usbeg children, very round and gay in their multi-coloured clothes, poured on to the balcony to do their afternoon drill. They looked healthy and insubordinate, and their red cheeks reminded me of fruit, ripe and on the point of falling. Above their shouts and their unruly footsteps, I heard a loud-speaker in one of the tea-houses, where peasants, shabby and somewhat sullen, drank tea out of handleless cups or slept on wooden couches. The clamour of the tinsmiths' alley provided a background of insistent noise. It had the same monotony as the hum of insects in a tropical forest.

Close to me, but invisible, somebody played upon a metal-stringed instrument. Only the market was silent. Without unnecessary words, the peasants, striped like hornets, sold and bought what seemed to me the last scourings of a rubbish heap. For three shillings, I procured a handful of apples not much larger than gooseberries, and I ate them with an enjoyment which surprised the Professor, while we wandered through the edge of Samarkand and over mud tracks towards Shah Zinde.

Another market spread like a Persian carpet, rich in colour, complicated in design, over the space between the grass-grown hill of tombs and a new mosque. Beyond it, at the top of a rough, green slope, with trees in the foreground, I saw a host of cupolas grey and without colour. It was beginning to rain. Under the trees peasants were cooking and eating their afternoon meal. The air smelt agreeably of meat and grease. Camels and donkeys filled the lane, which was inches deep in dust. While the driver argued with countrymen as obstinate as himself, I got out and walked over the hill, where women were gathering wood and dung for fires. Under my feet were innumerable tombs. Some of them burst through the grass. Others moulded it into swelling shapes. Piled as it were on top of the nameless graves, so softly rising above trees, were the domes of Shah Zinde, differently shaped and sized, but all clay-coloured. They looked like soap bubbles blown into a grey sky.

The correct approach to this burial place of "the living king," Shah Zinde, and his successors, is by means of a flight of steps rising steeply out of the lane.

Finding, at that time, no other entrance, I went down between the abandoned tombs of Afro Siab, that mountain of the dead, and climbed again, with the Professor panting behind me, through a glazed portal, with to the left a very lovely diwan or reception chamber, its roof carved and its beams glittering with blue, red and gold, and in front the narrow street of tombs. As one enters this cool and shadowed way, the façades of what appear to be miniature mosques stand up on either side. There are ten of

them, all different and all exquisitely coloured. A blue dome sur-
mounts the grave of Tamerlane's nurse or foster-mother. Mosaics
of Persian design, carvings, inlay, a lovely riot of colour, softened
by time, for the first building dates from 1326, ornament the little
mausoleums of Tamerlane's son Zade and of his first wife Turkan. And here is the charm of the place. It is all so small. After the
mighty Registan and the colossal destruction of Bibi Khanoum,
it is a relief to find space limited by ordinary proportions.

Between walls faced deliberately with enamel, we walked without words, glancing now and then into the reception chamber of
a tomb, admiring the design of Turkan Ali, the simplicity of Emir
Hussein, until the little street turned sharply and the walls lost
their colour.

Three more tombs that were houses all to themselves, another
gateway and a tree whose bark is naturally regarded as holy, and
then we came to a miniature court. I held my breath. Here at
last was the beauty of which I had dreamed when, years ago, in
Meshed, I saw the beginning of the "Golden Road" that leads to
Samarkand. For the court must have been steeped in sea-water. All
the blues from turquoise to the deepest sapphire were reflected
in the incomparable mosaics and this deep, quiet pool of cou-
lour contrasted or blended with the rich browns and golds of the
earthen walls. Sea and sand with sunshine caught between them, I
thought, and was reluctant to leave the warmly glowing court for
the dimness of the little mosques which clustered round. There
was Kutluk with the pale carved pillars and Nuri, most exquisitely tiled, called after the wife and daughter of Tamerlane, and,
at the end of the court, completing the toll of "the great dead,"
Sayed Ahmed.

Under the delicate dome of the portico, an old man prayed,
with his shoes beside him. A few Mullahs who had been drinking tea came with us, through a succession of chambers hung

with horses' tails, symbolic of a sacrifice, banners and tattered red
stuff, till we stood behind a grille and looked at the tomb of Shah
Zinde, who converted the Trans-Oxus regions to Islam, and was
eventually defeated and killed by the Nestorian Christians. Legend has it that his whip flowered into the two trees that shelter
the court, that his horse escaped, leaving its tail behind, and that
the Saint himself, decapitated, continued to roll into a well, taking with him his head, and thus saving his place in paradise.

Books by Rosita Forbes

Nonfiction

Unconducted Wanderers. London & New York: John Lane, 1919.

The Secret of the Sahara: Kufara. London: Cassell, 1921; New York: Doran, 1921.

El Raisuni: The Sultan of the Mountains—His Life Story as Told to Rosita Forbes. London: Butterworth, 1924; *The Sultan of the Mountains: The Life Story of Raisuli*. New York: Holt, 1924.

From Red Sea to Blue Nile: Abyssinian Adventure. London: Cassell, 1925; New York: Macaulay, 1925. Revised as *From Red Sea to Blue Nile: A Thousand Miles of Ethiopia*. New York: Furman, 1935; London: Cassell, 1936.

Adventure: Being a Gipsy Salad—Some Incidents, Excitements and Impressions of Twelve Highly-Seasoned Years. London: Cassell, 1928; New York: Houghton Mifflin, 1928.

Conflict: Angora to Afghanistan. London: Cassell, 1931; New York: Stokes, 1931.

Eight Republics in Search of a Future: Evolution and Revolution in South America. London: Cassell, 1933; New York: Stokes, 1934.

Women Called Wild. London: Grayson & Grayson, 1935; New York: Dutton, 1937.

Forbidden Road: Kabul to Samarkand. London: Cassell, 1937; New York: Dutton, 1937. Republished as *Russian Road to India: By Kabul and Samarkand*. London: Cassell, 1940.

These Are Real People. London: Jenkins, 1937; New York: Dutton, 1939.

Women of All Lands: Their Charm, Culture and Characteristics (editor). London: Amalgamated, 1939.

India of the Princes. London: Gifford, 1939; New York: Dutton, 1941.

A Unicorn in the Bahamas. London: Jenkins, 1939; New York: Dutton, 1940.

The Prodigious Caribbean: Columbus to Roosevelt. London: Cassell, 1940.

These Men I Knew. London: Hutchinson, 1940; New York: Ryerson, 1940.

Gypsy in the Sun. London: Cassell, 1944; New York: Dutton, 1944.

Appointment with Destiny. London, Cassell, 1946; New York: Dutton, 1946; abridged, with *Gypsy in the Sun*, as *Appointment in the Sun*. London: Cassell, 1949.

Henry Morgan, Pirate. New York: Reynall & Hitchcock, 1946; *Sir Henry Morgan, Pirate & Pioneer*. London: Cassell, 1946.

Islands in the Sun. London: Evans, 1949.

Novels

The Jewel in the Lotus: A Novel. London: Cassell, 1922.

Quest: The Story of Anne, Three Men and Some Arabs. London: Cassell, 1922; New York: Holt, 1923.

A Fool's Hell. London: Butterworth, 1923; New York: Holt, 1924.

If the Gods Laugh. London: Butterworth, 1925; New York: Macaulay, 1926.

Sirocco. London: Butterworth, 1927; *Pursuit*. New York: Macaulay, 1928.

Account Rendered and King's Mate. London: Cassell, 1928; *Account Rendered*. New York: Macaulay, 1929.

The Cavaliers of Death. London: Butterworth, 1930; New York: Macaulay, 1930.

One Flesh. London: Cassell, 1930; New York: Putnam, 1930.

Ordinary People. London: Cassell, 1931; *Promise You Won't Marry Me*. New York: Stokes, 1932.

The Extraordinary House. London: Cassell, 1934; New York: Stokes, 1934.

The Golden Vagabond. London: Cassell, 1936.

About the Editor

M argaret Bald is the author of *Banned Books: Literature Suppressed on Religious Grounds* and the co-author of *120 Banned Books: Censorship Histories of World Literature* and *100 Banned Books: Censorship Histories of World Literature*. She has been a freelance journalist and foreign correspondent, managing editor of *World Press Review* magazine, and an editorial consultant to the United Nations. She is managing editor at a social policy research organization and lives with her family in Brooklyn, New York.

Photograph by Metin Oner.